# Memoirs of Marguerite De Valois, Queen of France, Wife of Henri Iv; of Madame De Pompadour of the Court of Louis Xv; and of Catherine De Medici, Queen of France, Wife of Henri Ii

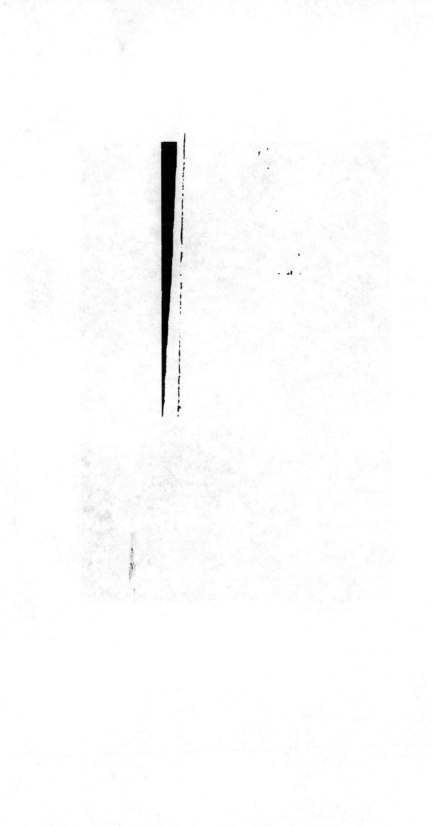

# MEMOIRS OF
# MARGUERITE DE VALOIS
*Queen of France, Wife of Henri IV*

## OF

# MADAME DE POMPADOUR
*Of the Court of Louis XV*

## AND OF

# CATHERINE DE MEDICI.
*Queen of France, Wife of Henri II*

*With a Special Introduction
and Illustrations*

NEW YORK
P F COLLIER & SON
PUBLISHERS

580754

# CONTENTS

## LETTER I

## LETTER II

## LETTER III

## LETTER IV

# CONTENTS

# INTRODUCTION

THE *Secret Memoirs* of Henry of Navarre's famous queen possess a value which the passage of time seems but to heighten. Emanating as they undoubtedly do from one of the chief actors in a momentous crisis in French history, and in the religious history of Europe as well, their importance as first-hand documents can hardly be overestimated. While the interest which attaches to their intimate discussions of people and manners of the day will appeal to the reader at the outset.

Marguerite de Valois was the French contemporary of Queen Elizabeth of England, and their careers furnish several curious points of parallel. Marguerite was the daughter of the famous Catherine de Médicis, and was given in marriage by her scheming mother to Henry of Navarre, whose ascendant Bourbon star threatened to eclipse (as afterwards it did) the waning house of Valois. Catherine had four sons, three of whom successively mounted the throne of France, but all were childless. Although the king of the petty state of Navarre was a Protestant, and Catherine was the most fanatical of Catholics, she made this marriage a pretext for welding the two houses; but actually it seems to have been a snare to lure him to Paris, for it was at this precise time that the bloody Massacre of St. Bartholomew's day was ordered. Henry himself escaped—it is said, through the protection of Marguerite, his bride,—but his adherents in the Protestant party were slain by the thousands. A wedded life begun under such sanguinary auspices was not destined to end happily. Indeed, their marriage resembled nothing so much as an armed truce, peaceable, and allowing both to pursue their several paths, and finally dissolved by mutual consent, in 1598, when Queen Marguerite was forty-five. The closing years of her life were spent in strict seclusion, at the Castle of Usson, in Auvergne, and it was at this time that she probably wrote her *Memoirs.*

In the original, the *Memoirs* are written in a clear vigorous French, and in epistolary form. Their first editor divided them into three sections, or books. As a whole they cover the secret history of the Court of France from the years 1565 to 1582—seventeen years of extraordinary interest, comprising, as they do, the Massacre of St. Bartholomew, already referred to, the formation of the famous League, the Peace of Sens, and the bitter religious persecutions which were at last ended by the Edict of Nantes issued after Henry of Navarre became Henry IV. of France. Besides the political bearing of the letters, they give a picturesque account of Court life at the end of the 16th century, the fashions and manners of the time, piquant descriptions, and amusing gossip, such as only a witty woman —as Marguerite certainly was—could inject into such subjects. The letters, indeed, abound in sprightly anecdote and small-talk, which yet have their value in lightening up the whole situation.

The period covered coincides very nearly with the first half of Marguerite's own life. Incidents of her girlhood are given, leading to more important matters, personal and political, up to the twenty-ninth year of her age. The letters end, therefore, some seven years prior to the death of her brother, Henry III. of France, and while she was still merely Queen of Navarre. It will always be a matter of regret that the latter half of her life was not likewise covered.

These *Memoirs* first appeared in printed form in
1628, thirteen years after their author's death. They
enjoyed great popularity, and in 1656 were translated
into English and published in London, with the following erroneous title: "The grand Cabinet Counsels
unlocked; or, the most faithful Transaction of Court
Affairs, and Growth and Continuance of the Civil
Wars in France, during the Reigns of Charles the last,
Henry III., and Henry IV., commonly called the
Great. Most excellently written, in the French
Tongue, by Margaret de Valois, Sister to the two first
Kings, and Wife of the last. Faithfully translated
by Robert Codrington, Master of Arts." Two years
later the work was again translated, this time under
the title of "Memorials of Court Affairs." The mis-
leading portion of Codrington's title is in regard to the
reign of Henry IV. As already shown, the letters
cease before that time, although chronicling many
events of his early career. The present careful trans-
lation has been made direct from the original, adhering
as closely as permissible to the rugged but clear-cut
verbal expressions of 16th century France.

Queen Marguerite herself is described by historians
and novelists as a singularly attractive woman, both
physically and mentally. Of a little above the average height, her figure was well-rounded and graceful,
her carriage dignified and commanding. One writer
thus describes her: "Her eyes were full, black, and
sparkling; she had bright, chestnut-coloured hair, and
a complexion fresh and blooming. Her skin was delicately white, and her neck admirably well formed; and
this so generally admired beauty, the fashion of dress,
in her time, admitted of being fully displayed." To
her personal charms were added a ready wit and pol-
ished manners. Her thoughts, whether spoken or
written, were always clearly and gracefully expressed.

In her retirement, at the close of her life, she often amused herself by writing verses which she set to music and afterwards sang, accompanying herself upon the lute, which she performed upon skilfully.

Regarding her personal character there has been diversity of opinion—as, indeed, there has been in the case of nearly every exalted personage. After her separation from the king, she was the subject of a scandalous attack, entitled *Le Divorce Satyrique, ou les Amours de la Reyne Marguerite de Valois;* but this anonymous libel was never seriously considered. M. Pierre de Bourdeville, Sieur de Brantôme (better known by the final name), who gives many facts concerning her later life in his *Anecdotes des Rois de France,* is a staunch adherent of hers. Ronsard, the Court poet, is also extravagant in his praises of her, but chiefly of her beauty. Numerous other poets and romancers have found her life a favourite subject. Meyerbeer's opera, *Les Huguenots,* is based upon her wedding, and the ensuing Massacre. Dumas's well-known novel, *Marguerite de Valois,* gives her a somewhat dubious reputation, as half-tool, half-agent for Catherine, and as the mistress of the historical La Mole. This doubtful phase, however, if true, was but in keeping with the fashion of the times. It is mentioned merely as a possible line completing the portrait of this brilliant woman, who lives again for us in the pages of her *Memoirs.*

## ON MARGUERITE DE VALOIS.

### QUEEN OF NAVARRE.

Dear native land! and you, proud castles! say
(Where grandsire,[1] father,[2] and three brothers[3] lay,
Who each, in turn, the crown imperial wore),
Me will you own, your daughter whom you bore?
Me, once your greatest boast and chiefest pride,
By Bourbon and Lorraine,[4] when sought a bride;
Now widowed wife,[5] a queen without a throne,
Midst rocks and mountains[6] wander I alone.
Nor yet hath Fortune vented all her spite,
But sets one up,[7] who now enjoys my right,
Points to the boy,[8] who henceforth claims the throne
And crown, a son of mine should call his own.
But ah, alas! for me 'tis now too late[9]
To strive 'gainst Fortune and contend with Fate;
Of those I slighted, can I beg relief?[10]
No; let me die the victim of my grief.
And can I then be justly said to live?
Dead in estate, do I then yet survive?
Last of the name, I carry to the grave
All the remains the House of Valois have.

[1] François I.  [2] Henri II.  [3] François II., Charles IX., and Henri III.
[4] Henri, King of Navarre, and Henri, Duc de Guise.
[5] Alluding to her divorce from Henri IV.  [6] The castle of Usson.
[7] Marie de' Medici, whom Henri married after his divorce from Marguerite.  [8] Louis XIII., the son of Henri and his queen, Marie de' Medici.
[9] Alluding to the differences betwixt Marguerite and Henri, her husband.
[10] This is said with allusion to the supposition that she was rather inclined to favour the suit of the Duc de Guise and reject Henri for a husband.

# THE MEMOIRS OF
# MARGUERITE DE VALOIS

## LETTER I

I SHOULD commend your work much more were I myself less praised in it; but I am unwilling to do so, lest my praises should seem rather the effect of self-love than to be founded on reason and justice. I am fearful that, like Themistocles, I should appear to admire their eloquence the most who are most forward to praise me. It is the usual frailty of our sex to be fond of flattery. I blame this in other women, and should wish not to be chargeable with it myself. Yet I confess that I take a pride in being painted by the hand of so able a master, however flattering the likeness may be. If I ever were possessed of the graces you have assigned to me, trouble and vexation render them no longer visible, and have even effaced them from my own recollection. So that I view myself in your Memoirs, and say, with old Madame de Rendan, who, not having consulted her glass since her husband's death, on seeing her own face in the mirror of another lady, exclaimed, " Who is this? " Whatever my friends tell me when they see me now, I am inclined to think proceeds from the partiality of their affection. I am sure that you yourself, when you consider more impartially what you have said,

will be induced to believe, according to these lines
of Du Bellay:

> " C'est chercher Rome en Rome,
> Et rien de Rome en Rome ne trouver."
>
> ('Tis to seek Rome, in Rome to go,
> And Rome herself at Rome not know.)

But as we read with pleasure the history of the Siege
of Troy, the magnificence of Athens, and other splendid cities, which once flourished, but are now so entirely destroyed that scarcely the spot whereon they
stood can be traced, so you please yourself with de-
scribing these excellences of beauty which are no
more, and which will be discoverable only in your
writings.

If you had taken upon you to contrast Nature and
Fortune, you could not have chosen a happier theme
upon which to descant, for both have made a trial of
their strength on the subject of your Memoirs. What
Nature did, you had the evidence of your own eyes to
vouch for, but what was done by Fortune, you know
only from hearsay; and hearsay, I need not tell you,
is liable to be influenced by ignorance or malice, and,
therefore, is not to be depended on. You will for
that reason, I make no doubt, be pleased to receive
these Memoirs from the hand which is most interested in the truth of them.

I have been induced to undertake writing my Memoirs the more from five or six observations which I
have had occasion to make upon your work, as you
appear to have been misinformed respecting certain
particulars. For example, in that part where mention is made of Pau, and of my journey in France;
likewise where you speak of the late Maréchal de
Biron, of Agen, and of the sally of the Marquis
de Camillac from that place.

These Memoirs might merit the honourable name of history from the truths contained in them, as I shall prefer truth to embellishment.  In fact, to embellish my story I have neither leisure nor ability; I shall, therefore, do no more than give a simple narration of events.  They are the labours of my evenings, and will come to you an unformed mass, to receive its shape from your hands, or as a chaos on which you have already thrown light.  Mine is a history most assuredly worthy to come from a man of honour, one who is a true Frenchman, born of illustrious parents, brought up in the Court of the Kings my father and brothers, allied in blood and friendship to the most virtuous and accomplished women of our times, of which society I have had the good fortune to be the bond of union.

I shall begin these Memoirs in the reign of Charles IX., and set out with the first remarkable event of my life which fell within my remembrance.  Herein I follow the example of geographical writers, who having described the places within their knowledge, tell you that all beyond them are sandy deserts, countries without inhabitants, or seas never navigated.  Thus I might say that all prior to the commencement of these Memoirs was the barrenness of my infancy, when we can only be said to vegetate like plants, or live, like brutes, according to instinct, and not as human creatures, guided by reason.  To those who had the direction of my earliest years I leave the task of relating the transactions of my infancy, if they find them as worthy of being recorded as the infantine exploits of Themistocles and Alexander,—the one exposing himself to be trampled on by the horses of a charioteer, who would not stop them when requested to do so, and the other refusing to run a race unless kings were to enter the contest against him.

Amongst such memorable things might be related the answer I made the King my father, a short time before the fatal accident which deprived France of peace, and our family of its chief glory. I was then about four or five years of age, when the King, placing me on his knee, entered familiarly into chat with me. There were, in the same room, playing and diverting themselves, the Prince de Joinville, since the great and unfortunate Duc de Guise, and the Marquis de Beaupréau, son of the Prince de la Roche-sur-Yon, who died in his fourteenth year, and by whose death his country lost a youth of most prom-ising talents. Amongst other discourse, the King asked which of the two Princes that were before me I liked best. I replied, " The Marquis." The King said, " Why so? He is not the handsomest." The Prince de Joinville was fair, with light-coloured hair, and the Marquis de Beaupréau brown, with dark hair. I answered, " Because he is the best behaved; whilst the Prince is always making mischief, and will be master over everybody."

This was a presage of what we have seen happen since, when the whole Court was infected with heresy, about the time of the Conference of Poissy. It was with great difficulty that I resisted and preserved my-self from a change of religion at that time. Many ladies and lords belonging to Court strove to convert me to Huguenotism. The Duc d'Anjou, since King Henri III. of France, then in his infancy, had been prevailed on to change his religion, and he often snatched my " Hours " out of my hand, and flung them into the fire, giving me Psalm Books and books of Huguenot prayers, insisting on my using them. I took the first opportunity to give them up to my gov-erness, Madame de Curton, whom God, out of his mercy to me, caused to continue steadfast in the Cathólic religion. She frequently took me to that pious, good man, the Cardinal de Tournon, who gave me good advice, and strengthened me in a perseverance in my religion, furnishing me with books and chaplets of beads in the room of those my brother Anjou took from me and burnt.

Many of my brother's most intimate friends had resolved on my ruin, and rated me severely upon my refusal to change, saying it proceeded from a childish obstinacy; that if I had the least understanding, and would listen, like other discreet persons, to the sermons that were preached, I should abjure my uncharitable bigotry; but I was, said they, as foolish as my governess. My brother Anjou added threats, and said the Queen my mother would give orders that I should be whipped. But this he said of his own head, for the Queen my mother did not, at that time, know of the errors he had embraced. As soon as it came to her knowledge, she took him to task, and severely reprimanded his governors, insisting upon their correcting him, and instructing him in the holy and ancient religion of his forefathers, from which she herself never swerved. When he used those menaces, as I have before related, I was a child seven or eight years old, and at that tender age would reply to him, "Well, get me whipped if you can; I will suffer whipping, and even death, rather than be damned."

I could furnish you with many other replies of the like kind, which gave proof of the early ripeness of my judgment and my courage; but I shall not trouble myself with such researches, choosing rather to begin these Memoirs at the time when I resided constantly with the Queen my mother.

Immediately after the Conference of Poissy, the civil wars commenced, and my brother Alençon and myself, on account of our youth, were sent to Amboise, whither all the ladies of the country repaired to us. With them came your aunt, Madame de Dampierre, who entered into a firm friendship with me, which was never interrupted until her death broke it off. There was likewise your cousin, the Duchesse de Rais, who had the good fortune to hear there of the death of her brute of a husband, killed at the battle of Dreux. The husband I mean was the first she had, named M. d'Annebaut, who was unworthy to have for a wife so accomplished and charming a woman as your cousin. She and I were not then so intimate friends as we have become since, and shall ever remain. The reason was that, though older than I, she was yet young, and young girls seldom take much notice of children, whereas your aunt was of an age when women admire their innocence and engaging simplicity.

I remained at Amboise until the Queen my mother was ready to set out on her grand progress, at which time she sent for me to come to her Court, which I did not quit afterwards.

Of this progress I will not undertake to give you a description, being still so young that, though the whole is within my recollection, yet the particular passages of it appear to me but as a dream, and are now lost. I leave this task to others, of riper years, as you were yourself. You can well remember the magnificence that was displayed everywhere, particularly at the baptism of my nephew, the Duc de Lorraine, at Bar-le-Duc; at the meeting of M. and Madame de Savoy, in the city of Lyons; the interview at Bayonne betwixt my sister, the Queen of Spain, the Queen my mother, and King Charles my brother. In your account of this interview you would not forget to make mention of the noble entertainment given by the Queen my mother, on an island, with the grand dances, and the form of the *salon*, which seemed appropriated by nature for such a purpose, it being a large meadow in the middle of the island, in the shape of an oval, surrounded on every side by tall spreading trees. In this meadow the Queen my mother had disposed a circle of niches, each of them large enough to contain a table of twelve covers. At one end a platform was raised, ascended by four steps formed of turf. Here their Majesties were seated at a table under a lofty canopy. The tables were all served by troops of shepherdesses dressed in cloth of gold and satin, after the fashion of the different provinces of France. These shepherdesses, during the passage of the superb boats from Bayonne to the island, were placed in separate bands, in a meadow on each side of the causeway, raised with turf; and whilst their Majesties and the company were passing through the great *salon*, they danced. On their passage by water, the barges were followed by other boats, having on board vocal and instrumental musicians, habited like Nereids, singing and playing the whole time. After landing, the shepherdesses I have mentioned before received the company in separate troops, with songs and dances, after the fashion and accompanied by the music of the provinces they represented,—the Poitevins playing on bagpipes; the Provençales on the viol and cymbal; the Burgundians and Champagners on the hautboy, bass viol, and tambourine; in like manner the Bretons and other provincialists. After the collation was served and the feast at an end, a large troop of musicians, habited like satyrs, was seen to come out of the opening of a rock, well lighted up, whilst nymphs were descending from the top in rich habits, who, as they came down, formed into a grand dance,—when, lo! fortune no longer favouring this brilliant festival, a sudden storm of rain came on, and all were glad to get off in the boats and make for town as fast as they could. The confusion in consequence of this precipitate retreat afforded as much matter to laugh at the next day as the splendour of the entertainment had excited admiration. In short, the festivity of this day was not forgotten, on one account or the other, amidst the variety of the like nature which succeeded it in the course of this progress.

## LETTER II

AT the time my magnanimous brother Charles reigned over France, and some few years after our return from the grand progress mentioned in my last letter, the Huguenots having renewed the war, a gentleman, despatched from my brother Anjou (afterwards Henri III. of France), came to Paris to inform the King and the Queen 'my mother that the Huguenot army was reduced to such an extremity that he hoped in a few days to force them to give him battle. He added his earnest wish for the honour of seeing them at Tours before that happened, so that, in case Fortune, envying him the glory he had already achieved at so early an age, should, on the so much looked-for day, after the good service he had done his religion and his King, crown the victory with his death, he might not have cause to regret leaving this world without the satisfaction of receiving their approbation of his conduct from their own mouths,—a satisfaction which would be more valuable, in his opinion, than the trophies he had gained by his two former victories.

I leave to your own imagination to suggest to you the impression which such a message from a dearly beloved son made on the mind of a mother who doted on all her children, and was always ready to sacrifice her own repose, nay, even her life, for their happiness.

She resolved immediately to set off and take the King with her. She had, besides myself, her usual small company of female attendants, together with Mesdames de Rais and de Sauves. She flew on the

wings of maternal affection, and reached Tours in
three days and a half.  A journey from Paris, made
with such precipitation, was not unattended with accidents and some inconveniences, of a nature to occasion much mirth and laughter.  The poor Cardinal de
Bourbon, who never quitted her, and whose temper of
mind, strength of body, and habits of life were ill
suited to encounter privations and hardships, suffered
greatly from this rapid journey.

We found my brother Anjou at Plessis-les-Tours,
with the principal officers of his army, who were the
flower of the princes and nobles of France.  In their
presence he delivered a harangue to the King, giving
a detail of his conduct in the execution of his charge,
beginning from the time he left the Court.  His discourse was framed with so much eloquence, and
spoken so gracefully, that it was admired by all present.  It appeared matter of astonishment that a youth
of sixteen should reason with all the gravity and powers of an orator of ripe years.  The comeliness of
his person, which at all times pleads powerfully in
favour of a speaker, was in him set off by the laurels
obtained in two victories.  In short, it was difficult to
say which most contributed to make him the admiration of all his hearers.

It is equally as impossible for me to describe in
words the feelings of my mother on this occasion, who
loved him above all her children, as it was for the
painter to represent on canvas the grief of Iphigenia's
father.  Such an overflow of joy would have been
discoverable in the looks and actions of any other
woman, but she had her passions so much under the
control of prudence and discretion that there was
nothing to be perceived in her countenance, or gathered from her words, of what she felt inwardly in
her mind.  She was, indeed, a perfect mistress of

herself, and regulated her discourse and her actions
by the rules of wisdom and sound policy, showing that
a person of discretion does upon all occasions only
what is proper to be done.  She did not amuse herself on this occasion with listening to the praises
which issued from every mouth, and sanction them
with her own approbation; but, selecting the chief
points in the speech relative to the future conduct of
the war, she laid them before the Princes and great
lords, to be deliberated upon, in order to settle a plan
of operations.

To arrange such a plan a delay of some days was
requisite.  During this interval, the Queen my mother
walking in the park with some of the Princes, my
brother Anjou begged me to take a turn or two with
him in a retired walk.  He then addressed me in the
following words: " Dear sister, the nearness of blood,
as well as our having been brought up together, naturally, as they ought, attach us to each other.  You
must already have discovered the partiality I have
had for you above my brothers, and I think that I
have perceived the same in you for me.  We have
been hitherto led to this by nature, without deriving
any other advantage from it than the sole pleasure of
conversing together.  So far might be well enough
for our childhood, but now we are no longer children.
You know the high situation in which, by the favour
of God and our good mother the Queen, I am here
placed.  You may be assured that, as you are the
person in the world whom I love and esteem the most,
you will always be a partaker of my advancement.
I know you are not wanting in wit and discretion,
and I am sensible you have it in your power to do
me service with the Queen our mother, and preserve
me in my present employments.  It is a great point
obtained for me, always to stand well in her favour.

I am fearful that my absence may be prejudicial to that purpose, and I must necessarily be at a distance from Court. Whilst I am away, the King my brother is with her, and has it in his power to insinuate himself into her good graces. This I fear, in the end, may be of disservice to me. The King my brother is growing older every day. He does not want for courage, and, though he now diverts himself with hunting, he may grow ambitious, and choose rather to chase men than beasts; in such a case I must resign to him my commission as his lieutenant. This would prove the greatest mortification that could happen to me, and I would even prefer death to it. Under such an apprehension I have considered of the means of prevention, and see none so feasible as having a confidential person about the Queen my mother, who shall always be ready to espouse and support my cause. I know no one so proper for that purpose as yourself, who will be, I doubt not, as attentive to my interest as I should be myself. You have wit, discretion, and fidelity, which are all that are wanting, provided you will be so kind as to undertake such a good office. In that case I shall have only to beg of you not to neglect attending her morning and evening, to be the first with her and the last to leave her. This will induce her to repose a confidence and open her mind to you. To make her the more ready to do this, I shall take every opportunity to commend your good sense and understanding, and to tell her that I shall take it kind in her to leave off treating you as a child, which, I shall say, will contribute to her own comfort and satisfaction. I am well convinced that she will listen to my advice. Do you speak to her with the same confidence as you do to me, and be assured that she will approve of it. It will conduce to your own happiness to obtain her favour. You may do yourself service

whilst you are labouring for my interest; and you may
rest satisfied that, after God, I shall think I owe all
the good fortune which may befall me to yourself."

This was entirely a new kind of language to me.
I had hitherto thought of nothing but amusements,
of dancing, hunting, and the like diversions; nay, I
had never yet discovered any inclination of setting
myself off to advantage by dress, and exciting an
admiration of my person and figure. I had no ambition of any kind, and had been so strictly brought
up under the Queen my mother that I scarcely durst
speak before her; and if she chanced to turn her eyes
towards me I trembled, for fear that I had done something to displease her. At the conclusion of my
brother's harangue, I was half inclined to reply to
him in the words of Moses, when he was spoken to
from the burning bush: " Who am I, that I should go
unto Pharaoh? Send, I pray thee, by the hand of him
whom thou wilt send."

However, his words inspired me with resolution
and powers I did not think myself possessed of before. I had naturally a degree of courage, and, as
soon as I recovered from my astonishment, I found
I was quite an altered person. His address pleased
me, and wrought in me a confidence in myself; and
I found I was become of more consequence than I
had ever conceived I had been. Accordingly, I replied to him thus: "Brother, if God grant me the
power of speaking to the Queen our mother as I have
the will to do, nothing can be wanting for your service, and you may expect to derive all the good you
hope from it, and from my solicitude and attention
for your interest. With respect to my undertaking
such a matter for you, you will soon perceive that
I shall sacrifice all the pleasures in this world to my
watchfulness for your service. You may perfectly

rely on me, as there is no one that honours or regards
you more than I do. Be well assured that I shall
act for you with the Queen my mother as zealously
as you would for yourself."

These sentiments were more strongly impressed
upon my mind than the words I made use of were
capable of conveying an idea of. This will appear
more fully in my following letters.

As soon as we were returned from walking, the
Queen my mother retired with me into her closet,
and addressed the following words to me: "Your
brother has been relating the conversation you have
had together; he considers you no longer as a child,
neither shall I. It will be a great comfort to me to
converse with you as I would with your brother. For
the future you will freely speak your mind, and have
no apprehensions of taking too great a liberty, for it
is what I wish." These words gave me a pleasure
then which I am now unable to express. I felt a
satisfaction and a joy which nothing before had ever
caused me to feel. I now considered the pastimes of
my childhood as vain amusements. I shunned the
society of my former companions of the same age. I
disliked dancing and hunting, which I thought beneath
my attention. I strictly complied with her agreeable
injunction, and never missed being with her at her
rising in the morning and going to rest at night.
She did me the honour, sometimes, to hold me in conversation for two and three hours at a time. God
was so gracious with me that I gave her great satisfaction; and she thought she could not sufficiently
praise me to those ladies who were about her. I
spoke of my brother's affairs to her, and he was constantly apprised by me of her sentiments and opinion;
so that he had every reason to suppose I was firmly
attached to his interest.

## LETTER III

I CONTINUED to pass my time with the Queen my mother, greatly to my satisfaction, until after the battle of Moncontour. By the same despatch that brought the news of this victory to the Court, my brother, who was ever desirous to be near the Queen my mother, wrote her word that he was about to lay siege to St. Jean d'Angely, and that it would be necessary that the King should be present whilst it was going on. She, more anxious to see him than he could be to have her near him, hastened to set out on the journey, taking me with her, and her customary train of attendants. I likewise experienced great joy upon the occasion, having no suspicion that any mischief awaited me. I was still young and without experience, and I thought the happiness I enjoyed was always to continue; but the malice of Fortune prepared for me at this interview a reverse that I little expected, after the fidelity with which I had discharged the trust my brother had reposed in me.

Soon after our last meeting, it seems, my brother Anjou had taken Le Guast to be near his person, who had ingratiated himself so far into his favour and confidence that he saw only with his eyes, and spoke but as he dictated. This evil-disposed man, whose whole life was one continued scene of wickedness, had perverted his mind and filled it with maxims of the most atrocious nature. He advised him to have no regard but for his own interest; neither to love nor put trust in any one; and not to promote the views or advan-

tage of either brother or sister. These and other
maxims of the like nature, drawn from the school of
Machiavelli, he was continually suggesting to him.
He had so frequently inculcated them that they were
strongly impressed on his mind, insomuch that, upon
our arrival, when, after the first compliments, my
mother began to open in my praise and express the
attachment I had discovered for him, this was his
reply, which he delivered with the utmost coldness:
" He was well pleased," he said, " to have succeeded
in the request he had made to me; but that prudence
directed us not to continue to make use of the same
expedients, for what was profitable at one time might
not be so at another." She asked him why he made
that observation. This question afforded the opportunity he wished for, of relating a story he had fabricated, purposely to ruin me with her.

He began with observing to her that I was grown
very handsome, and that M. de Guise wished to marry
me; that his uncles, too, were very desirous of such a
match; and, if I should entertain a like passion for
him, there would be danger of my discovering to him
all she said to me; that she well knew the ambition
of that house, and how ready they were, on all occasions, to circumvent ours. It would, therefore, be
proper that she should not, for the future, communicate any matter of State to me, but, by degrees,
withdraw her confidence.

I discovered the evil effects proceeding from this
pernicious advice on the very same evening. I remarked an unwillingness on her part to speak to me
before my brother; and, as soon as she entered into
discourse with him, she commanded me to go to bed.
This command she repeated two or three times. I
quitted her closet, and left them together in conversation; but, as soon as he was gone, I returned and en-

treated her to let me know if I had been so unhappy as to have done anything, through ignorance, which had given her offence. She was at first inclined to dissemble with me; but at length she said to me thus: " Daughter, your brother is prudent and cautious; you ought not to be displeased with him for what he does, and you must believe what I shall tell you is right and proper." She then related the conversation she had with my brother, as I have just written it; and she then ordered me never to speak to her in my brother's presence.

These words were like so many daggers plunged into my breast. In my disgrace, I experienced as much grief as I had before joy on being received into her favour and confidence. I did not omit to say everything to convince her of my entire ignorance of what my brother had told her. I said it was a matter I had never heard mentioned before; and that, had I known it, I should certainly have made her immediately acquainted with it. All I said was to no purpose; my brother's words had made the first impression; they were constantly present in her mind, and outweighed probability and truth. When I discovered this, I told her that I felt less uneasiness at being deprived of my happiness than I did joy when I had acquired it; for my brother had taken it from me, as he had given it. He had given it without reason; he had taken it away without cause. He had praised me for discretion and prudence when I did not merit it, and he suspected my fidelity on grounds wholly imaginary and fictitious. I concluded with assuring her that I should never forget my brother's behaviour on this occasion.

Hereupon she flew into a passion and commanded me not to make the least show of resentment at his behaviour. From that hour she gradually withdrew her favour from me. Her son became the god of her idolatry, at the shrine of whose will she sacrificed everything.

The grief which I inwardly felt was very great and overpowered all my faculties, until it wrought so far on my constitution as to contribute to my receiving the infection which then prevailed in the army. A few days after I fell sick of a raging fever, attended with purple spots, a malady which carried off numbers, and, amongst the rest, the two principal physicians belonging to the King and Queen, Chappelain and Castelan. Indeed, few got over the disorder after being attacked with it.

In this extremity the Queen my mother, who partly guessed the cause of my illness, omitted nothing that might serve to remove it; and, without fear of consequences, visited me frequently. Her goodness contributed much to my recovery; but my brother's hypocrisy was sufficient to destroy all the benefit I received from her attention, after having been guilty of so treacherous a proceeding. After he had proved so ungrateful to me, he came and sat at the foot of my bed from morning to night, and appeared as anxiously attentive as if we had been the most perfect friends. My mouth was shut up by the command I had received from the Queen our mother, so that I only answered his dissembled concern with sighs, like Burrus in the presence of Nero, when he was dying by the poison administered by the hands of that tyrant. The sighs, however, which I vented in my brother's presence, might convince him that I attributed my sickness rather to his ill offices than to the prevailing contagion.

God had mercy on me, and supported me through this dangerous illness. After I had kept my bed a fortnight, the army changed its quarters, and I was conveyed away with it in a litter. At the end of each day's march, I found King Charles at the door of my quarters, ready, with the rest of the good gentlemen belonging to the Court, to carry my litter up to my bedside. In this manner I came to Angers from St. Jean d'Angely, sick in body, but more sick in mind. Here, to my misfortune, M. de Guise and his uncles had arrived before me. This was a circumstance which gave my good brother great pleasure, as it afforded a colourable appearance to his story. I soon discovered the advantage my brother would make of it to increase my already too great mortification; for he came daily to see me, and as constantly brought M. de Guise into my chamber with him. He pretended the sincerest regard for De Guise, and, to make him believe it, would take frequent opportunities of embracing him, crying out at the same time, "Would to God you were my brother!" This he often put in practice before me, which M. de Guise seemed not to comprehend; but I, who knew his malicious designs, lost all patience, yet did not dare to reproach him with his hypocrisy.

As soon as I was recovered, a treaty was set on foot for a marriage betwixt the King of Portugal and me, an ambassador having been sent for that purpose. The Queen my mother commanded me to prepare to give the ambassador an audience; which I did accordingly. My brother had made her believe that I was averse to this marriage; accordingly, she took me to task upon it, and questioned me on the subject, expecting she should find some cause to be angry with me. I told her my will had always been guided by her own, and that whatever she thought right for me to do, I should do it. She answered me, angrily, according as she had been wrought upon, that I did not speak the sentiments of my heart, for she well knew that the Cardinal de Lorraine had persuaded me. into a promise of having his nephew. I begged her to forward this match with the King of Portugal, and I would convince her of my obedience to her commands. Every day some new matter was reported to incense her against me. All these were machinations worked up by the mind of Le Guast. In short, I was constantly receiving some fresh mortification, so that I hardly passed a day in quiet. On one side, the King of Spain was using his utmost endeavours to break off the match with Portugal, and M. de Guise, continuing at Court, furnished grounds for persecuting me on the other. Still, not a single person of the Guises ever mentioned a word to me on the subject; and it was well known that, for more than a twelvemonth, M. de Guise had been paying his addresses to the Princesse de Porcian; but the slow progress made in bringing this match to a conclusion was said to be owing to his designs upon me.

As soon as I made this discovery I resolved to write to my sister, Madame de Lorraine, who had a great influence in the House of Porcian, begging her to use her endeavours to withdraw M. de Guise from Court, and make him conclude his match with the Princess, laying open to her the plot which had been concerted to ruin the Guises and me. She readily saw through it, came immediately to Court, and concluded the match, which delivered me from the aspersions cast on my character, and convinced the Queen my mother that what I had told her was the real truth. This at the same time stopped the mouths of my enemies and gave me some repose.

At length the King of Spain, unwilling that the King of Portugal should marry out of his family, broke off the treaty which had been entered upon for my marriage with him.

# LETTER IV

SOME short time after this a marriage was projected betwixt the Prince of Navarre, now our renowned King Henri IV., and me.

The Queen my mother, as she sat at table, discoursed for a long time upon the subject with M. de Meru, the House of Montmorency having first proposed the match. After the Queen had risen from table, he told me she had commanded him to mention it to me. I replied that it was quite unnecessary, as I had no will but her own; however, I should wish she would be pleased to remember that I was a Catholic, and that I should dislike to marry any one of a contrary persuasion.

Soon after this the Queen sent for me to attend her in her closet. She there informed me that the Montmorencys had proposed this match to her, and that she was desirous to learn my sentiments upon it. I answered that my choice was governed by her pleasure, and that I only begged her not to forget that I was a good Catholic.

This treaty was in negotiation for some time after this conversation, and was not finally settled until the arrival of the Queen of Navarre, his mother, at Court, where she died soon after.

Whilst the Queen of Navarre lay on her death-bed, a circumstance happened of so whimsical a nature that, though not of consequence to merit a place in the history, it may very well deserve to be related by me to you. Madame de Nevers, whose oddities you well know, attended the Cardinal de Bourbon,

A—3                    33

Madame de Guise, the Princesse de Condé, her sisters, and myself to the late Queen of Navarre's apartments, whither we all went to pay those last duties which her rank and our nearness of blood demanded of us. We found the Queen in bed with her curtains undrawn, the chamber not disposed with the pomp and ceremonies of our religion, but after the simple manner of the Huguenots; that is to say, there were no priests, no cross, nor any holy water. We kept ourselves at some distance from the bed, but Madame de Nevers, whom you know the Queen hated more than any woman besides, and which she had shown both in speech and by actions,—Madame de Nevers, I say, approached the bedside, and, to the great astonishment of all present, who well knew the enmity subsisting betwixt them, took the Queen's hand, with many low curtseys, and kissed it; after which, making another curtsey to the very ground, she retired and rejoined us.

A few months after the Queen's death, the Prince of Navarre, or rather, as he was then styled, the King, came to Paris in deep mourning, attended by eight hundred gentlemen, all in mourning habits. He was received with every honour by King Charles and the whole Court, and, in a few days after his arrival, our marriage was solemnised with all possible magnificence; the King of Navarre and his retinue putting off their mourning and dressing themselves in the most costly manner. The whole Court, too, was richly attired; all which you can better conceive than I am able to express. For my own part, I was set out in a most royal manner; I wore a crown on my head with the *coët*, or regal close gown of ermine, and I blazed in diamonds. My blue-coloured robe had a train to it of four ells in length, which was supported by three princesses. A platform had been raised, some height from the ground, which led from the Bishop's palace to the Church of Notre-Dame. It was hung with cloth of gold; and below it stood the people in throngs to view the procession, stifling with heat.7 We were received at the church door by the Cardinal de Bourbon, who officiated for that day, and pronounced the nuptial benediction. After this we proceeded on the same platform to the tribune which separates the nave from the choir, where was a double staircase, one leading into the choir, the other through the nave to the church door. The King of Navarre passed by the latter and went out of church.

But fortune, which is ever changing, did not fail soon to disturb the felicity of this union. This was occasioned by the wound received by the Admiral, which had wrought the Huguenots up to a degree of desperation. The Queen my mother was reproached on that account in such terms by the elder Pardaillan and some other principal Huguenots, that she began to apprehend some evil design. M. de Guise and my brother the King of Poland, since Henri III. of France, gave it as their advice to be beforehand with the Huguenots. King Charles was of a contrary opinion. He had a great esteem for M. de La Roche-foucauld, Teligny, La Noüe, and some other leading men of the same religion; and, as I have since heard him say, it was with the greatest difficulty he could be prevailed upon to give his consent, and not before he had been made to understand that his own life and the safety of his kingdom depended upon it.

The King having learned that Maurevel had made an attempt upon the Admiral's life, by firing a pistol at him through a window,—in which attempt he failed, having wounded the Admiral only in the shoulder,—and supposing that Maurevel had done this at the instance of M. de Guise, to revenge the death of

his father, whom the Admiral had caused to be killed
in the same manner by Poltrot, he was so much incensed against M. de Guise that he declared with an
oath that he would make an example of him; and,
indeed, the King would have put M. de Guise under
an arrest, if he had not kept out of his sight the
whole day. The Queen my mother used every argument to convince King Charles that what had been
done was for the good of the State; and this because, as I observed before, the King had so great a
regard for the Admiral, La Noue, and Teligny, on
account of their bravery, being himself a prince of a
gallant and noble spirit, and esteeming others in
whom he found a similar disposition. Moreover,
these designing men had insinuated themselves into
the King's favour by proposing an expedition to Flanders, with a view of extending his dominions and ag-
grandising his power, propositions which they well
knew would secure to themselves an influence over his
royal and generous mind.

Upon this occasion, the Queen my mother represented to the King that the attempt of M. de Guise
upon the Admiral's life was excusable in a son who,
being denied justice, had no other means of avenging
his father's death. Moreover, the Admiral, she said,
had deprived her by assassination, during his minority
and her regency, of a faithful servant in the person of
Charri, commander of the King's body-guard, which
rendered him deserving of the like treatment.

Notwithstanding that the Queen my mother spoke
thus to the King, discovering by her expressions and
in her looks all the grief which she inwardly felt on
the recollection of the loss of persons who had been
useful to her; yet, so much was King Charles inclined
to save those who, as he thought, would one day be
serviceable to him, that he still persisted in his deter-

mination to punish M. de Guise, for whom he ordered
strict search to be made.

At length Pardaillan, disclosing by his menaces,
during the supper of the Queen my mother, the evil
intentions of the Huguenots, she plainly perceived that
things were brought to so near a crisis, that, unless
steps were taken that very night to prevent it, the
King and herself were in danger of being assassinated.
She, therefore, came to the resolution of declaring to
King Charles his real situation. For this purpose she
thought of the Maréchal de Rais as the most proper
person to break the matter to the King, the Marshal
being greatly in his favour and confidence.

Accordingly, the Marshal went to the King in his
closet, between the hours of nine and ten, and told
him he was come as a faithful servant to discharge
his duty, and lay before him the danger in which he
stood, if he persisted in his resolution of punishing
M. de Guise, as he ought now to be informed that the
attempt made upon the Admiral's life was not set on
foot by him alone, but that his (the King's) brother
the King of Poland, and the Queen his mother, had
their shares in it; that he must be sensible how much
the Queen lamented Charri's assassination, for which
she had great reason, having very few servants about
her upon whom she could rely, and as it happened
during the King's minority,—at the time, moreover,
when France was divided between the Catholics and
the Huguenots, M. de Guise being at the head of the
former, and the Prince de Condé of the latter, both
alike striving to deprive him of his crown; that
through Providence, both his crown and kingdom had
been preserved by the prudence and good conduct of
the Queen Regent, who in this extremity found herself
powerfully aided by the said Charri, for which reason
she had vowed to avenge his death; that, as to the

Admiral, he must be ever considered as dangerous to the State, and whatever show he might make of affection for his Majesty's person, and zeal for his service in Flanders, they must be considered as mere pretences, which he used to cover his real design of reducing the kingdom to a state of confusion.

The Marshal concluded with observing that the original intention had been to make away with the Admiral only, as the most obnoxious man in the kingdom; but Maurevel having been so unfortunate as to fail in his attempt, and the Huguenots becoming desperate enough to resolve to take up arms, with design to attack, not only M. de Guise, but the Queen his mother, and his brother the King of Poland, supposing them, as well as his Majesty, to have commanded Maurevel to make his attempt, he saw nothing but cause of alarm for his Majesty's safety,—as well on the part of the Catholics, if he persisted in his resolution to punish M. de Guise, as of the Huguenots, for the reasons which he had just laid before him.

# LETTER V

KING CHARLES, a prince of great prudence, always paying a particular deference to his mother, and being much attached to the Catholic religion, now convinced of the intentions of the Huguenots, adopted a sudden resolution of following his mother's counsel, and putting himself under the safeguard of the Catholics. It was not, however, without extreme regret that he found he had it not in his power to save Teligny, La Nouë, and M. de La Rochefoucauld.

He went to the apartments of the Queen his mother, and sending for M. de Guise and all the Princes and Catholic officers, the "Massacre of St. Bartholomew" was that night resolved upon.

Immediately every hand was at work; chains were drawn across the streets, the alarm-bells were sounded, and every man repaired to his post, according to the orders he had received, whether it was to attack the Admiral's quarters, or those of the other Huguenots. M. de Guise hastened to the Admiral's, and Besme, a gentleman in the service of the former, a German by birth, forced into his chamber, and having slain him with a dagger, threw his body out of a window to his master.

I was perfectly ignorant of what was going forward. I observed every one to be in motion: the Huguenots, driven to despair by the attack upon the Admiral's life, and the Guises, fearing they should not have justice done them, whispering all they met in the ear.

The Huguenots were suspicious of me because I
was a Catholic, and the Catholics because I was married to the King of Navarre, who was a Huguenot.
This being the case, no one spoke a syllable of the
matter to me.

At night, when I went into the bedchamber of the
Queen my mother, I placed myself on a coffer, next
my sister Lorraine, who, I could not but remark,
appeared greatly cast down. The Queen my mother
was in conversation with some one, but, as soon as
she espied me, she bade me go to bed. As I was
taking leave, my sister seized me by the hand and
stopped me, at the same time shedding a flood of
tears: "For the love of God," cried she, "do not
stir out of this chamber!" I was greatly alarmed
at this exclamation; perceiving which, the Queen my
mother called my sister to her, and chid her very
severely. My sister replied it was sending me away
to be sacrificed; for, if any discovery should be made,
I should be the first victim of their revenge. The
Queen my mother made answer that, if it pleased
God, I should receive no hurt, but it was necessary
I should go, to prevent the suspicion that might arise
from my staying.

I perceived there was something on foot which I
was not to know, but what it was I could not make
out from anything they said.

The Queen again bade me go to bed in a peremp-
tory tone. My sister wished me a good night, her
tears flowing apace, but she did not dare to say a
word more; and I left the bedchamber more dead
than alive.

As soon as I reached my own closet, I threw
myself upon my knees and prayed to God to take
me into his protection and save me; but from whom
or what, I was ignorant. Hereupon the King my

husband, who was already in bed, sent for me. I went to him, and found the bed surrounded by thirty or forty Huguenots, who were entirely unknown to me; for I had been then but a very short time married. Their whole discourse, during the night, was upon what had happened to the Admiral, and they all came to a resolution of the next day demanding justice of the King against M. de Guise; and, if it was refused, to take it themselves.

For my part, I was unable to sleep a wink the whole night, for thinking of my sister's tears and distress, which had greatly alarmed me, although I had not the least knowledge of the real cause. As soon as day broke, the King my husband said he would rise and play at tennis until King Charles was risen, when he would go to him immediately and demand justice. He left the bedchamber, and all his gentlemen followed.

As soon as I beheld it was broad day, I apprehended all the danger my sister had spoken of was over; and being inclined to sleep, I bade my nurse make the door fast, and I applied myself to take some repose. In about an hour I was awakened by a violent noise at the door, made with both hands and feet, and a voice calling out, "Navarre! Navarre!" My nurse, supposing the King my husband to be at the door, hastened to open it, when a gentleman, named M. de Teian, ran in, and threw himself immediately upon my bed. He had received a wound in his arm from a sword, and another by a pike, and was then pursued by four archers, who followed him into the bedchamber. Perceiving these last, I jumped out of bed, and the poor gentleman after me, holding me fast by the waist. I did not then know him; neither was I sure that he came to do me no harm, or whether the archers were in pursuit of him or me.

In this situation I screamed aloud, and he cried out
likewise, for our fright was mutual.   At length, by
God's providence, M. de Nançay, captain of the guard,
came into the bedchamber, and, seeing me thus surrounded, though he could not help pitying me, he was
scarcely able to refrain from laughter.   However, he
reprimanded the archers very severely for their indiscretion, and drove them out of the chamber.   At my
request he granted the poor gentleman his life, and I
had him put to bed in my closet, caused his wounds to
be dressed, and did not suffer him to quit my apartment until he was perfectly cured.   I changed my
shift, because it was stained with the blood of this
man, and, whilst I was doing so, De Nançay gave
me an account of the transactions of the foregoing
night, assuring me that the King my husband was
safe, and actually at that moment in the King's bedchamber.   He made me muffle myself up in a cloak,
and conducted me to the apartment of my sister,
Madame de Lorraine, whither I arrived more than
half dead.   As we passed through the antechamber,
all the doors of which were wide open, a gentleman
of the name of Bourse, pursued by archers, was run
through the body with a pike, and fell dead at my
feet.   As if I had been killed by the same stroke, I
fell, and was caught by M. de Nançay before I
reached the ground.   As soon as I recovered from this
fainting-fit, I went into my sister's bedchamber, and
was immediately followed by M. de Mioflano, first
gentleman to the King my husband, and Armagnac,
his first *valet de chambre,* who both came to beg me
to save their lives.   I went and threw myself on my
knees before the King and the Queen my mother, and
obtained the lives of both of them.

Five or six days afterwards, those who were engaged in this plot, considering that it was incomplete

whilst the King my husband and the Prince de Condé remained alive, as their design was not only to dispose of the Huguenots, but of the Princes of the blood likewise; and knowing that no attempt could be made on my husband whilst I continued to be his wife, devised a scheme which they suggested to the Queen my mother for divorcing me from him. Accordingly, one holiday, when I waited upon her to chapel, she charged me to declare to her, upon my oath, whether I believed my husband to be like other men. " Because," said she, " if he is not, I can easily procure you a divorce from him." I begged her to believe that I was not sufficiently competent to answer such a question, and could only reply, as the Roman lady did to her husband, when he chid her for not informing him of his stinking breath, that, never having approached any other man near enough to know a difference, she thought all men had been alike in that respect. " But," said I, " Madame, since you have put the question to me, I can only declare I am content to remain as I am;" and this I said because I suspected the design of separating me from my husband was in order to work some mischief against him.

## LETTER VI

WE accompanied the King of Poland as far
as Beaumont. For some months before he
quitted France, he had used every endeavour to efface from my mind the ill offices he had so
ungratefully done me. He solicited to obtain the same
place in my esteem which he held during our infancy; and, on taking leave of me, made me confirm it by oaths and promises. His departure from
France, and King Charles's sickness, which happened
just about the same time, excited the spirit of the two
factions into which the kingdom was divided, to form
a variety of plots. The Huguenots, on the death of
the Admiral, had obtained from the King my husband, and my brother Alençon, a written obligation
to avenge it. Before St. Bartholomew's Day, they
had gained my brother over to their party, by the
hope of securing Flanders for him. They now persuaded my husband and him to leave the King and
Queen on their return, and pass into Champagne,
there to join some troops which were in waiting to
receive them.

M. de Miossans, a Catholic gentleman, having received an intimation of this design, considered it so
prejudicial to the interests of the King his master,
that he communicated it to me with the intention of
frustrating a plot of so much danger to themselves
and to the State. I went immediately to the King
and the Queen my mother, and informed them that
I had a matter of the utmost importance to lay before

them; but that I could not declare it unless they would be pleased to promise me that no harm should ensue from it to such as I should name to them, and that they would put a stop to what was going forward without publishing their knowledge of it. Having obtained my request, I told them that my brother Alençon and the King my husband had an intention, on the very next day, of joining some Huguenot troops, which expected them, in order to fulfil the engagement they had made upon the Admiral's death; and for this their intention, I begged they might be excused, and that they might be prevented from going away without any discovery being made that their designs had been found out. All this was granted me, and measures were so prudently taken to stay them, that they had not the least suspicion that their intended evasion was known. Soon after, we arrived at St. Germain, where we stayed some time, on account of the King's indisposition. All this while my brother Alençon used every means he could devise to ingratiate himself with me, until at last I promised him my friendship, as I had before done to my brother the King of Poland. As he had been brought up at a distance from Court, we had hitherto known very little of each other, and kept ourselves at a distance. Now that he had made the first advances, in so respectful and affectionate a manner, I resolved to receive him into a firm friendship, and to interest myself in whatever concerned him, without prejudice, however, to the interests of my good brother King Charles, whom I loved more than any one besides, and who continued to entertain a great regard for me, of which he gave me proofs as long as he lived.

Meanwhile King Charles was daily growing worse, and the Huguenots constantly forming new plots.

They were very desirous to get my brother the Duc d'Alençon and the King my husband away from Court. I got intelligence, from time to time, of their designs; and, providentially, the Queen my mother defeated their intentions when a day had been fixed on for the arrival of the Huguenot troops at St. Germain. To avoid this visit, we set off the night before for Paris, two hours after midnight, putting King Charles in a litter, and the Queen my mother taking my brother and the King my husband with her in her own carriage.

They did not experience on this occasion such mild treatment as they had hitherto done, for the King going to the Wood of Vincennes, they were not permitted to set foot out of the palace. This misunderstanding was so far from being mitigated by time, that the mistrust and discontent were continually increasing, owing to the insinuations and bad advice offered to the King by those who wished the ruin and downfall of our house. To such a height had these jealousies risen that the Maréchaux de Montmorency and de Cossé were put under a close arrest, and La Mole and the Comte de Donas executed. Matters were now arrived at such a pitch that commissioners were appointed from the Court of Parliament to hear and determine upon the case of my brother and the King my husband.

My husband, having no counsellor to assist him, desired me to draw up his defence in such a manner that he might not implicate any person, and, at the same time, clear my brother and himself from any criminality of conduct. With God's help I accomplished this task to his great satisfaction, and to the surprise of the commissioners, who did not expect to find them so well prepared to justify themselves.

As it was apprehended, after the death of La Mole

and the Comte de Donas, that their lives were likewise in danger, I had resolved to save them at the hazard of my own ruin with the King, whose favour I entirely enjoyed at that time. I was suffered to pass to and from them in my coach, with my women, who were not even required by the guard to unmask, nor was my coach ever searched. This being the case, I had intended to convey away one of them disguised in a female habit. But the difficulty lay in settling betwixt themselves which should remain behind in prison, they being closely watched by their guards, and the escape of one bringing the other's life into hazard. Thus they could never agree upon the point, each of them wishing to be the person I should deliver from confinement.

But Providence put a period to their imprisonment by a means which proved very unfortunate for me. This was no other than the death of King Charles, who was the only stay and support of my life,—a brother from whose hands I never received anything but good; who, during the persecution I underwent at Angers, through my brother Anjou, assisted me with all his advice and credit. In a word, when I lost King Charles, I lost everything.

## LETTER VII

AFTER this fatal event, which was as unfortunate for France as for me, we went to Lyons to give the meeting to the King of Poland, now Henri III. of France. The new King was as much governed by Le Guast as ever, and had left this intriguing, mischievous man behind in France to keep his party together. Through this man's insinuations he had conceived the most confirmed jealousy of my brother Alençon. He suspected that I was the bond that connected the King my husband and my brother, and that, to dissolve their union, it would be necessary to create a coolness between me and my husband, and to work up a quarrel of rivalship betwixt them both by means of Madame de Sauves, whom they both visited. This abominable plot, which proved the source of so much disquietude and unhappiness, as well to my brother as myself, was as artfully conducted as it was wickedly designed.

Many have held that God has great personages more immediately under his protection, and that minds of superior excellence have bestowed on them a good genius, or secret intelligencer, to apprise them of good, or warn them against evil. Of this number I might reckon the Queen my mother, who has had frequent intimations of the kind; particularly the very night before the tournament which proved so fatal to the King my father, she dreamed that she saw him wounded in the eye, as it really happened; upon which she awoke, and begged him not to run a

48

course that day, but content himself with looking on.
Fate prevented the nation from enjoying so much
happiness as it would have done had he followed her
advice. Whenever she lost a child, she beheld a bright
flame shining before her, and would immediately cry
out, "God save my children!" well knowing it was
the harbinger of the death of some one of them, which
melancholy news was sure to be confirmed very shortly
after. During her very dangerous illness at Metz,
where she caught a pestilential fever, either from the
coal fires, or by visiting some of the nunneries which
had been infected, and from which she was restored to
health and to the kingdom through the great skill
and experience of that modern Æsculapius, M. de
Castillan her physician—I say, during that illness, her
bed being surrounded by my brother King Charles,
my brother and sister Lorraine, several members of
the Council, besides many ladies and princesses, not
choosing to quit her, though without hopes of her
life, she was heard to cry out, as if she saw the
battle of Jarnac: "There! see how they flee! My
son, follow them to victory! Ah, my son falls! O
my God, save him! See there! the Prince de Condé
is dead!" All who were present looked upon these
words as proceeding from her delirium, as she knew
that my brother Anjou was on the point of giving
battle, and thought no more of it. On the night
following, M. de Losses brought the news of the battle; and, it being supposed that she would be pleased
to hear of it, she was awakened, at which she appeared to be angry, saying: "Did I not know it
yesterday?" It was then that those about her
recollected what I have now related, and concluded
that it was no delirium, but one of those revelations
made by God to great and illustrious persons. Ancient
history furnishes many examples of the like kind

amongst the pagans, as the apparition of Brutus and many others, which I shall not mention, it not being my intention to illustrate these Memoirs with such narratives, but only to relate the truth, and that with as much expedition as I am able, that you may be the sooner in possession of my story.

I am far from supposing that I am worthy of these divine admonitions; nevertheless, I should accuse myself of ingratitude towards my God for the benefits I have received, which I esteem myself obliged to acknowledge whilst I live; and I further believe myself bound to bear testimony of his goodness and power, and the mercies he hath shown me, so that I can declare no extraordinary accident ever befell me, whether fortunate or otherwise, but I received some warning of it, either by dream or in some other way, so that I may say with the poet—

> "De mon bien, ou mon mal,
> Mon esprit m'est oracle."
>
> (Whate'er of good or ill befell,
> My mind was oracle to tell.)

And of this I had a convincing proof on the arrival of the King of Poland, when the Queen my mother went to meet him. Amidst the embraces and compliments of welcome in that warm season, crowded as we were together and stifling with heat, I found a universal shivering come over me, which was plainly perceived by those near me. It was with difficulty I could conceal what I felt when the King, having saluted the Queen my mother, came forward to salute me. This secret intimation of what was to happen thereafter made a strong impression on my mind at the moment, and I thought of it shortly after, when I discovered that the King had conceived a hatred of me through the malicious suggestions of Le Guast, who had made him believe, since the King's death, that I espoused my brother Alençon's party during his absence, and cemented a friendship betwixt the King my husband and him.

## LETTER VIII

A N opportunity was diligently sought by my enemies to effect their design of bringing about a
misunderstanding betwixt my brother Alençon,
the King my husband, and me, by creating a jealousy
of me in my husband, and in my brother and husband, on account of their mutual love for Madame de
Sauves.

One afternoon, the Queen my mother having retired
to her closet to finish some despatches which were
likely to detain her there for some time, Madame de
Nevers, your kinswoman, Madame de Rais, another
of your relations, Bourdeille, and Surgères asked me
whether I would not wish to see a little of the city.
Whereupon Mademoiselle de Montigny, the niece of
Madame Usez, observing to us that the Abbey of
St. Pierre was a beautiful convent, we all resolved
to visit it. She then begged to go with us, as she
said she had an aunt in that convent, and as it was
not easy to gain admission into it, except in the company of persons of distinction. Accordingly, she went
with us; and there being six of us, the carriage was
crowded. Over and above those I have mentioned,
there was Madame de Curton, the lady of my bedchamber, who always attended me. Liancourt, first
esquire to the King, and Camille placed themselves
on the steps of Torigni's carriage, supporting themselves as well as they were able, making themselves
merry on the occasion, and saying they would go and
see the handsome nuns, too. I look upon it as ordered
by Divine Providence that I should have Mademoiselle

de Montigny with me, who was not well acquainted
with any lady of the company, and that the two
gentlemen just mentioned, who were in the confidence
of King Henri, should likewise be of the party, as
they were able to clear me of the calumny intended
to be fixed upon me.

Whilst we were viewing the convent, my carriage
waited for us in the square. In the square many gentlemen belonging to the Court had their lodgings.
My carriage was easily to be distinguished, as it was
gilt and lined with yellow velvet trimmed with silver.
We had not come out of the convent when the King
passed through the square on his way to see Quelus,
who was then sick. He had with him the King my
husband, D'O——, and the fat fellow Ruffé.

The King, observing no one in my carriage, turned
to my husband and said: " There is your wife's coach,
and that is the house where Bidé lodges. Bidé is
sick, and I will engage my word she is gone upon a
visit to him. Go," said he to Ruffé, " and see whether
she is not there." In saying this, the King addressed
himself to a proper tool for his malicious purpose, for
this fellow Ruffé was entirely devoted to Le Guast.
I need not tell you he did not find me there; however, knowing the King's intention, he, to favour it,
said loud enough for the King my husband to hear
him: " The birds have been there, but they are now
flown." This furnished sufficient matter for conversation until they reached home.

Upon this occasion, the King my husband displayed
all the good sense and generosity of temper for which
he is remarkable. He saw through the design, and
he despised the maliciousness of it. The King my
brother was anxious to see the Queen my mother
before me, to whom he imparted the pretended discovery, and she, whether to please a son on whom she

doted, or whether she really gave credit to the story, had related it to some ladies with much seeming anger.

Soon afterwards I returned with the ladies who had accompanied me to St. Pierre's, entirely ignorant of what had happened. I found the King my husband in our apartments, who began to laugh on seeing me, and said: "Go immediately to the Queen your mother, but I promise you you will not return very well pleased." I asked him the reason, and what had happened. He answered: "I shall tell you nothing; but be assured of this, that I do not give the least credit to the story, which I plainly perceive to be fabricated in order to stir up a difference betwixt us two, and break off the friendly intercourse between your brother and me."

Finding I could get no further information on the subject from him, I went to the apartment of the Queen my mother. I met M. de Guise in the antechamber, who was not displeased at the prospect of a dissension in our family, hoping that he might make some advantage of it. He addressed me in these words: "I waited here expecting to see you, in order to inform you that some ill office has been done you with the Queen." He then told me the story he had learned of D'O——, who, being intimate with your kinswoman, had informed M. de Guise of it, that he might apprise us.

I went into the Queen's bedchamber, but did not find my mother there. However, I saw Madame de Nemours, the rest of the princesses, and other ladies, who all exclaimed on seeing me: "Good God! the Queen your mother is in such a rage; we would advise you, for the present, to keep out of her sight."

"Yes," said I, "so I would, had I been guilty of

what the King has reported; but I assure you all I
am entirely innocent, and must therefore speak with
her and clear myself."

I then went into her closet, which was separated
from the bedchamber by a slight partition only, so
that our whole conversation could be distinctly heard.
She no sooner set eyes upon me than she flew into a
great passion, and said everything that the fury of
her resentment suggested. I related to her the whole
truth, and begged to refer her to the company which
attended me, to the number of ten or twelve persons,
desiring her not to rely on the testimony of those more
immediately about me, but examine Mademoiselle
Montigny, who did not belong to me, and Liancourt
and Camille, who were the King's servants.

She would not hear a word I had to offer, but continued to rate me in a furious manner; whether it
was through fear, or affection for her son, or whether
she believed the story in earnest, I know not. When
I observed to her that I understood the King had
done me this ill office in her opinion, her anger
was redoubled, and she endeavoured to make me believe that she had been informed of the circumstance
by one of her own *valets de chambre,* who had himself seen me at the place. Perceiving that I gave no
credit to this account of the matter, she became more
and more incensed against me.

All that was said was perfectly heard by those in
the next room. At length I left her closet, much
chagrined; and returning to my own apartments, I
found the King my husband there, who said to me:
" Well, was it not as I told you? "

He, seeing me under great concern, desired me not
to grieve about it, adding that " Liancourt and Camille
would attend the King that night in his bedchamber,
and relate the affair as it really was; and to-morrow,"

continued he, "the Queen your mother will receive
you in a very different manner."

"But, monsieur," I replied, "I have received too
gross an affront in public to forgive those who were
the occasion of it; but that is nothing when compared
with the malicious intention of causing so heavy a misfortune to befall me as to create a variance betwixt
you and me."

"But," said he, "God be thanked, they have failed
in it."

"For that," answered I, "I am the more beholden
to God and your amiable disposition. However," continued I, "we may derive this good from it, that it
ought to be a warning to us to put ourselves upon our
guard against the King's stratagems to bring about
a disunion betwixt you and my brother, by causing a
rupture betwixt you and me."

Whilst I was saying this, my brother entered the
apartment, and I made them renew their protestations
of friendship. But what oaths or promises can prevail against love! This will appear more fully in the
sequel of my story.

An Italian banker, who had concerns with my
brother, came to him the next morning, and invited
him, the King my husband, myself, the princesses,
and other ladies, to partake of an entertainment in
a garden belonging to him. Having made it a constant rule, before and after I married, as long as I
remained in the Court of the Queen my mother, to
go to no place without her permission, I waited on
her, at her return from mass, and asked leave to be
present at this banquet. She refused to give any leave,
and said she did not care where I went. I leave you
to judge, who know my temper, whether I was not
greatly mortified at this rebuff.

Whilst we were enjoying this entertainment, the

King, having spoken with Liancourt, Camille, and Mademoiselle Montigny, was apprised of the mistake which the malice or misapprehension of Ruffé had led him into. Accordingly, he went to the Queen my mother and related the whole truth, entreating her to remove any ill impressions that might remain with me, as he perceived that I was not deficient in point of understanding, and feared that I might be induced to engage in some plan of revenge.

When I returned from the banquet before mentioned, I found that what the King my husband had foretold was come to pass; for the Queen my mother sent for me into her back closet, which was adjoining the King's, and told me that she was now acquainted with the truth, and found I had not deceived her with a false story. She had discovered, she said, that there was not the least foundation for the report her *valet de chambre* had made, and should dismiss him from her service as a bad man. As she perceived by my looks that I saw through this disguise, she said everything she could think of to persuade me to a belief that the King had not mentioned it to her. She continued her arguments, and I still appeared incredulous. At length the King entered the closet, and made many apologies, declaring he had been imposed on, and assuring me of his most cordial friendship and esteem; and thus matters were set to rights again.

# LETTER IX

AFTER staying some time at Lyons, we went to Avignon. Le Guast, not daring to hazard any fresh imposture, and finding that my conduct afforded no ground for jealousy on the part of my husband, plainly perceived that he could not, by that means, bring about a misunderstanding betwixt my brother and the King my husband. He therefore resolved to try what he could effect through Madame de Sauves. In order to do this, he obtained such an influence over her that she acted entirely as he directed; insomuch that, by his artful instructions, the passion which these young men had conceived, hitherto wavering and cold, as is generally the case at their time of life, became of a sudden so violent that ambition and every obligation of duty were at once absorbed by their attentions to this woman.

This occasioned such a jealousy betwixt them that, though her favours were divided with M. de Guise, Le Guast, De Souvray, and others, any one of whom she preferred to the brothers-in-law, such was the infatuation of these last, that each considered the other as his only rival.

To carry on De Guast's sinister designs, this woman persuaded the King my husband that I was jealous of her, and on that account it was that I joined with my brother. As we are ready to give ear and credit to those we love, he believed all she said. From this time he became distant and reserved towards me, shunning my presence as much as possible; whereas, before, he was open and communi-

cative to me as to a sister, well knowing that I yielded
to his pleasure in all things, and was far from
harbouring jealousy of any kind.

What I had dreaded, I now perceived had come to
pass. This was the loss of his favour and good
opinion; to preserve which I had studied to gain his
confidence by a ready compliance with his wishes,
well knowing that mistrust is the sure forerunner of
hatred.

I now turned my mind to an endeavour to wean
my brother's affection from Madame de Sauves, in
order to counterplot Le Guast in his design to bring
about a division, and thereby to effect our ruin. I
used every means with my brother to divert his
passion; but the fascination was too strong, and my
pains proved ineffectual. In anything else, my brother
would have suffered himself to be ruled by me; but
the charms of this Circe, aided by that sorcerer, Le
Guast, were too powerful to be dissolved by my advice.
So far was he from profiting by my counsel that he
was weak enough to communicate it to her. So blind
are lovers!

Her vengeance was excited by this communication,
and she now entered more fully into the designs of
Le Guast. In consequence, she used all her art to
make the King my husband conceive an aversion for
me; insomuch that he scarcely ever spoke with me.
He left her late at night, and, to prevent our meeting
in the morning, she directed him to come to her at
the Queen's levée, which she duly attended; after
which he passed the rest of the day with her. My
brother likewise followed her with the greatest assiduity, and she had the artifice to make each of them
think that he alone had any place in her esteem.
Thus was a jealousy kept up betwixt them, and, in
consequence, disunion and mutual ruin!

We made a considerable stay at Avignon, whence we proceeded through Burgundy and Champagne to Rheims, where the King's marriage was celebrated. From Rheims we came to Paris, things going on in their usual train, and Le Guast prosecuting his designs with all the success he could wish. At Paris my brother was joined by Bussi, whom he received with all the favour which his bravery merited. He was inseparable from my brother, in consequence of which I frequently saw him, for my brother and I were always together, his household being equally at my devotion as if it were my own. Your aunt, remarking this harmony betwixt us, has often told me that it called to her recollection the times of my uncle, M. d'Orléans, and my aunt, Madame de Savoie.

Le Guast thought this a favourable circumstance to complete his design. Accordingly, he suggested to Madame de Sauves to make my husband believe that it was on account of Bussi that I frequented my brother's apartments so constantly.

The King my husband, being fully informed of all my proceedings from persons in his service who attended me everywhere, could not be induced to lend an ear to this story. Le Guast, finding himself foiled in this quarter, applied to the King, who was well inclined to listen to the tale, on account of his dislike to my brother and me, whose friendship for each other was unpleasing to him.

Besides this, he was incensed against Bussi, who, being formerly attached to him, had now devoted himself wholly to my brother,—an acquisition which, on account of the celebrity of Bussi's fame for parts and valour, redounded greatly to my brother's honour, whilst it increased the malice and envy of his enemies.

The King, thus worked upon by Le Guast, mentioned it to the Queen my mother, thinking it would

have the same effect on her as the tale which was
trumped up at Lyons. But she, seeing through the
whole design, showed him the improbability of the
story, adding that he must have some wicked people
about him, who could put such notions in his head,
observing that I was very unfortunate to have fallen
upon such evil times. "In my younger days," said
she, "we were allowed to converse freely with all the
gentlemen who belonged to the King our father,
the Dauphin, and M. d'Orléans, your uncles. It was
common for them to assemble in the bedchamber of
Madame Marguerite, your aunt, as well as in mine,
and nothing was thought of it. Neither ought it to
appear strange that Bussi sees my daughter in the
presence of her husband's servants. They are not
shut up together. Bussi is a person of quality, and
holds the first place in your brother's family. What
grounds are there for such a calumny? At Lyons
you caused me to offer her an affront, which I fear
she will never forget."

The King was astonished to hear his mother talk
in this manner, and interrupted her with saying:
"Madame, I only relate what I have heard."

"But who is it," answered she, "that tells you all
this? I fear no one that intends you any good, but
rather one that wishes to create divisions amongst
you all."

As soon as the King had left her she told me all
that had passed, and said: "You are unfortunate to
live in these times." Then calling your aunt, Madame
de Dampierre, they entered into a discourse concerning the pleasures and innocent freedoms of the times
they had seen, when scandal and malevolence were
unknown at Court.

Le Guast, finding this plot miscarry, was not long
in contriving another. He addressed himself for this

purpose to certain gentlemen who attended the King my husband. These had been formerly the friends of Bussi, but, envying the glory he had obtained, were now become his enemies. Under the mask of zeal for their master, they disguised the envy which they harboured in their breasts. They entered into a design of assassinating Bussi as he left my brother to go to his own lodgings, which was generally at a late hour. They knew that he was always accompanied home by fifteen or sixteen gentlemen, belonging to my brother, and that, notwithstanding he wore no sword, having been lately wounded in the right arm, his presence was sufficient to inspire the rest with courage.

In order, therefore, to make sure work, they resolved on attacking him with two or three hundred men, thinking that night would throw a veil over the disgrace of such an assassination.

Le Guast, who commanded a regiment of guards, furnished the requisite number of men, whom he disposed in five or six divisions, in the street through which he was to pass. Their orders were to put out the torches and *flambeaux,* and then to fire their pieces, after which they were to charge his company, observing particularly to attack one who had his right arm slung in a scarf.

Fortunately they escaped the intended massacre, and, fighting their way through, reached Bussi's lodgings, one gentleman only being killed, who was particularly attached to M. de Bussi, and who was probably mistaken for him, as he had his arm likewise slung in a scarf.

An Italian gentleman, who belonged to my brother, left them at the beginning of the attack, and came running back to the Louvre. As soon as he reached my brother's chamber door, he cried out aloud:

" Bussi is assassinated!" My brother was going out, but I, hearing the cry of assassination, left my chamber, by good fortune not being undressed, and stopped my brother. I then sent for the Queen my mother to come with all haste in order to prevent him from going out, as he was resolved to do, regardless of what might happen. It was with difficulty we could stay him, though the Queen my mother represented the hazard he ran from the darkness of the night, and his ignorance of the nature of the attack, which might have been purposely designed by Le Guast to take away his life. Her entreaties and persuasions would have been of little avail if she had not used her authority to order all the doors to be barred, and taken the resolution of remaining where she was until she had learned what had really happened.

Bussi, whom God had thus miraculously preserved, with that presence of mind which he was so remarkable for in time of battle and the most imminent danger, considering within himself when he reached home the anxiety of his master's mind should he have received any false report, and fearing he might expose himself to hazard upon the first alarm being given (which certainly would have been the case, if my mother had not interfered and prevented it), immediately despatched one of his people to let him know every circumstance.

The next day Bussi showed himself at the Louvre without the least dread of enemies, as if what had happened had been merely the attack of a tournament. My brother exhibited much pleasure at the sight of Bussi, but expressed great resentment at such a daring attempt to deprive him of so brave and valuable a servant, a man whom Le Guast durst not attack in any other way than by a base assassination.

## LETTER X

THE Queen my mother, a woman endowed with the greatest prudence and foresight of any one I ever knew, apprehensive of evil consequences from this affair, and fearing a dissension betwixt her two sons, advised my brother to fall upon some pretence for sending Bussi away from Court. In this advice I joined her, and through our united counsel and request, my brother was prevailed upon to give his consent. I had every reason to suppose that Le Guast would take advantage of the rencounter to foment the coolness which already existed betwixt my brother and the King my husband into an open rupture. Bussi, who implicitly followed my brother's directions in everything, departed with a company of the bravest noblemen that were about the latter's person.

Bussi was now removed from the machinations of Le Guast, who likewise failed in accomplishing a design he had long projected,—to disunite the King my husband and me.

One night my husband was attacked with a fit, and continued insensible for the space of an hour,—occasioned, I supposed, by his excesses with women, for I never knew anything of the kind to happen to him before. However, as it was my duty so to do, I attended him with so much care and assiduity that, when he recovered, he spoke of it to every one, declaring that, if I had not perceived his indisposition and called for the help of my women, he should not have survived the fit.

From this time he treated me with more kindness, and the cordiality betwixt my brother and him was again revived, as if I had been the point of union at which they were to meet, or the cement that joined them together.

Le Guast was now at his wit's end for some fresh contrivance to breed disunion in the Court.

He had lately persuaded the King to remove from about the person of the Queen-consort, a princess of the greatest virtue and most amiable qualities, a female attendant of the name of Changi, for whom the Queen entertained a particular esteem, as having been brought up with her. Being successful in this measure, he now thought of making the King my husband send away Torigni, whom I greatly regarded.

The argument he used with the King was, that young princesses ought to have no favourites about them.

The King, yielding to this man's persuasions, spoke of it to my husband, who observed that it would be a matter that would greatly distress me; that if I had an esteem for Torigni it was not without cause, as she had been brought up with the Queen of Spain and me from our infancy; that, moreover, Torigni was a young lady of good understanding, and had been of great use to him during his confinement at Vincennes; that it would be the greatest ingratitude in him to overlook services of such a nature, and that he remembered well when his Majesty had expressed the same sentiments.

Thus did he defend himself against the performance of so ungrateful an action. However, the King listened only to the arguments of Le Guast, and told my husband that he should have no more love for him if he did not remove Torigni from about me the very next morning.

He was forced to comply, greatly contrary to his will, and, as he has since declared to me, with much regret. Joining entreaties to commands, he laid his injunctions on me accordingly.

How displeasing this separation was I plainly discovered by the many tears I shed on receiving his orders. It was in vain to represent to him the injury done to my character by the sudden removal of one who had been with me from my earliest years, and was so greatly in my esteem and confidence; he could not give an ear to my reasons, being firmly bound by the promise he had made to the King.

Accordingly, Torigni left me that very day, and went to the house of a relation, M. Chastelas. I was so greatly offended with this fresh indignity, after so many of the kind formerly received, that I could not help yielding to resentment; and my grief and concern getting the upper hand of my prudence, I exhibited a great coolness and indifference towards my husband. Le Guast and Madame de Sauves were successful in creating a like indifference on his part, which, coinciding with mine, separated us altogether, and we neither spoke to each other nor slept in the same bed.

A few days after this, some faithful servants about the person of the King my husband remarked to him the plot which had been concerted with so much artifice to lead him to his ruin, by creating a division, first betwixt him and my brother, and next betwixt him and me, thereby separating him from those in whom only he could hope for his principal support. They observed to him that already matters were brought to such a pass that the King showed little regard for him, and even appeared to despise him.

They afterwards addressed themselves to my brother, whose situation was not in the least mended since the departure of Bussi, Le Guast causing fresh indignities to be offered him daily. They represented to him that the King my husband and he were both circumstanced alike, and equally in disgrace, as Le Guast had everything under his direction; so that both of them were under the necessity of soliciting, through him, any favours which they might want of the King, and which, when demanded, were constantly refused them with great contempt. Moreover, it was become dangerous to offer them service, as it was inevitable ruin for any one to do so.

" Since, then," said they, " your dissensions appear to be so likely to prove fatal to both, it would be advisable in you both to unite and come to a determination of leaving the Court; and, after collecting together your friends and servants, to require from the King an establishment suitable to your ranks." They observed to my brother that he had never yet been put in possession of his appanage, and received for his subsistence only some certain allowances, which were not regularly paid him, as they passed through the hands of Le Guast, and were at his disposal, to be discharged or kept back, as he judged proper. They concluded with observing that, with regard to the King my husband, the government of Guyenne was taken out of his hands; neither was he permitted to visit that or any other of his dominions.

It was hereupon resolved to pursue the counsel now given, and that the King my husband and my brother should immediately withdraw themselves from Court. My brother made me acquainted with this resolution, observing to me, as my husband and he were now friends again, that I ought to forget all that had passed; that my husband had declared to him that he was sorry things had so happened, that we had been outwitted by our enemies, but that he was resolved, from henceforward, to show me every attention and give me every proof of his love and esteem, and he concluded with begging me to make my husband every show of affection, and to be watchful for their interest during their absence.

It was concerted betwixt them that my brother should depart first, making off in a carriage in the best manner he could; that, in a few days afterwards, the King my husband should follow, under pretence of going on a hunting party. They both expressed their concern that they could not take me with them, assuring me that I had no occasion to have any apprehensions, as it would soon appear that they had no design to disturb the peace of the kingdom, but merely to ensure the safety of their own persons, and to settle their establishments. In short, it might well be supposed that, in their present situation, they had reason to apprehend danger to themselves from such as had evil designs against their family.

Accordingly, as soon as it was dusk and before the King's supper-time, my brother changed his cloak, and concealing the lower part of his face to his nose in it, left the palace, attended by a servant who was little known, and went on foot to the gate of St. Honoré, where he found Simier waiting for him in a coach, borrowed of a lady for the purpose.

My brother threw himself into it, and went to a house about a quarter of a league out of Paris, where horses were stationed ready; and at the distance of about a league farther, he joined a party of two or three hundred horsemen of his servants, who were awaiting his coming. My brother was not missed till nine o'clock, when the King and the Queen my mother asked me the reason he did not come to sup with them as usual, and if I knew of his being indisposed. I told them I had not seen him since noon. There-

upon they sent to his apartments. Word was brought
back that he was not there. Orders were then given
to inquire at the apartments of the ladies whom he
was accustomed to visit. He was nowhere to be
found. There was now a general alarm. The King
flew into a great passion, and began to threaten me.
He then sent for all the Princes and the great officers
of the Court; and giving orders for a pursuit to be
made, and to bring him back, dead or alive, cried out:
" He is gone to make war against me; but I will
show him what it is to contend with a king of my
power."

Many of the Princes and officers of State remonstrated against these orders, which they observed
ought to be well weighed. They said that, as their
duty directed, they were willing to venture their lives
in the King's service; but to act against his brother
they were certain would not be pleasing to the King
himself; that they were well convinced his brother
would undertake nothing that should give his Majesty
displeasure, or be productive of danger to the realm;
that perhaps his leaving the Court was owing to some
disgust, which it would be more advisable to send
and inquire into. Others, on the contrary, were for
putting the King's orders into execution; but, whatever expedition they could use, it was day before
they set off; and as it was then too late to overtake
my brother, they returned, being only equipped for
the pursuit.

I was in tears the whole night of my brother's departure, and the next day was seized with a violent
cold, which was succeeded by a fever that confined
me to my bed.

Meanwhile my husband was preparing for his departure, which took up all the time he could spare
from his visits to Madame de Sauves; so that he

did not think of me. He returned as usual at two or three in the morning, and, as we had separate beds, I seldom heard him; and in the morning, before I was awake, he went to my mother's levée, where he met Madame de Sauves, as usual.

This being the case, he quite forgot his promise to my brother of speaking to me; and when he went away, it was without taking leave of me.

The King did not show my husband more favour after my brother's evasion, but continued to behave with his former coolness. This the more confirmed him in the resolution of leaving the Court, so that in a few days, under the pretence of hunting, he went away.

## LETTER XI

THE King, supposing that I was a principal instrument in aiding the Princes in their desertion, was greatly incensed against me, and his rage became at length so violent that, had not the Queen my mother moderated it, I am inclined to think my life had been in danger. Giving way to her counsel, he became more calm, but insisted upon a guard being placed over me, that I might not follow the King my husband, neither have communication with any one, so as to give the Princes intelligence of what was going on at Court. The Queen my mother gave her consent to this measure, as being the least violent, and was well pleased to find his anger cooled in so great a degree. She, however, requested that she might be permitted to discourse with me, in order to reconcile me to a submission to treatment of so different a kind from what I had hitherto known. At the same time she advised the King to consider that these troubles might not be lasting; that everything in the world bore a double aspect; that what now appeared to him horrible and alarming, might, upon a second view, assume a more pleasing and tranquil look; that, as things changed, so should measures change with them; that there might come a time when he might have occasion for my services; that, as prudence counselled us not to repose too much confidence in our friends, lest they should one day become our enemies, so was it advisable to conduct ourselves in such a manner to our enemies as if we had hopes they should hereafter become our friends. By such prudent remonstrances did the Queen my mother restrain the King from proceeding to extremities with me, as he would otherwise possibly have done.

Le Guast now endeavoured to divert his fury to another object, in order to wound me in a most sensitive part. He prevailed on the King to adopt a design for seizing Torigni, at the house of her cousin Chastelas, and, under pretence of bringing her before the King, to drown her in a river which they were to cross. The party sent upon this errand was admitted by Chastelas, not suspecting any evil design, without the least difficulty, into his house. As soon as they had gained admission they proceeded to execute the cruel business they were sent upon, by fastening Torigni with cords and locking her up in a chamber, whilst their horses were baiting. Meantime, according to the French custom, they crammed themselves, like gluttons, with the best eatables the house afforded. Chastelas, who was a man of discretion, was not displeased to gain time at the expense of some part of his substance, considering that the suspension of a sentence is a prolongation of life, and that during this respite the King's heart might relent, and he might countermand his former orders. With these considerations he was induced to submit, though it was in his power to have called for assistance to repel this violence. But God, who hath constantly regarded my afflictions and afforded me protection against the malicious designs of my enemies, was pleased to order poor Torigni to be delivered by means which I could never have devised had I been acquainted with the plot, of which I was totally ignorant. Several of the domestics, male as well as female, had left the house in a fright, fearing the insolence and rude treatment of this troop of soldiers, who behaved as riot-ously as if they were in a house given up to pillage. Some of these, at the distance of a quarter of a league from the house, by God's providence, fell in with Ferté and Avantigni, at the head of their troops, in number about two hundred horse, on their march to join my brother. Ferté, remarking a labourer, whom he knew to belong to Chastelas, apparently in great distress, inquired of him what was the matter, and whether he had been ill-used by any of the soldiery. The man related to him all he knew, and in what state he had left his master's house. Hereupon Ferté and Avantigni resolved, out of regard to me, to effect Torigni's deliverance, returning thanks to God for having afforded them so favourable an opportunity of testifying the respect they had always entertained towards me.

Accordingly, they proceeded to the house with all expedition, and arrived just at the moment these soldiers were setting Torigni on horseback, for the purpose of conveying her to the river wherein they had orders to plunge her. Galloping into the courtyard, sword in hand, they cried out: "Assassins, if you dare to offer that lady the least injury, you are dead men!" So saying, they attacked them and drove them to flight, leaving their prisoner behind, nearly as dead with joy as she was before with fear and apprehension. After returning thanks to God and her deliverers for so opportune and unexpected a rescue, she and her cousin Chastelas set off in a carriage, under the escort of their rescuers, and joined my brother, who, since he could not have me with him, was happy to have one so dear to me about him. She remained under my brother's protection as long as any danger was apprehended, and was treated with as much respect as if she had been with me.

Whilst the King was giving directions for this

notable expedition, for the purpose of sacrificing
Torigni to his vengeance, the Queen my mother,
who had not received the least intimation of it,
came to my apartment as I was dressing to go
abroad, in order to observe how I should be received
after what had passed at Court, having still some
alarms on account of my husband and brother. I
had hitherto confined myself to my chamber, not
having perfectly recovered my health, and, in reality,
being all the time as much indisposed in mind as in
body.

My mother, perceiving my intention, addressed me
in these words: " My child, you are giving yourself
unnecessary trouble in dressing to go abroad. Do
not be alarmed at what I am going to tell you. Your
own good sense will dictate to you that you ought not
to be surprised if the King resents the conduct of your
brother and husband, and as he knows the love and
friendship that exist between you three, should suppose that you were privy to their design of leaving the
Court. He has, for this reason, resolved to detain
you in it, as a hostage for them. He is sensible how
much you are beloved by your husband, and thinks he
can hold no pledge that is more dear to him. On this
account it is that the King has ordered his guards to
be placed, with directions not to suffer you to leave
your apartments. He has done this with the advice
of his counsellors, by whom it was suggested that, if
you had your free liberty, you might be induced to
advise your brother and husband of their delibera-
tions. I beg you will not be offended with these
measures, which, if it so please God, may not be of
long continuance. I beg, moreover, you will not be
displeased with me if I do not pay you frequent visits,
as I should be unwilling to create any suspicions in
the King's mind. However, you may rest assured that

I shall prevent any further steps from being taken
that may prove disagreeable to you, and that I shall
use my utmost endeavours to bring about a reconciliation betwixt your brothers."

I represented to her, in reply, the great indignity
that was offered to me by putting me under arrest;
that it was true my brother had all along communicated to me the just cause he had to be dissatisfied,
but that, with respect to the King my husband, from
the time Torigni was taken from me we had not
spoken to each other; neither had he visited me during my indisposition, nor did he even take leave of me
when he left Court. "This," says she, "is nothing at
all; it is merely a trifling difference betwixt man and
wife, which a few sweet words, conveyed in a letter,
will set to rights. When, by such means, he has
regained your affections, he has only to write to you
to come to him, and you will set off at the very first
opportunity. Now, this is what the King my son
wishes to prevent."

## LETTER XII

THE Queen my mother left me, saying these words. For my part, I remained a close prisoner, without a visit from a single person, none of my most intimate friends daring to come near me, through the apprehension that such a step might prove injurious to their interests. Thus it is ever in Courts. Adversity is solitary, while prosperity dwells in a crowd; the object of persecution being sure to be shunned by his nearest friends and dearest connections. The brave Grillon was the only one who ventured to visit me, at the hazard of incurring disgrace. He came five or six times to see me, and my guards were so much astonished at his resolution, and awed by his presence, that not a single Cerberus of them all would venture to refuse him entrance to my apartments.

Meanwhile, the King my husband reached the States under his government. Being joined there by his friends and dependents, they all represented to him the indignity offered to me by his quitting the Court without taking leave of me. They observed to him that I was a princess of good understanding, and that it would be for his interest to regain my esteem; that, when matters were put on their former footing, he might derive to himself great advantage from my presence at Court. Now that he was at a distance from his Circe, Madame de Sauves, he could listen to good advice. Absence having abated the force of her charms, his eyes were opened; he discovered the plots and machinations of our enemies, and clearly perceived that a rupture could not but tend to the ruin of us both.

Accordingly, he wrote me a very affectionate letter, wherein he entreated me to forget all that had passed betwixt us, assuring me that from thenceforth he would ever love me, and would give me every demonstration that he did so, desiring me to inform him of what was going on at Court, and how it fared with me and my brother. My brother was in Champagne and the King my husband in Gascony, and there had been no communication betwixt them, though they were on terms of friendship.

I received this letter during my imprisonment, and it gave me great comfort under that situation. Although my guards had strict orders not to permit me to set pen to paper, yet, as necessity is said to be the mother of invention, I found means to write many letters to him.

Some few days after I had been put under arrest, my brother had intelligence of it, which chagrined him so much that, had not the love of his country prevailed with him, the effects of his resentment would have been shown in a cruel civil war, to which purpose he had a sufficient force entirely at his devotion. He was, however, withheld by his patriotism, and contented himself with writing to the Queen my mother, informing her that, if I was thus treated, he should be driven upon some desperate measure. She, fearing the consequence of an open rupture, and dreading lest, if blows were once struck, she should be deprived of the power of bringing about a reconciliation betwixt the brothers, represented the consequences to the King, and found him well disposed to lend an ear to her reasons, as his anger was now cooled by the apprehensions of being attacked in Gascony, Dauphiny, Languedoc, and Poitou, with all the strength of the Huguenots under the King my husband.

Besides the many strong places held by the Huguenots, my brother had an army with him in Champagne, composed chiefly of nobility, the bravest and best in France. The King found, since my brother's departure, that he could not, either by threats or rewards, induce a single person among the princes and great lords to act against him, so much did every one fear to intermeddle in this quarrel, which they considered as of a family nature; and after having maturely reflected on his situation, he acquiesced in my mother's opinion, and begged her to fall upon some means of reconciliation. She thereupon proposed going to my brother and taking me with her. To the measure of taking me, the King had an objection, as he considered me as the hostage for my husband and brother. She then agreed to leave me behind, and set off without my knowledge of the matter. At their interview, my brother represented to the Queen my mother that he could not but be greatly dissatisfied with the King after the many mortifications he had received at Court; that the cruelty and injustice of confining me hurt him equally as if done to himself; observing, moreover, that, as if my arrest were not a sufficient mortification, poor Torigni must be made to suffer; and concluding with the declaration of his firm resolution not to listen to any terms of peace until I was restored to my liberty, and reparation made me for the indignity I had sustained. The Queen my mother being unable to obtain any other answer, returned to Court and acquainted the King with my brother's determination. Her advice was to go back again with me, for going without me, she said, would answer very little purpose; and if I went with her in disgust, it would do more harm than good. Besides, there was reason to fear, in that case, I should insist upon going to my husband. " In short," says she, "my daughter's guard must be removed, and she must be satisfied in the best way we can."

The King agreed to follow her advice, and was now, on a sudden, as eager to reconcile matters betwixt us as she was herself. Hereupon I was sent for, and when I came to her, she informed me that she had paved the way for peace; that it was for the good of the State, which she was sensible I must be as desirous to promote as my brother; that she had it now in her power to make a peace which would be as satisfactory as my brother could desire, and would put us entirely out of the reach of Le Guast's machinations, or those of any one else who might have an influence over the King's mind. She observed that, by assisting her to procure a good understanding betwixt the King and my brother, I should relieve her from that cruel disquietude under which she at present laboured, as, should things come to an open rupture, she could not but be grieved, whichever party prevailed, as they were both her sons. She therefore expressed her hopes that I would forget the injuries I had received, and dispose myself to concur in a peace, rather than join in any plan of revenge. She assured me that the King was sorry for what had happened; that he had even expressed his regret to her with tears in his eyes, and had declared that he was ready to give me every satisfaction. I replied that I was willing to sacrifice everything for the good of my brothers and of the State; that I wished for nothing so much as peace, and that I would exert myself to the utmost to bring it about.

As I uttered these words, the King came into the closet, and, with a number of fine speeches, endeavoured to soften my resentment and to recover my friendship, to which I made such returns as might show him I harboured no ill-will for the injuries I

had received. I was induced to such behaviour rather
out of contempt, and because it was good policy to let
the King go away satisfied with me.

Besides, I had found a secret pleasure, during my
confinement, from the perusal of good books, to which
I had given myself up with a delight I never before
experienced. I consider this as an obligation I owe
to fortune, or, rather, to Divine Providence, in order
to prepare me, by such efficacious means, to bear up
against the misfortunes and calamities that awaited
me. By tracing nature in the universal book which
is opened to all mankind, I was led to the knowledge
of the Divine Author. Science conducts us, step by
step, through the whole range of creation, until we ar-
rive, at length, at God. Misfortune prompts us to
summon our utmost strength to oppose grief and recover tranquillity, until at length we find a powerful
aid in the knowledge and love of God, whilst prosperity hurries us away until we are overwhelmed by
our passions. My captivity and its consequent soli-
tude afforded me the double advantage of exciting a
passion for study, and an inclination for devotion, advantages I had never experienced during the vanities
and splendour of my prosperity.

As I have already observed, the King, discovering
in me no signs of discontent, informed me that the
Queen my mother was going into Champagne to have
an interview with my brother, in order to bring about
a peace, and begged me to accompany her thither
and to use my best endeavours to forward his views,
as he knew my brother was always well disposed to
follow my counsel; and he concluded with saying
that the peace, when accomplished, he should ever
consider as being due to my good offices, and should
esteem himself obliged to me for it. I promised to
exert myself in so good a work, which I plainly per-

ceived was both for my brother's advantage and the benefit of the State.

The Queen my mother and I set off for Sens the next day. The conference was agreed to be held in a gentleman's château, at a distance of about a league from that place. My brother was waiting for us, accompanied by a small body of troops and the principal Catholic noblemen and princes of his army. Amongst these were the Duc Casimir and Colonel Poux, who had brought him six thousand German horse, raised by the Huguenots, they having joined my brother, as the King my husband and he acted in conjunction.

The treaty was continued for several days, the conditions of peace requiring much discussion, especially such articles of it as related to religion. With respect to these, when at length agreed upon, they were too much to the advantage of the Huguenots, as it appeared afterwards, to be kept; but the Queen my mother gave in to them, in order to have a peace, and that the German cavalry before mentioned might be disbanded. She was, moreover, desirous to get my brother out of the hands of the Huguenots; and he was himself as willing to leave them, being always a very good Catholic, and joining the Huguenots only through necessity.

One condition of the peace was, that my brother should have a suitable establishment. My brother likewise stipulated for me, that my marriage portion should be assigned in lands, and M. de Beauvais, a commissioner on his part, insisted much upon it. My mother, however, opposed it, and persuaded me to join her in it, assuring me that I should obtain from the King all I could require. Thereupon I begged I might not be included in the articles of peace, observing that I would rather owe whatever I was to receive to the particular favour of the King and the Queen my mother, and should, besides, consider it as more secure when obtained by such means.

The peace being thus concluded and ratified on both sides, the Queen my mother prepared to return. At this instant I received letters from the King my husband, in which he expressed a great desire to see me, begging me, as soon as peace was agreed on, to ask leave to go to him. I communicated my husband's wish to the Queen my mother, and added my own entreaties. She expressed herself greatly averse to such a measure, and used every argument to set me against it. She observed that, when I refused her proposal of a divorce after St. Bartholomew's Day, she gave way to my refusal, and commended me for it, because my husband was then converted to the Catholic religion; but now that. he had abjured Catholicism, and was turned Huguenot again, she could not give her consent that I should go to him. When I still insisted upon going, she burst into a flood of tears, and said, if I did not return with her, it would prove her ruin; that the King would believe it was her doing; that she had promised to bring me back with her; and that, when my brother returned to Court, which would be soon, she would give her consent.

We now returned to Paris, and found the King well satisfied that we had made a peace; though not, however, pleased with the articles concluded in favour of the Huguenots. He therefore resolved within himself, as soon as my brother should return to Court, to find some pretext for renewing the war. These advantageous conditions were, indeed, only granted the Huguenots to get my brother out of their hands, who was detained near two months, being employed in disbanding his German horse and the rest of his army.

## LETTER XIII

AT length my brother returned to Court, accompanied by all the Catholic nobility who had followed his fortunes. The King received him very graciously, and showed, by his reception of him, how much he was pleased at his return. Bussi, who returned with my brother, met likewise with a gracious reception. Le Guast was now no more, having died under the operation of a particular regimen ordered for him by his physician. He had given himself up to every kind of debauchery; and his death seemed the judgment of the Almighty on one whose body had long been perishing, and whose soul had been made over to the prince of demons as the price of assistance through the means of diabolical magic, which he constantly practised. The King, though now without this instrument of his malicious contrivances, turned his thoughts entirely upon the destruction of the Huguenots. To effect this, he strove to engage my brother against them, and thereby make them his enemies; and that I might be considered as another enemy, he used every means to prevent me from going to the King my husband. Accordingly he showed every mark of attention to both of us, and manifested an inclination to gratify all our wishes.

After some time, M. de Duras arrived at Court, sent by the King my husband to hasten my departure. Hereupon, I pressed the King greatly to think well of it, and give me his leave. He, to colour his refusal, told me he could not part with me at present, as I was the chief ornament of his Court; that he must keep me a little longer, after which he would accompany me himself on my way as far as Poitiers. With this answer and assurance, he sent M. de Duras back. These excuses were purposely framed in order to gain time until everything was prepared for declaring war against the Huguenots, and, in consequence, against the King my husband, as he fully designed to do.

As a pretence to break with the Huguenots, a report was spread abroad that the Catholics were dissatisfied with the Peace of Sens, and thought the terms of it too advantageous for the Huguenots. This rumour succeeded, and produced all that discontent amongst the Catholics intended by it. A league was formed in the provinces and great cities, which was joined by numbers of the Catholics. M. de Guise was named as the head of all. This was well known to the King, who pretended to be ignorant of what was going forward, though nothing else was talked of at Court.

The States were convened to meet at Blois. Previous to the opening of this assembly, the King called my brother to his closet, where were present the Queen my mother and some of the King's counsellors. He represented the great consequence the Catholic league was to his State and authority, even though they should appoint De Guise as the head of it; that such a measure was of the highest importance to them both, meaning my brother and himself; that the Catholics had very just reason to be dissatisfied with the peace, and that it behoved him, addressing himself to my brother, rather to join the Catholics than the Huguenots, and this from conscience as well as interest. He concluded his address to my brother with conjuring him, as a son of France and a good

Catholic, to assist him with his aid and counsel in this critical juncture, when his crown and the Catholic religion were both at stake. He further said that, in order to get the start of so formidable a league, he ought to form one himself, and become the head of it, as well to show his zeal for religion as to prevent the Catholics from uniting under any other leader. He then proposed to declare himself the head of a league, which should be joined by my brother, the princes, nobles, governors, and others holding offices under the Government. Thus was my brother reduced to the necessity of making his Majesty a tender of his services for the support and maintenance of the Catholic religion.

The King, having now obtained assurances of my brother's assistance in the event of a war, which was his sole view in the league which he had formed with so much art, assembled together the princes and chief noblemen of his Court, and, calling for the roll of the league, signed it first himself, next calling upon my brother to sign it, and, lastly, upon all present.

The next day the States opened their meeting, when the King, calling upon the Bishops of Lyons, Ambrune, Vienne, and other prelates there present, for their advice, was told that, after the oath taken at his coronation, no oath made to heretics could bind him, and therefore he was absolved from his engagements with the Huguenots.

This declaration being made at the opening of the assembly, and war declared against the Huguenots, the King abruptly dismissed from Court the Huguenot, Genisac, who had arrived a few days before, charged by the King my husband with a commission to hasten my departure. The King very sharply told him that his sister had been given to a Catholic, and not to a Huguenot; and that if the King my

husband expected to have me, he must declare himself a Catholic.

Every preparation for war was made, and nothing
else talked of at Court; and, to make my brother still
more obnoxious to the Huguenots, he had the command of an army given him.  Genisac came and informed me of the rough message he had been dismissed with.  Hereupon I went directly to the closet
of the Queen my mother, where I found the King.
I expressed my resentment at being deceived by him,
and at being cajoled by his promise to accompany me
from Paris to Poitiers, which, as it now appeared,
was a mere pretence.  I represented that I did not
marry by my own choice, but entirely agreeable to
the advice of King Charles, the Queen my mother,
and himself; that, since they had given him to me for
a husband, they ought not to hinder me from partak-
ing of his fortunes; that I was resolved to go to him,
and that if I had not their leave, I would get away
how I could, even at the hazard of my life.  The King
answered: " Sister, it is not now a time to importune
me for leave.  I acknowledge that I have, as you say,
hitherto prevented you from going, in order to forbid
it altogether.  From the time the King of Navarre
changed his religion, and again became a Huguenot,
I have been against your going to him.  What the
Queen my mother and I are doing is for your good.
I am determined to carry on a war of extermination
until this wretched religion of the Huguenots, which
is of so mischievous a nature, is no more.  Consider,
my sister, if you, who are a Catholic, were once in
their hands, you would become a hostage for me, and
prevent my design.  And who knows but they might
seek their revenge upon me by taking away your life?
No, you shall not go amongst them; and if you leave
us in the manner you have now mentioned, rely upon

it that you will make the Queen your mother and me your bitterest enemies, and that we shall use every means to make you feel the effects of our resentment; and, moreover, you will make your husband's situation worse instead of better."

I went from this audience with much dissatisfaction, and, taking advice of the principal persons of both sexes belonging to Court whom I esteemed my friends, I found them all of opinion that it would be exceedingly improper for me to remain in a Court now at open variance with the King my husband. They recommended me not to stay at Court whilst the war lasted, saying it would be more honourable for me to leave the kingdom under the pretence of a pilgrimage, or a visit to some of my kindred. The Princesse de Roche-sur-Yon was amongst those I consulted upon the occasion, who was on the point of setting off for Spa to take the waters there.

My brother was likewise present at the consultation, and brought with him Mondoucet, who had been to Flanders in quality of the King's agent, whence he was just returned to represent to the King the discontent that had arisen amongst the Flemings on account of infringements made by the Spanish Government on the French laws. He stated that he was commissioned by several nobles, and the municipalities of several towns, to declare how much they were inclined in their hearts towards France, and how ready they were to come under a French government. Mondoucet, perceiving the King not inclined to listen to his representation, as having his mind wholly occupied by the war he had entered into with the Huguenots, whom he was resolved to punish for having joined my brother, had ceased to move in it further to the King, and addressed himself on the subject to my brother. My brother, with that princely spirit which led him to undertake great achievements, readily lent an ear to Mondoucet's proposition, and promised to engage in it, for he was born rather to conquer than to keep what he conquered. Mondoucet's proposition was the more pleasing to him as it was not unjust,—it being, in fact, to recover to France what had been usurped by Spain.

Mondoucet had now engaged himself in my brother's service, and was to return to Flanders under a pretence of accompanying the Princesse de Roche-sur-Yon in her journey to Spa; and as this agent perceived my counsellors to be at a loss for some pretence for my leaving Court and quitting France during the war, and that at first Savoy was proposed for my retreat, then Lorraine, and then Our Lady of Loretto, he suggested to my brother that I might be of great use to him in Flanders, if, under the colour of any complaint, I should be recommended to drink the Spa waters, and go with the Princesse de Roche-sur-Yon. My brother acquiesced in this opinion, and came up to me, saying: "Oh, Queen! you need be no longer at a loss for a place to go to. I have observed that you have frequently an erysipelas on your arm, and you must accompany the Princess to Spa. You must say your physicians had ordered those waters for the complaint; but when they did so, it was not the season to take them. That season is now approaching, and you hope to have the King's leave to go there."

My brother did not deliver all he wished to say at that time, because the Cardinal de Bourbon was present, whom he knew to be a friend to the Guises and to Spain. However, I saw through his real design, and that he wished me to promote his views in Flanders.

The company approved of my brother's advice, and the Princesse de Roche-sur-Yon heard the proposal with great joy, having a great regard for me. She promised to attend me to the Queen my mother when I should ask her consent.

The next day I found the Queen alone, and represented to her the extreme regret I experienced in finding that a war was inevitable betwixt the King my husband and his Majesty, and that I must continue in a state of separation from my husband; that, as long as the war lasted, it was neither decent nor honourable for me to stay at Court, where I must be in one or other, or both, of these cruel situations: either that the King my husband should believe that I continued in it out of inclination, and think me deficient in the duty I owed him; or that his Majesty should entertain suspicions of my giving intelligence to the King my husband. Either of these cases, I observed, could not but prove injurious to me. I therefore prayed her not to take it amiss if I desired to remove myself from Court, and from becoming so unpleasantly situated; adding that my physicians had for some time recommended me to take the Spa waters for an erysipelas—to which I had been long subject—on my arm; the season for taking these waters was now approaching, and that if she approved of it, I would use the present opportunity, by which means I should be at a distance from Court, and show my husband that, as I could not be with him, I was unwilling to remain amongst his enemies. I further expressed my hopes that, through her prudence, a peace might be effected in a short time betwixt the King my husband and his Majesty, and that my husband might be restored to the favour he formerly enjoyed; that whenever I learned the news of so joyful an event, I would renew my solicitations to be permitted to go to my husband. In the meantime, I should hope for her permission to have the honour of accompanying the Princesse de Roche-sur-Yon, there present, in her journey to Spa.

She approved of what I proposed, and expressed her satisfaction that I had taken so prudent a resolution. She observed how much she was chagrined when she found that the King, through the evil persuasions of the bishops, had resolved to break through the conditions of the last peace, which she had concluded in his name. She saw already the ill effects of this hasty proceeding, as it had removed from the King's Council many of his ablest and best servants. This gave her, she said, much concern, as it did likewise to think I could not remain at Court without offending my husband, or creating jealousy and suspicion in the King's mind. This being certainly what was likely to be the consequence of my staying, she would advise the King to give me leave to set out on this journey.

She was as good as her word, and the King discoursed with me on the subject without exhibiting the smallest resentment. Indeed, he was well pleased now that he had prevented me from going to the King my husband, for whom he had conceived the greatest animosity.

He ordered a courier to be immediately despatched to Don John of Austria,—who commanded for the King of Spain in Flanders,—to obtain from him the necessary passports for a free passage in the countries under his command, as I should be obliged to cross a part of Flanders to reach Spa, which is in the bishopric of Liège.

All matters being thus arranged, we separated in a few days after this interview. The short time my brother and I remained together was employed by him in giving me instructions for the commission I had undertaken to execute for him in Flanders. The

King and the Queen my mother set out for Poitiers, to be near the army of M. de Mayenne, then besieging Brouage, which place being reduced, it was intended to march into Gascony and attack the King my husband.

My brother had the command of another army, ordered to besiege Issoire and some other towns, which he soon after took.

For my part, I set out on my journey to Flanders accompanied by the Princesse de Roche-sur-Yon, Madame de Tournon, the lady of my bedchamber, Madame de Moüy of Picardy, Madame de Chastelaine, De Millon, Mademoiselle d'Atric, Mademoiselle de Tournon, and seven or eight other young ladies. My male attendants were the Cardinal de Lenoncourt, the Bishop of Langres, and M. de Moüy, Seigneur de Picardy, at present father-in-law to the brother of Queen Louise, called the Comte de Chaligny, with my principal steward of the household, my chief esquires, and the other gentlemen of my establishment.

## LETTER XIV

THE cavalcade that attended me excited great curiosity as it passed through the several towns in the course of my journey, and reflected no small degree of credit on France, as it was splendidly set out, and made a handsome appearance. I travelled in a litter raised with pillars. The lining of it was Spanish velvet, of a crimson colour, embroidered in various devices with gold and different coloured silk thread. The windows were of glass, painted in devices. The lining and windows had, in the whole, forty devices, all different and alluding to the sun and its effects. Each device had its motto, either in the Spanish or Italian language. My litter was followed by two others; in the one was the Princesse de Roche-sur-Yon, and in the other Madame de Tournon, my lady of the bedchamber. After them followed ten maids of honour, on horseback, with their governess; and, last of all, six coaches and chariots, with the rest of the ladies and all our female attendants.

I took the road of Picardy, the towns in which province had received the King's orders to pay me all due honours. Being arrived at Le Catelet, a strong place, about three leagues distant from the frontier of the Cambrésis, the Bishop of Cambray (an ecclesiastical State acknowledging the King of Spain only as a guarantee) sent a gentleman to inquire of me at what hour I should leave the place, as he intended to meet me on the borders of his territory.

Accordingly I found him there, attended by a number of his people, who appeared to be true Flemings, and to have all the rusticity and unpolished manners of their country. The Bishop was of the House of Barlemont, one of the principal families in Flanders. All of this house have shown themselves Spaniards at heart, and at that time were firmly attached to Don John. The Bishop received me with great politeness and not a little of the Spanish ceremony.

Although the city of Cambray is not so well built as some of our towns in France, I thought it, notwithstanding, far more pleasant than many of these, as the streets and squares are larger and better disposed. The churches are grand and highly ornamented, which is, indeed, common to France; but what I admired, above all, was the citadel, which is the finest and best constructed in Christendom. The Spaniards experienced it to be strong whilst my brother had it in his possession. The governor of the citadel at this time was a worthy gentleman named M. d'Ainsi, who was, in every respect, a polite and well-accomplished man, having the carriage and behaviour of one of our most perfect courtiers, very different from the rude incivility which appears to be the characteristic of a Fleming.

The Bishop gave us a grand supper, and after supper a ball, to which he had invited all the ladies of the city. As soon as the ball was opened he withdrew, in accordance with the Spanish ceremony; but M. d'Ainsi did the honours for him, and kept me company during the ball, conducting me afterwards to a collation, which, considering his command at the citadel, was, I thought, imprudent. *I speak from experience, having been taught, to my cost, and contrary to my desire, the caution and vigilance necessary to be observed in keeping such places.* As my regard for my brother was always predominant in me, I continually had his instructions in mind, and now thought I had a fair opportunity to open my commission and forward his views in Flanders, this town of Cambray, and especially the citadel, being, as it were, a key to that country. Accordingly I employed all the talents God had given me to make M. d'Ainsi a friend to France, and attach him to my brother's interest. Through God's assistance I succeeded with him, and so much was M. d'Ainsi pleased with my conversation that he came to the resolution of soliciting the Bishop, his master, to grant him leave to accompany me as far as Namur, where Don John of Austria was in waiting to receive me, observing that he had a great desire to witness so splendid an interview. This *Spanish* Fleming, the Bishop, had the weakness to grant M. d'Ainsi's request, who continued following in my train for ten or twelve days. During this time he took every opportunity of discoursing with me, and showed that, in his heart, he was well disposed to embrace the service of France, wishing no better master than the Prince my brother, and declaring that he heartily despised being under the command of his Bishop, who, though his sovereign, was not his superior by birth, being born a private gentleman like himself, and, in every other respect, greatly his inferior.

Leaving Cambray, I set out to sleep at Valenciennes, the chief city of a part of Flanders called by the same name. Where this country is divided from Cambrésis (as far as which I was conducted by the Bishop of Cambray), the Comte de Lalain, M. de Montigny his brother, and a number of gentlemen, to the amount of two or three hundred, came to meet me.

Valenciennes is a town inferior to Cambray in

point of strength, but equal to it for the beauty of its
squares, and churches,—the former ornamented with
fountains, as the latter are with curious clocks. The
ingenuity of the Germans in the construction of their
clocks was a matter of great surprise to all my
attendants, few amongst whom had ever before
seen clocks exhibiting a number of moving figures,
and playing a variety of tunes in the most agreeable
manner.

The Comte de Lalain, the governor of the city,
invited the lords and gentlemen of my train to a banquet, reserving himself to give an entertainment to
the ladies on our arrival at Mons, where we should
find the Countess his wife, his sister-in-law Madame
d'Aurec, and other ladies of distinction. Accordingly
the Count, with his attendants, conducted us thither
the next day. He claimed a relationship with the King
my husband, and was, in reality, a person who carried
great weight and authority. He was much dissatisfied with the Spanish Government, and had conceived
a great dislike for it since the execution of Count
Egmont, who was his near kinsman.

Although he had hitherto abstained from entering
into the league with the Prince of Orange and the
Huguenots, being himself a steady Catholic, yet he
had not admitted of an interview with Don John,
neither would he suffer him, nor any one in the interest of Spain, to enter upon his territories. Don
John was unwilling to give the Count any umbrage,
lest he should force him to unite the Catholic League
of Flanders, called the League of the States, to that
of the Prince of Orange and the Huguenots, well
foreseeing that such a union would prove fatal to the
Spanish interest, as other governors have since experienced. With this disposition of mind, the Comte
de Lalain thought he could not give me sufficient

demonstrations of the joy he felt by my presence;
and he could not have shown more honour to his
natural prince, nor displayed greater marks of zeal
and affection.

On our arrival at Mons, I was lodged in his house,
and found there the Countess his wife, and a Court
consisting of eighty or a hundred ladies of the city
and country. My reception was rather that of their
sovereign lady than of a foreign princess. The Flemish ladies are naturally lively, affable, and engaging.
The Comtesse de Lalain is remarkably so, and is,
moreover, a woman of great sense and elevation of
mind, in which particular, as well as in air and countenance, she carries a striking resemblance to the
lady your cousin. We became immediately intimate,
and commenced a firm friendship at our first meeting. When the supper hour came, we sat down to a
banquet, which was succeeded by a ball; and this
rule the Count observed as long as I stayed at Mons,
which was, indeed, longer than I intended. It had
been my intention to stay at Mons one night only, but
the Count's obliging lady prevailed on me to pass a
whole week there. I strove to excuse myself from so
long a stay, imagining it might be inconvenient to
them; but whatever I could say availed nothing with
the Count and his lady, and I was under the necessity
of remaining with them eight days. The Countess
and I were on so familiar a footing that she stayed in
my bedchamber till a late hour, and would not have
left me then had she not imposed upon herself a task
very rarely performed by persons of her rank, which,
however, placed the goodness of her disposition in the
most amiable light. In fact, she gave suck to her
infant son; and one day at table, sitting next me,
whose whole attention was absorbed in the promotion
of my brother's interest,—the table being the place

where, according to the custom of the country, all are familiar and ceremony is laid aside,—she, dressed out in the richest manner and blazing with diamonds, gave the breast to her child without rising from her seat, the infant being brought to the table as superbly habited as its nurse, the mother. She performed this maternal duty with so much good humour, and with a gracefulness peculiar to herself, that this charitable office—which would have appeared disgusting and been considered as an affront if done by some others of equal rank—gave pleasure to all who sat at table, and, accordingly, they signified their approbation by their applause.

The tables being removed, the dances commenced in the same room wherein we had supped, which was magnificent and large. The Countess and I sitting side by side, I expressed the pleasure I received from her conversation, and that I should place this meeting amongst the happiest events of my life. "Indeed," said I, "I shall have cause to regret that it ever did take place, as I shall depart hence so unwillingly, there being so little probability of our meeting again soon. Why did Heaven deny our being born in the same country!"

This was said in order to introduce my brother's business. She replied: "This country did, indeed, formerly belong to France, and our lawyers now plead their causes in the French language. The greater part of the people here still retain an affection for the French nation. For my part," added the Countess, "I have had a strong attachment to your country ever since I have had the honour of seeing you. This country has been long in the possession of the House of Austria, but the regard of the people for that house has been greatly weakened by the death of Count Egmont, M. de Horne, M. de Mon-

tigny, and others of the same party, some of them our
near relations, and all of the best families of the
country. We entertain the utmost dislike for the
Spanish Government, and wish for nothing so much
as to throw off the yoke of their tyranny; but, as the
country is divided betwixt different religions, we are
at a loss how to effect it. If we could unite, we
should soon drive out the Spaniards; but this division
amongst ourselves renders us weak. Would to God
the King your brother would come to a resolution
of reconquering this country, to which he has an
ancient claim! We should all receive him with open
arms."

This was a frank declaration, made by the Countess
without premeditation, but it had been long agitated
in the minds of the people, who considered that it
was from France they were to hope for redress from
the evils with which they were afflicted. I now found
I had as favourable an opening as I could wish for
to declare my errand. I told her that the King of
France my brother was averse to engaging in foreign war, and the more so as the Huguenots in his
kingdom were too strong to admit of his sending any
large force out of it. "My brother Alençon," said
I, "has sufficient means, and might be induced to
undertake it. He has equal valour, prudence, and
benevolence with the King my brother or any of
his ancestors. He has been bred to arms, and is
esteemed one of the bravest generals of these times.
He has the command of the King's army against
the Huguenots, and has lately taken a well-fortified
town, called Issoire, and some other places that were
in their possession. You could not invite to your
assistance a prince who has it so much in his power
to give it; being not only a neighbour, but having
a kingdom like France at his devotion, whence he

may expect to derive the necessary aid and succour. The Count your husband may be assured that if he do my brother this good office he will not find him ungrateful, but may set what price he pleases upon his meritorious service. My brother is of a noble and generous disposition, and ready to requite those who do him favours. He is, moreover, an admirer of men of honour and gallantry, and accordingly is followed by the bravest and best men France has to boast of. I am in hopes that a peace will soon be reëstablished with the Huguenots, and expect to find it so on my return to France. If the Count your husband think as you do, and will permit me to speak to him on the subject, I will engage to bring my brother over to the proposal, and, in that case, your country in general, and your house in particular, will be well satisfied with him. If, through your means, my brother should establish himself here, you may depend on seeing me often, there being no brother or sister who has a stronger affection for each other."

The Countess appeared to listen to what I said with great pleasure, and acknowledged that she had not entered upon this discourse without design. She observed that, having perceived I did her the honour to have some regard for her, she had resolved within herself not to let me depart out of the country without explaining to me the situation of it, and begging me to procure the aid of France to relieve them from the apprehensions of living in a state of perpetual war or of submitting to Spanish tyranny. She thereupon entreated me to allow her to relate our present conversation to her husband, and permit them both to confer with me on the subject the next day. To this I readily gave my consent.

Thus we passed the evening in discourse upon the

object of my mission, and I observed that she took a singular pleasure in talking upon it in all our succeeding conferences when I thought proper to introduce it. The ball being ended, we went to hear vespers at the church of the Canonesses, an order of nuns of which we have none in France. These are young ladies who are entered in these communities at a tender age, in order to improve their fortunes till they are of an age to be married. They do not all sleep under the same roof, but in detached houses within an enclosure. In each of these houses are three, four, or perhaps six young girls, under the care of an old woman. These governesses, together with the abbess, are of the number of such as have never been married. These girls never wear the habit of the order but in church; and the service there ended, they dress like others, pay visits, frequent balls, and go where they please. They were constant visitors at the Count's entertainments, and danced at his balls.

The Countess thought the time long until the night, when she had an opportunity of relating to the Count the conversation she had with me, and the opening of the business. The next morning she came to me, and brought her husband with her. He entered into a detail of the grievances the country laboured under, and the just reasons he had for ridding it of the tyranny of Spain. In doing this, he said, he should not consider himself as acting against his natural sovereign, because he well knew he ought to look for him in the person of the King of France. He explained to me the means whereby my brother might establish himself in Flanders, having possession of Hainault, which extended as far as Brussels. He said the difficulty lay in securing the Cambrésis, which is situated betwixt Hainault and Flanders. It would, therefore, be necessary to engage M. d'Ainsi in the business. To this I replied that, as he was his neighbour and friend, it might be better that he should open the matter to him; and I begged he would do so. I next assured him that he might have the most perfect reliance on the gratitude and friendship of my brother, and be certain of receiving as large a share of power and authority as such a service done by a person of his rank merited. Lastly, we agreed upon an interview betwixt my brother and M. de Montigny, the brother of the Count, which was to take place at La Fère, upon my return, when this business should be arranged. During the time I stayed at Mons, I said all I could to confirm the Count in this resolution, in which I found myself seconded by the Countess.

The day of my departure was now arrived, to the great regret of the ladies of Mons, as well as myself. The Countess expressed herself in terms which showed she had conceived the warmest friendship for me, and made me promise to return by way of that city. I presented the Countess with a diamond bracelet, and to the Count I gave a riband and diamond star of considerable value. But these presents, valuable as they were, became more so, in their estimation, as I was the donor.

Of the ladies, none accompanied me from this place, except Madame d'Aurec. She went with me to Namur, where I slept that night, and where she expected to find her husband and the Duc d'Arscot, her brother-in-law, who had been there since the peace betwixt the King of Spain and the States of Flanders. For though they were both of the party of the States, yet the Duc d'Arscot, being an old courtier and having attended King Philip in Flanders and England, could not withdraw himself from Court and the society of the great. The Comte de Lalain, with all his nobles, conducted me two leagues beyond his government, and until he saw Don John's company in the distance advancing to meet me. He then took his leave of me, being unwilling to meet Don John; but M. d'Ainsi stayed with me, as his master, the Bishop of Cambray, was in the Spanish interest.

This gallant company having left me, I was soon after met by Don John of Austria, preceded by a great number of running footmen, and escorted by only twenty or thirty horsemen. He was attended by a number of noblemen, and amongst the rest the Duc d'Arscot, M. d'Aurec, the Marquis de Varenbon, and the younger Balençon, governor, for the King of Spain, of the county of Burgundy. These last two, who are brothers, had ridden post to meet me. Of Don John's household there was only Louis de Gonzago of any rank. He called himself a relation of the Duke of Mantua; the others were mean-looking people, and of no consideration. Don John alighted from his horse to salute me in my litter, which was opened for the purpose. I returned the salute after the French fashion to him, the Duc d'Arscot, and M. d'Aurec. After an exchange of compliments, he mounted his horse, but continued in discourse with me until we reached the city, which was not before it grew dark, as I set off late, the ladies of Mons keeping me as long as they could, amusing themselves with viewing my litter, and requiring an explanation of the different mottoes and devices. However, as the Spaniards excel in preserving good order, Namur appeared with particular advantage, for the streets were well lighted, every house being illuminated, so that the blaze exceeded that of daylight.

Our supper was served to us in our respective apart-

ments, Don John being unwilling, after the fatigue
of so long a journey, to incommode us with a banquet.  The house in which I was lodged had been
newly furnished for the purpose of receiving me.  It
consisted of a magnificent large *salon,* with a private
apartment, consisting of lodging rooms and closets,
furnished in the most costly manner, with furniture
of every kind, and hung with the richest tapestry of
velvet and satin, divided into compartments by col-
umns of silver embroidery, with knobs of gold, all
wrought in the most superb manner.  Within these
compartments were figures in antique habits, embroidered in gold and silver.

The Cardinal de Lenoncourt, a man of taste and
curiosity, being one day in these apartments with the
Duc d'Arscot, who, as I have before observed, was an
ornament to Don John's Court, remarked to him that
this furniture seemed more proper for a great king
than a young unmarried prince like Don John.  To
which the Duc d'Arscot replied that it came to him
as a present, having been sent to him by a bashaw
belonging to the Grand Seignior, whose sons he had
made prisoners in a signal victory obtained over the
Turks.  Don John having sent the bashaw's sons back
without ransom, the father, in return, made him a
present of a large quantity of gold, silver, and silk
stuffs, which he caused to be wrought into tapestry
at Milan, where there are curious workmen in this
way; and he had the Queen's bedchamber hung with
tapestry representing the battle in which he had so
gloriously defeated the Turks.

The next morning Don John conducted us to chapel,
where we heard mass celebrated after the Spanish
manner, with all kinds of music, after which we par-
took of a banquet prepared by Don John.  He and
I were seated at a separate table, at a distance of three

yards from which stood the great one, of which the honours were done by Madame d'Aurec.  At this table the ladies and principal lords took their seats. Don John was served with drink by Louis de Gonzago, kneeling.  The tables being removed, the ball was opened, and the dancing continued the whole afternoon.  The evening was spent in conversation betwixt Don John and me, who told me I greatly resembled the Queen his mistress, by whom he meant the late Queen my sister, and for whom he professed to have entertained a very high esteem.  In short, Don John manifested, by every mark of attention and politeness, as well to me as to my attendants, the very great pleasure he had in receiving me.

The boats which were to convey me upon the Meuse to Liège not all being ready, I was under the necessity of staying another day.  The morning was passed as that of the day before.  After dinner, we embarked on the river in a very beautiful boat, surrounded by others having on board musicians playing on hautboys, horns, and violins, and landed at an island where Don John had caused a collation to be prepared in a large bower formed with branches of ivy, in which the musicians were placed in small recesses, playing on their instruments during the time of supper.  The tables being removed, the dances began, and lasted till it was time to return, which I did in the same boat that conveyed me thither, and which was that provided for my voyage.

The next morning Don John conducted me to the boat, and there took a most polite and courteous leave, charging M. and Madame d'Aurec to see me safe to Huy, the first town belonging to the Bishop of Liège, where I was to sleep.  As soon as Don John had gone on shore, M. d'Ainsi, who remained in the boat, and who had the Bishop of Cambray's permission to go to Namur only, took leave of me with many protestations of fidelity and attachment to my brother and myself.

But Fortune, envious of my hitherto prosperous journey, gave me two omens of the sinister events of my return.

The first was the sudden illness which attacked Mademoiselle de Tournon, the daughter of the lady of my bedchamber, a young person, accomplished, with every grace and virtue, and for whom I had the most perfect regard. No sooner had the boat left the shore than this young lady was seized with an alarming disorder, which, from the great pain attending it, caused her to scream in the most doleful manner. The physicians attributed the cause to spasms of the heart, which, notwithstanding the utmost exertions of their skill, carried her off a few days after my arrival at Liège. As the history of this young lady is remarkable, I shall relate it in my next letter.

The other omen was what happened to us at Huy, immediately upon our arrival there. This town is built on the declivity of a mountain, at the foot of which runs the river Meuse. As we were about to land, there fell a torrent of rain, which, coming down the steep sides of the mountain, swelled the river instantly to such a degree that we had only time to leap out of the boat and run to the top, the flood reaching the very highest street, next to where I was to lodge. There we were forced to put up with such accommodation as could be procured in the house, as it was impossible to remove the smallest article of our baggage from the boats, or even to stir out of the house we were in, the whole city being under water. However, the town was as suddenly relieved from this calamity as it had been afflicted with it, for, on the next morning, the whole inundation had ceased, the waters having run off, and the river being confined within its usual channel.

Leaving Huy, M. and Madame d'Aurec returned to Don John at Namur, and I proceeded, in the boat, to sleep that night at Liège.

## LETTER XV

THE Bishop of Liège, who is the sovereign of the city and province, received me with all the cordiality and respect that could be expected from a personage of his dignity and great accomplishments. He was, indeed, a nobleman endowed with singular prudence and virtue, agreeable in his person and conversation, gracious and magnificent in his carriage and behaviour, to which I may add that he spoke the French language perfectly.

He was constantly attended by his chapter, with several of his canons, who are all sons of dukes, counts, or great German lords. The bishopric is itself a sovereign State, which brings in a considerable revenue, and includes a number of fine cities. The bishop is chosen from amongst the canons, who must be of noble descent, and resident one year. The city is larger than Lyons, and much resembles it, having the Meuse running through it. The houses in which the canons reside have the appearance of noble palaces. The streets of the city are regular and spacious, the houses of the citizens well built, the squares large, and ornamented with curious fountains. The churches appear as if raised entirely of marble, of which there are considerable quarries in the neighbourhood; they are all of them ornamented with beautiful clocks, and exhibit a variety of moving figures.

The Bishop received me as I landed from the boat, and conducted me to his magnificent residence, ornamented with delicious fountains and gardens, set off with galleries, all painted, superbly gilt, and enriched with marble, beyond description.

The spring which affords the waters of Spa being distant no more than three or four leagues from the city of Liège, and there being only a village, consisting of three or four small houses, on the spot, the Princesse de Roche-sur-Yon was advised by her physicians to stay at Liège and have the waters brought to her, which they assured her would have equal efficacy, if taken after sunset and before sunrise, as if drunk at the spring. I was well pleased that she resolved to follow the advice of the doctors, as we were more comfortably lodged and had an agreeable society; for, besides his Grace (so the bishop is styled, as a king is addressed his Majesty, and a prince his Highness), the news of my arrival being spread about, many lords and ladies came from Germany to visit me. Amongst these was the Countess d'Aremberg, who had the honour to accompany Queen Elizabeth to Mezières, to which place she came to marry King Charles my brother, a lady very high in the estimation of the Empress, the Emperor, and all the princes in Christendom. With her came her sister the Landgravine, Madame d'Aremberg her daughter, M. d'Aremberg her son, a gallant and accomplished nobleman, the perfect image of his father, who brought the Spanish succours to King Charles my brother, and returned with great honour and additional reputation. This meeting, so honourable to me, and so much to my satisfaction, was damped by the grief and concern occasioned by the loss of Mademoiselle de Tournon, whose story, being of a singular nature, I shall now relate to you, agreeably to the promise I made in my last letter.

I must begin with observing to you that Madame

de Tournon, at this time lady of my bedchamber, had several daughters, the eldest of whom married M. de Balençon, governor, for the King of Spain, in the county of Burgundy.  This daughter, upon her marriage, had solicited her mother to admit of her taking her sister, the young lady whose story I am now about to relate, to live with her, as she was going to a country strange to her, and wherein she had no relations.  To this her mother consented; and the young lady, being universally admired for her modesty and graceful accomplishments, for which she certainly deserved admiration, attracted the notice of the Marquis de Varenbon.  The Marquis, as I before mentioned, is the brother of M. de Balençon, and was intended for the Church; but, being violently enamoured of Mademoiselle de Tournon (who, as he lived in the same house, he had frequent opportunities of seeing), he now begged his brother's permission to marry her, not having yet taken orders.  The young lady's family, to whom he had likewise communicated his wish, readily gave their consent, but his brother refused his, strongly advising him to change his resolution and put on the gown.

Thus were matters situated when her mother, Madame de Tournon, a virtuous and pious lady, thinking she had cause to be offended, ordered her daughter to leave the house of her sister, Madame de Balençon, and come to her.  The mother, a woman of a violent spirit, not considering that her daughter was grown up and merited a mild treatment, was continually scolding the poor young lady, so that she was for ever with tears in her eyes.  Still, there was nothing to blame in the young girl's conduct, but such was the severity of the mother's disposition.  The daughter, as you may well suppose, wished to be from under the mother's tyrannical government, and was accordingly delighted with the thoughts of attending me in this journey to Flanders, hoping, as it happened, that she should meet the Marquis de Varenbon somewhere on the road, and that, as he had now abandoned all thoughts of the Church, he would renew his proposal of marriage, and take her from her mother.

I have before mentioned that the Marquis de Varenbon and the younger Balençon joined us at Namur. Young Balençon, who was far from being so agreeable as his brother, addressed himself to the young lady, but the Marquis, during the whole time we stayed at Namur, paid not the least attention to her, and seemed as if he had never been acquainted with her.

The resentment, grief, and disappointment occasioned by a behaviour so slighting and unnatural was necessarily stifled in her breast, as decorum and her sex's pride obliged her to appear as if she disregarded it; but when, after taking leave, all of them left the boat, the anguish of her mind, which she had hitherto suppressed, could no longer be restrained, and, labouring for vent, it stopped her respiration, and forced from her those lamentable outcries which I have already spoken of. Her youth combated for eight days with this uncommon disorder, but at the expiration of that time she died, to the great grief of her mother, as well as myself. I say of her mother, for, though she was so rigidly severe over this daughter, she tenderly loved her.

The funeral of this unfortunate young lady was solemnized with all proper ceremonies, and conducted in the most honourable manner, as she was descended from a great family, allied to the Queen my mother. When the day of interment arrived, four of my gentlemen were appointed bearers, one of whom was named La Boëssière. This man had entertained a secret passion for her, which he never durst declare on account of the inferiority of his family and station. He was now destined to bear the remains of her, dead, for whom he had long been dying, and was now as near dying for her loss as he had before been for her love. The melancholy procession was marching slowly along, when it was met by the Marquis de Varenbon, who had been the sole occasion of it. We had not left Namur long when the Marquis reflected upon his cruel behaviour towards this unhappy young lady; and his passion (wonderful to relate) being revived by the absence of her who inspired it, though scarcely alive while she was present, he had resolved to come and ask her of her mother in marriage. He made no doubt, perhaps, of success, as he seldom failed in enterprises of love; witness the great lady he has since obtained for a wife, in opposition to the will of her family. He might, besides, have flattered himself that he should easily have gained a pardon from her by whom he was beloved, according to the Italian proverb, " Che la forza d'amore non riguarda al delitto " (Lovers are not criminal in the estimation of one another). Accordingly, the Marquis solicited Don John to be despatched to me on some errand, and arrived, as I said before, at the very instant the corpse of this ill-fated young lady was being borne to the grave. He was stopped by the crowd occasioned by this solemn procession. He contemplates it for some time. He observes a long train of persons in mourning, and remarks the coffin to be covered with a white pall, and that there are chaplets of flowers laid upon the coffin. He inquires whose funeral it is. The answer he receives is, that it is the funeral of a young lady. Unfortunately for him, this reply fails to satisfy his curiosity. He makes up to one who led the procession, and eagerly asks the name of the young lady they are proceeding to bury. When, oh, fatal answer! Love, willing to avenge the victim of his ingratitude and neglect, suggests a reply which had nearly deprived him of life. He no sooner hears the name of Mademoiselle de Tournon pronounced than he falls from his horse in a swoon. He is taken up for dead, and conveyed to the nearest house, where he lies for a time insensible; his soul, no doubt, leaving his body to obtain pardon from her whom he had hastened to a premature grave, to return to taste the bitterness of death a second time.

Having performed the last offices to the remains of this poor young lady, I was unwilling to discompose the gaiety of the society assembled here on my account by any show of grief. Accordingly, I joined the Bishop, or, as he is called, his Grace, and his canons, in their entertainments at different houses, and in gardens, of which the city and its neighbourhood afforded a variety. I was every morning attended by a numerous company to the garden, in which I drank the waters, the exercise of walking being recommended to be used with them. As the physician who advised me to take them was my own brother, they did not fail of their effect with me; and for these six or seven years which are gone over my head since I drank them, I have been free from any complaint of erysipelas on my arm. From this garden we usually proceeded to the place where we were invited to dinner. After dinner we were amused with a ball; from the ball we went to some convent, where we heard vespers; from vespers to supper, and that over, we had another ball, or music on the river.

## LETTER XVI

IN this manner we passed the six weeks, which is the usual time for taking these waters, at the expiration of which the Princesse de Roche-sur-Yon was desirous to return to France; but Madame d'Aurec, who just then returned to us from Namur, on her way to rejoin her husband in Lorraine, brought us news of an extraordinary change of affairs in that town and province since we had passed through it.

It appeared from this lady's account that, on the very day we left Namur, Don John, after quitting the boat, mounted his horse under pretence of taking the diversion of hunting, and, as he passed the gate of the castle of Namur, expressed a desire of seeing it; that, having entered, he took possession of it, notwithstanding he held it for the States, agreeably to a convention. Don John, moreover, arrested the persons of the Duc d'Arscot and M. d'Aurec, and also made Madame d'Aurec a prisoner. After some remonstrances and entreaties, he had set her husband and brother-in-law at liberty, but detained her as a hostage for them. In consequence of these measures, the whole country was in arms. The province of Namur was divided into three parties: the first whereof was that of the States, or the Catholic party of Flanders; the second that of the Prince of Orange and the Huguenots; the third, the Spanish party, of which Don John was the head.

By letters which I received just at this time from my brother, through the hands of a gentleman named

Lescar, I found I was in great danger of falling into
the hands of one or other of these parties.

These letters informed me that, since my departure
from Court, God had dealt favourably with my
brother, and enabled him to acquit himself of the command of the army confided to him, greatly to the
benefit of the King's service; so that he had taken all
the towns and driven the Huguenots out of the provinces, agreeably to the design for which the army
was raised; that he had returned to the Court at
Poitiers, where the King stayed during the siege of
Brouage, to be near to M. de Mayenne, in order to
afford him whatever succours he stood in need of;
that, as the Court is a Proteus, forever putting on a
new face, he had found it entirely changed, so that
he had been no more considered than if he had done
the King no service whatever; and that Bussi, who
had been so graciously looked upon before and during this last war, had done great personal service, and
had lost a brother at the storming of Issoire, was very
coolly received, and even as maliciously persecuted as
in the time of Le Guast; in consequence of which
either he or Bussi experienced some indignity or other.
He further mentioned that the King's favourites had
been practising with his most faithful servants,
Maugiron, La Valette, Mauléon, and Hivarrot, and
several other good and trusty men, to desert him,
and enter into the King's service; and, lastly, that the
King had repented of giving me leave to go to Flanders, and that, to counteract my brother, a plan was
laid to intercept me on my return, either by the Spaniards, for which purpose they had been told that I
had treated for delivering up the country to him, or
by the Huguenots, in revenge of the war my brother
had carried on against them, after having formerly
assisted them.

This intelligence required to be well considered, as there seemed to be an utter impossibility of avoiding both parties. I had, however, the pleasure to think that two of the principal persons of my company stood well with either one or another party. The Cardinal de Lenoncourt had been thought to favour the Huguenot party, and M. Descartes, brother to the Bishop of Lisieux, was supposed to have the Spanish interest at heart. I communicated our difficult situation to the Princesse de Roche-sur-Yon and Madame de Tournon, who, considering that we could not reach La Fère in less than five or six days, answered me, with tears in their eyes, that God only had it in his power to preserve us, that I should recommend myself to his protection, and then follow such measures as should seem advisable. They observed that, as one of them was in a weak state of health, and the other advanced in years, I might affect to make short journeys on their account, and they would put up with every inconvenience to extricate me from the danger I was in.

I next consulted with the Bishop of Liège, who most certainly acted towards me like a father, and gave directions to the grand master of his household to attend me with his horses as far as I should think proper. As it was necessary that we should have a passport from the Prince of Orange, I sent Mondoucet to him to obtain one, as he was acquainted with the Prince and was known to favour his religion. Mondoucet did not return, and I believe I might have waited for him until this time to no purpose. I was advised by the Cardinal de Lenoncourt and my first esquire, the Chevalier Salviati, who were of the same party, not to stir without a passport; but, as I suspected a plan was laid to entrap me, I resolved to set out the next morning.

They now saw that this pretence was insufficient to detain me; accordingly, the Chevalier Salviati prevailed with my treasurer, who was secretly a Huguenot, to declare he had not money enough in his hands to discharge the expenses we had incurred at Liège, and that, in consequence, my horses were detained. I afterwards discovered that this was false, for, on my arrival at La Fère, I called for his accounts, and found he had then a balance in his hands which would have enabled him to pay the expenses of my family for six or seven weeks. The Princesse de Roche-sur-Yon, incensed at the affront put upon me, and seeing the danger I incurred by staying, advanced the money that was required, to their great confusion; and I took my leave of his Grace the Bishop, presenting him with a diamond worth three thousand crowns, and giving his domestics gold chains and rings. Having thus taken our leave, we proceeded to Huy, without any other passport than God's good providence.

This town, as I observed before, belongs to the Bishop of Liège, but was now in a state of tumult and confusion, on account of the general revolt of the Low Countries, the townsmen taking part with the Netherlanders, notwithstanding the bishopric was a neutral State. On this account they paid no respect to the grand master of the Bishop's household, who accompanied us, but, knowing Don John had taken the castle of Namur in order, as they supposed, to intercept me on my return, these brutal people, as soon as I had got into my quarters, rang the alarm-bell, drew up their artillery, placed chains across the streets, and kept us thus confined and separated the whole night, giving us no opportunity to expostulate with them on such conduct. In the morning we were suffered to leave the town without further molestation, and the streets we passed through were lined with armed men.

From there we proceeded to Dinant, where we intended to sleep; but, unfortunately for us, the townspeople had on that day chosen their burghermasters, a kind of officers like the consuls in Gascony and France. In consequence of this election, it was a day of tumult, riot, and debauchery; every one in the town was drunk, no magistrate was acknowledged. In a word, all was in confusion. To render our situation still worse, the grand master of the Bishop's household had formerly done the town some ill office, and was considered as its enemy. The people of the town, when in their sober senses, were inclined to favour the party of the States, but under the influence of Bacchus they paid no regard to any party, not even to themselves.

As soon as I had reached the suburbs, they were alarmed at the number of my company, quitted the bottle and glass to take up their arms, and immediately shut the gates against me. I had sent a gentleman before me, with my harbinger and quartermasters, to beg the magistrates to admit me to stay one night in the town, but I found my officers had been put under an arrest. They bawled out to us from within, to tell us their situation, but could not make themselves heard. At length I raised myself up in my litter, and, taking off my mask, made a sign to a townsman nearest me, of the best appearance, that I was desirous to speak with him. As soon as he drew near me, I begged him to call out for silence, which being with some difficulty obtained, I represented to him who I was, and the occasion of my journey; that it was far from my intention to do them harm; but, to prevent any suspicions of the kind, I only begged to be admitted to go into their city with my women, and as few others of my attendants as they thought proper, and that we might be permitted to stay there for one night, whilst the rest of my company remained within the suburbs.

They agreed to this proposal, and opened their gates for my admission. I then entered the city with the principal persons of my company, and the grand master of the Bishop's household. This reverend personage, who was eighty years of age, and wore a beard as white as snow, which reached down to his girdle,—this venerable old man, I say, was no sooner recognized by the drunken and armed rabble than he was accosted with the grossest abuse, and it was with difficulty they were restrained from laying violent hands upon him. At length I got him into my lodgings, but the mob fired at the house, the walls of which were only of plaster. Upon being thus attacked, I inquired for the master of the house, who, fortunately, was within. I entreated him to speak from the window, to some one without, to obtain permission for my being heard. I had some difficulty to get him to venture doing so. At length, after much bawling from the window, the burghermasters came to speak to me, but were so drunk that they scarcely knew what they said. I explained to them that I was entirely ignorant that the grand master of the Bishop's household was a person to whom they had a dislike, and I begged them to consider the consequences of giving offence to a person like me, who was a friend of the principal lords of the States, and I assured them that the Comte de Lalain, in particular, would be greatly displeased when he should hear how I had been received there.

The name of the Comte de Lalain produced an instant effect, much more than if I had mentioned all the sovereign princes I was related to. The principal person amongst them asked me, with some hesitation and stammering, if I was really a particular friend

of the Count's.   Perceiving that to claim kindred with
the Count would do me more service than being related to all the Powers in Christendom, I answered
that I was both a friend and a relation.   They then
made me many apologies and *congés*, stretching forth
their hands in token of friendship; in short, they now
behaved with as much civility as before with rudeness.
They begged my pardon for what had happened, and
promised that the good old man, the grand master of
the Bishop's household, should be no more insulted,
but be suffered to leave the city quietly, the next
morning, with me.

As soon as morning came, and while I was preparing to go to hear mass, there arrived the King's agent
to Don John, named Du Bois, a man much attached
to the Spanish interest.  He informed me that he had
received orders from the King my brother to conduct
me in safety on my return.  He said that he had prevailed on Don John to permit Barlemont to escort me
to Namur with a troop of cavalry, and begged me to
obtain leave of the citizens to admit Barlemont and
his troop to enter the town, that they might receive
my orders.

Thus had they concerted a double plot; the one to
get possession of the town, the other of my person.
I saw through the whole design, and consulted with
the Cardinal de Lenoncourt, communicating to him
my suspicions.  The Cardinal was as unwilling to fall
into the hands of the Spaniards as I could be; he
therefore thought it advisable to acquaint the townspeople with the plot, and make our escape from the
city by another road, in order to avoid meeting Barlemont's troop.  It was agreed betwixt us that the
Cardinal should keep Du Bois in discourse, whilst I
consulted the principal citizens in another apartment.
Accordingly, I assembled as many as I could, to

whom I represented that if they admitted Barlemont and his troop within the town, he would most certainly take possession of it for Don John. I gave it as my advice to make a show of defence, to declare they would not be taken by surprise, and to offer to admit Barlemont, and no one else, within their gates. They resolved to act according to my counsel, and offered to serve me at the hazard of their lives. They promised to procure me a guide, who should conduct me by a road by following which I should put the river betwixt me and Don John's forces, whereby I should be out of his reach, and could be lodged in houses and towns which were in the interest of the States only.

This point being settled, I despatched them to give admission to M. de Barlemont, who, as soon as he entered within the gates, begged hard that his troop might come in likewise. Hereupon, the citizens flew into a violent rage, and were near putting him to death. They told him that if he did not order his men out of sight of the town, they would fire upon them with their great guns. This was done with design to give me time to leave the town before they could follow in pursuit of me. M. de Barlemont and the agent, Du Bois, used every argument they could devise to persuade me to go to Namur, where they said Don John waited to receive me.

I appeared to give way to their persuasions, and, after hearing mass and taking a hasty dinner, I left my lodgings, escorted by two or three hundred armed citizens, some of them engaging Barlemont and Du Bois in conversation. We all took the way to the gate which opens to the river, and directly opposite to that leading to Namur. Du Bois and his colleague told me I was not going the right way, but I continued talking, and as if I did not hear them. But when we reached the gate I hastened into the boat, and my people after me. M. de Barlemont and the agent Du Bois, calling out to me from the bank, told me I was doing very wrong and acting directly contrary to the King's intention, who had directed that I should return by way of Namur.

In spite of all their remonstrances we crossed the river with all possible expedition, and, during the two or three crossings which were necessary to convey over the litters and horses, the citizens, to give me the more time to escape, were debating with Barlemont and Du Bois concerning a number of grievances and complaints, telling them, in their coarse language, that Don John had broken the peace and falsified his engagements with the States; and they even rehearsed the old quarrel of the death of Egmont, and, lastly, declared that if the troop made its appearance before their walls again, they would fire upon it with their artillery.

I had by this means sufficient time to reach a secure distance, and was, by the help of God and the assistance of my guide, out of all apprehensions of danger from Barlemont and his troop.

I intended to lodge that night in a strong castle, called Fleurines, which belonged to a gentleman of the Party of the States, whom I had seen with the Comte de Lalain. Unfortunately for me, the gentleman was absent, and his lady only was in the castle. The courtyard being open, we entered it, which put the lady into such a fright that she ordered the bridge to be drawn up, and fled to the strong tower. Nothing we could say would induce her to give us entrance. In the meantime, three hundred gentlemen, whom Don John had sent off to intercept our passage, and take possession of the castle of Fleurines, judging that I should take up my quarters there, made their appearance upon an eminence, at the distance of about a thousand yards. They, seeing our carriages in the courtyard, and supposing that we ourselves had taken to the strong tower, resolved to stay where they were that night, hoping to intercept me the next morning.

In this cruel situation were we placed, in a courtyard surrounded by a wall by no means strong, and shut up by a gate equally as weak and as capable of being forced, remonstrating from time to time with the lady, who was deaf to all our prayers and entreaties.

Through God's mercy, her husband, M. de Fleurines, himself appeared just as night approached. We then gained instant admission, and the lady was greatly reprimanded by her husband for her incivility and indiscreet behaviour. This gentleman had been sent by the Comte de Lalain, with directions to conduct me through the several towns belonging to the States, the Count himself not being able to leave the army of the States, of which he had the chief command, to accompany me.

This was as favourable a circumstance for me as I could wish; for, M. de Fleurines offering to accompany me into France, the towns we had to pass through being of the party of the States, we were everywhere quietly and honourably received. I had only the mortification of not being able to visit Mons, agreeably to my promise made to the Comtesse de Lalain, not passing nearer to it than Nivelle, seven long leagues distant from it. The Count being at Antwerp, and the war being hottest in the neighbourhood of Mons, I thus was prevented seeing either of them on my return. I could only write to the Countess by a servant of the gentleman who was now my conductor. As soon as she learned I was at Nivelle, she sent some gentlemen, natives of the part of Flan-

ders I was in, with a strong injunction to see me safe
on the frontier of France.

I had to pass through the Cambrésis, partly in favour of Spain and partly of the States. Accordingly,
I set out with these gentlemen, to lodge at Cateau-
Cambrésis. There they took leave of me, in order
to return to Mons, and by them I sent the Countess a
gown of mine, which had been greatly admired by her
when I wore it at Mons; it was of black satin, curiously embroidered, and cost nine hundred crowns.

When I arrived at Cateau-Cambrésis, I had intelligence sent me that a party of the Huguenot troops
had a design to attack me on the frontiers of Flanders
and France. This intelligence I communicated to a
few only of my company, and prepared to set off an
hour before daybreak. When I sent for my litters
and horses, I found much such a kind of delay from
the Chevalier Salviati as I had before experienced at
Liège, and suspecting it was done designedly, I left
my litter behind, and mounted on horseback, with
such of my attendants as were ready to follow me.
By this means, with God's assistance, I escaped being
waylaid by my enemies, and reached Catelet at ten in
the morning. From there I went to my house at La
Fère, where I intended to reside until I learned that
peace was concluded upon.

At La Fère I found a messenger in waiting from
my brother, who had orders to return with all expedition, as soon as I arrived, and inform him of it.
My brother wrote me word, by that messenger, that
peace was concluded, and the King returned to Paris;
that, as to himself, his situation was rather worse
than better; that he and his people were daily receiving some affront or other, and continual quarrels were
excited betwixt the King's favourites and Bussi and
my brother's principal attendants. This, he added,

had made him impatient for my return, that he might come and visit me.

I sent his messenger back, and immediately after, my brother sent Bussi and all his household to Angers, and, taking with him fifteen or twenty attendants, he rode post to me at La Fère. It was a great satisfaction to me to see one whom I so tenderly loved and greatly honoured, once more. I considered it amongst the greatest felicities I ever enjoyed, and, accordingly, it became my chief study to make his residence here agreeable to him. He himself seemed delighted with this change of situation, and would willingly have continued in it longer had not the noble generosity of his mind called him forth to great achievements. The quiet of our Court, when compared with that he had just left, affected him so powerfully that he could not but express the satisfaction he felt by frequently exclaiming, "Oh, Queen! how happy I am with you. My God! your society is a paradise wherein I enjoy every delight, and I seem to have lately escaped from hell, with all its furies and tortures!"

# LETTER XVII

WE passed nearly two months together, which appeared to us only as so many days. I gave him an account of what I had done for him in Flanders, and the state in which I had left the business. He approved of the interview with the Comte de Lalain's brother in order to settle the plan of operations and exchange assurances. Accordingly, the Comte de Montigny arrived, with four or five other leading men of the county of Hainault. One of these was charged with a letter from M. d'Ainsi, offering his services to my brother, and assuring him of the citadel of Cambray. M. de Montigny delivered his brother's declaration and engagement to give up the counties of Hainault and Artois, which included a number of fine cities. These offers made and accepted, my brother dismissed them with presents of gold medals, bearing his and my effigies, and every assurance of his future favour; and they returned to prepare everything for his coming. In the meanwhile my brother considered on the necessary measures to be used for raising a sufficient force, for which purpose he returned to the King, to prevail with him to assist him in this enterprise.

As I was anxious to go to Gascony, I made ready for the journey, and set off for Paris, my brother meeting me at the distance of one day's journey.

At St. Denis I was met by the King, the Queen my mother, Queen Louise, and the whole Court. It

was at St. Denis that I was to stop and dine, and
there it was that I had the honour of the meeting
I have just mentioned.

I was received very graciously, and most sumptuously entertained. I was made to recount the
particulars of my triumphant journey to Liège, and
perilous return. The magnificent entertainments I had
received excited their admiration, and they rejoiced
at my narrow escapes. With such conversation I
amused the Queen my mother and the rest of the
company in her coach, on our way to Paris, where,
supper and the ball being ended, I took an opportunity, when I saw the King and the Queen my
mother together, to address them.

I expressed my hopes that they would not now
oppose my going to the King my husband; that now,
by the peace, the chief objection to it was removed,
and if I delayed going, in the present situation of affairs, it might be prejudicial and discreditable to
me. Both of them approved of my request, and commended my resolution. The Queen my mother added
that she would accompany me on my journey, as it
would be for the King's service that she did so. She
said the King must furnish me with the necessary
means for the journey, to which he readily assented.
I thought this a proper time to settle everything, and
prevent another journey to Court, which would be no
longer pleasing after my brother left it, who was now
pressing his expedition to Flanders with all haste.
I therefore begged the Queen my mother to recollect
the promise she had made my brother and me as soon
as peace was agreed upon, which was that, before my
departure for Gascony, I should have my marriage
portion assigned to me in lands. She said that she
recollected it well, and the King thought it very reasonable, and promised that it should be done. I en-

treated that it might be concluded speedily, as I wished to set off, with their permission, at the beginning of the next month.    This, too, was granted me, but granted after the mode of the Court; that is to say, notwithstanding my constant solicitations, instead of despatch, I experienced only delay; and thus it continued for five or six months in negotiation.

My brother met with the like treatment, though he was continually urging the necessity for his setting out for Flanders, and representing that his expedition was for the glory and advantage of France,—for its glory, as such an enterprise would, like Piedmont, prove a school of war for the young nobility, wherein future Montlucs, Brissacs, Termes, and Bellegardes would be bred, all of them instructed in these wars, and afterwards, as field-marshals, of the greatest service to their country; and it would be for the advantage of France, as it would prevent civil wars; for Flanders would then be no longer a country wherein such discontented spirits as aimed at novelty could assemble to brood over their malice and hatch plots for the disturbance of their native land.

These representations, which were both reasonable and consonant with truth, had no weight when put into the scale against the envy excited by this advancement of my brother's fortune.    Accordingly, every delay was used to hinder him from collecting his forces together, and stop his expedition to Flanders.    Bussi and his other dependents were offered a thousand indignities.    Every stratagem was tried, by day as well as by night, to pick quarrels with Bussi,— now by Quélus, at another time by Grammont,—with the hope that my brother would engage in them.    This was unknown to the King; but Maugiron, who had engrossed the King's favour, and who had quitted my brother's service, sought every means to ruin him,

as it is usual for those who have given offence to hate
the offended party.

Thus did this man take every occasion to brave
and insult my brother; and relying upon the countenance and blind affection shown him by the King,
had leagued himself with Quélus, Saint-Luc, Saint-
Maigrin, Grammont, Mauléon, Hivarrot, and other
young men who enjoyed the King's favour. As those
who are favourites find a number of followers at
Court, these licentious young courtiers thought they
might do whatever they pleased. Some new dispute
betwixt them and Bussi was constantly starting.
Bussi had a degree of courage which knew not how
to give way to any one; and my brother, unwilling to
give umbrage to the King, and foreseeing that such
proceedings would not forward his expedition, to
avoid quarrels and, at the same time, to promote his
plans, resolved to despatch Bussi to his duchy of
Alençon, in order to discipline such troops as he
should find there. My brother's amiable qualities
excited the jealousy of Maugiron and the rest of his
cabal about the King's person, and their dislike for
Bussi was not so much on his own account as because
he was strongly attached to my brother. The slights
and disrespect shown to my brother were remarked
by every one at Court; but his prudence, and the
patience natural to his disposition, enabled him to
put up with their insults, in hopes of finishing the
business of his Flemish expedition, which would remove him to a distance from them and their machinations. This persecution was the more mortifying
and discreditable as it even extended to his servants,
whom they strove to injure by every means they
could employ. M. de la Chastre at this time had a
lawsuit of considerable consequence decided against
him, because he had lately attached himself to my

brother. At the instance of Maugiron and Saint-Luc, the King was induced to solicit the cause in favour of Madame de Sénetaire, their friend. M. de la Chastre, being greatly injured by it, complained to my brother of the injustice done him, with all the concern such a proceeding may be supposed to have occasioned.

About this time Saint-Luc's marriage was celebrated. My brother resolved not to be present at it, and begged of me to join him in the same resolution. The Queen my mother was greatly uneasy on account of the behaviour of these young men, fearing that, if my brother did not join them in this festivity, it might be attended with some bad consequence, especially as the day was likely to produce scenes of revelry and debauch; she, therefore, prevailed on the King to permit her to dine on the wedding-day at St. Maur, and take my brother and me with her. This was the day before Shrove Tuesday; and we returned in the evening, the Queen my mother having well lectured my brother, and made him consent to appear at the ball, in order not to displease the King.

But this rather served to make matters worse than better, for Maugiron and his party began to attack him with such insolent speeches as would have offended any one of far less consequence. They said he needed not to have given himself the trouble of dressing, for he was not missed in the afternoon; but now, they supposed, he came at night at the most suitable time; with other allusions to the meanness of his figure and smallness of stature. All this was addressed to the bride, who sat near him, but spoken out on purpose that he might hear it. My brother, perceiving this was purposely said to provoke an answer and occasion his giving offence to the King, removed from his seat full of resentment; and, consulting with M. de la Chastre, he came to the resolution of leaving the Court in a few days on a hunting party. He still thought his absence might stay their malice, and afford him an opportunity the more easily of settling his preparations for the Flemish expedition with the King. He went immediately to the Queen my mother, who was present at the ball, and was extremely sorry to learn what had happened, and imparted her resolution, in his absence, to solicit the King to hasten his expedition to Flanders. M. de Villequier being present, she bade him acquaint the King with my brother's intention of taking the diversion of hunting a few days; which she thought very proper herself, as it would put a stop to the disputes which had arisen betwixt him and the young men, Maugiron, Saint-Luc, Quélus, and the rest.

My brother retired to his apartment, and, considering his leave as granted, gave orders to his domestics to prepare to set off the next morning for St. Germain, where he should hunt the stag for a few days. He directed the grand huntsman to be ready with the hounds, and retired to rest, thinking to withdraw awhile from the intrigues of the Court, and amuse himself with the sports of the field. M. de Villequier, agreeably to the command he had received from the Queen my mother, asked for leave, and obtained it. The King, however, staying in his closet, like Rehoboam, with his council of five or six young men, they suggested suspicions in his mind respecting my brother's departure from Court. In short, they worked upon his fears and apprehensions so greatly, that he took one of the most rash and inconsiderate steps that was ever decided upon in our time; which was to put my brother and all his principal servants under an arrest. This measure was executed with as much indiscretion as it had been resolved upon. The King, under this agitation of mind, late as it was, hastened to the Queen my mother, and seemed as if there was a general alarm and the enemy at the gates, for he exclaimed on seeing her: "How could you, Madame, think of asking me to let my brother go hence? Do you not perceive how dangerous his going will prove to my kingdom? Depend upon it that this hunting is merely a pretence to cover some treacherous design. I am going to put him and his people under an arrest, and have his papers examined. I am sure we shall make some great discoveries."

At the time he said this he had with him the Sieur de Cossé, captain of the guard, and a number of Scottish archers. The Queen my mother, fearing, from the King's haste and trepidation, that some mischief might happen to my brother, begged to go with him. Accordingly, undressed as she was, wrapping herself up in a night-gown, she followed the King to my brother's bedchamber. The King knocked at the door with great violence, ordering it to be immediately opened, for that he was there himself. My brother started up in his bed, awakened by the noise, and, knowing that he had done nothing that he need fear, ordered Cangé, his *valet de chambre,* to open the door. The King entered in a great rage, and asked him when he would have done plotting against him. "But I will show you," said he, "what it is to plot against your sovereign." Hereupon he ordered the archers to take away all the trunks, and turn the *valets de chambre* out of the room. He searched my brother's bed himself, to see if he could find any papers concealed in it. My brother had that evening received a letter from Madame de Sauves, which he kept in his hand, unwilling that it should be seen. The King endeavoured to force it from him. He refused to part with it, and earnestly entreated the

King would not insist upon seeing it. This only excited the King's anxiety the more to have it in his
possession, as he now supposed it to be the key to
the whole plot, and the very document which would
at once bring conviction home to him. At length, the
King having got it into his hands, he opened it in
the presence of the Queen my mother, and they were
both as much confounded, when they read the con-
tents, as Cato was when he obtained a letter from
Cæsar, in the Senate, which the latter was unwilling
to give up; and which Cato, supposing it to contain
a conspiracy against the Republic, found to be no
other than a love-letter from his own sister.

But the shame of this disappointment served only
to increase the King's anger, who, without conde-
scending to make a reply to my brother, when repeatedly asked what he had been accused of, gave him in
charge of M. de Cossé and his Scots, commanding
them not to admit a single person to speak with
him.

It was one o'clock in the morning when my brother
was made a prisoner in the manner I have now
related. He feared some fatal event might succeed
these violent proceedings, and he was under the greatest concern on my account, supposing me to be under
a like arrest. He observed M. de Cossé to be much
affected by the scene he had been witness to, even to
shedding tears. As the archers were in the room he
would not venture to enter into discourse with him,
but only asked what was become of me. M. de Cossé
answered that I remained at full liberty. My brother
then said it was a great comfort to him to hear that
news; "but," added he, "as I know she loves me so
entirely that she would rather be confined with me
than have her liberty whilst I was in confinement, I
beg you will go to the Queen my mother, and desire

her to obtain leave for my sister to be with me." He did so, and it was granted.

The reliance which my brother displayed upon this occasion in the sincerity of my friendship and regard for him conferred so great an obligation in my mind that, though I have received many particular favours since from him, this has always held the foremost place in my grateful remembrance.

By the time he had received permission for my being with him, daylight made its appearance. Seeing this, my brother begged M. de Cossé to send one of his archers to acquaint me with his situation, and beg me to come to him.

## LETTER XVIII

I WAS ignorant of what had happened to my brother, and when the Scottish archer came into my bedchamber, I was still asleep. He drew the curtains of the bed, and told me, in his broken French, that my brother wished to see me. I stared at the man, half awake as I was, and thought it a dream. After a short pause, and being thoroughly awakened, I asked him if he was not a Scottish archer. He answered me in the affirmative. "What!" cried I, "has my brother no one else to send a message by?" He replied he had not, for all his domestics had been put under an arrest. He then proceeded to relate, as well as he could explain himself, the events of the preceding night, and the leave granted my brother for my being with him during his imprisonment.

The poor fellow, observing me to be much affected by this intelligence, drew near, and whispered me to this purport: "Do not grieve yourself about this matter; I know a way of setting your brother at liberty, and you may depend upon it, that I will do it; but, in that case, I must go off with him." I assured him that he might rely upon being as amply rewarded as he could wish for such assistance, and, huddling on my clothes, I followed him alone to my brother's apartments. In going thither, I had occasion to traverse the whole gallery, which was filled with people, who, at another time, would have pressed forward to pay their respects to me; but, now that Fortune seemed to frown upon me, they all avoided me, or appeared as if they did not see me.

Coming into my brother's apartments, I found him not at all affected by what had happened; for such was the constancy of his mind, that his arrest had wrought no change, and he received me with his usual cheerfulness.  He ran to meet me, and taking me in his arms, he said:

"Queen! I beg you to dry up your tears; in my present situation, nothing can grieve me so much as to find you under any concern; for my own part, I am so conscious of my innocence and the integrity of my conduct, that I can defy the utmost malice of my enemies.  If I should chance to fall the victim of their injustice, my death would prove a more cruel punishment to them than to me, who have courage sufficient to meet it in a just cause.  It is not death I fear, because I have tasted sufficiently of the calamities and evils of life, and am ready to leave this world, which I have found only the abode of sorrow; but the circumstance I dread most is, that, not finding me sufficiently guilty to doom me to death, I shall be condemned to a long, solitary imprisonment; though I should even despise their tyranny in that respect, could I but have the assurance of being comforted by your presence."

These words, instead of stopping my tears, only served to make them stream afresh.  I answered, sobbing, that my life and fortune were at his devotion; that the power of God alone could prevent me from affording him my assistance under every extremity; that, if he should be transported from that place, and I should be withheld from following him, I would kill myself on the spot.

Changing our discourse, we framed a number of conjectures on what might be the probable cause of the King's angry proceedings against him, but found ourselves at a loss what to assign them to.

Whilst we were discussing this matter the hour came for opening the palace gates, when a simple young man belonging to Bussi presented himself for entrance. Being stopped by the guard and questioned as to whither he was going, he, panic-struck, replied he was going to M. de Bussi, his master. This answer was carried to the King, and gave fresh grounds for suspicion. It seems my brother, supposing he should not be able to go to Flanders for some time, and resolving to send Bussi to his duchy of Alençon as I have already mentioned, had lodged him in the Louvre, that he might be near him to take instructions at every opportunity.

L'Archant, the general of the guard, had received the King's commands to make a search in the Louvre for him and Simier, and put them both under arrest. He entered upon this business with great unwillingness, as he was intimate with Bussi, who was accustomed to call him " father." L'Archant, going to Simier's apartment, arrested him; and though he judged Bussi was there too, yet being unwilling to find him, he was going away. Bussi, however, who had concealed himself under the bed, as not knowing to whom the orders for his arrest might be given, finding he was to be left there, and sensible that he should be well treated by L'Archant, called out to him, as he was leaving the room, in his droll manner:

" What, papa, are you going without me? Don't you think I am as great a rogue as that Simier?"

" Ah, son," replied L'Archant, " I would much rather have lost my arm than have met with you!"

Bussi, being a man devoid of all fear, observed that it was a sign that things went well with him; then, turning to Simier, who stood trembling with fear, he jeered him upon his pusillanimity. L'Archant removed them both, and set a guard over them; and, in the next place, proceeded to arrest M. de la Chastre, whom he took to the Bastille.

Meanwhile M. de l'Oste was appointed to the command of the guard which was set over my brother. This was a good sort of old man, who had been appointed governor to the King my husband, and loved me as if I had been his own child. Sensible of the injustice done to my brother and me, and lamenting the bad counsel by which the King was guided, and being, moreover, willing to serve us, he resolved to deliver my brother from arrest. In order to make his intention known to us he ordered the Scottish archers to wait on the stairs without, keeping only two whom he could trust in the room. Then taking me aside, he said:

"There is not a good Frenchman living who does not bleed at his heart to see what we see. I have served the King your father, and I am ready to lay down my life to serve his children. I expect to have the guard of the Prince your brother, wherever he shall chance to be confined; and, depend upon it, at the hazard of my life, I will restore him to his liberty. But," added he, "that no suspicions may arise that such is my design, it will be proper that we be not seen together in conversation; however, you may rely upon my word."

This afforded me great consolation; and, assuming a degree of courage hereupon, I observed to my brother that we ought not to remain there without knowing for what reason we were detained, as if we were in the Inquisition; and that to treat us in such a manner was to consider us as persons of no account. I then begged M. de l'Oste to entreat the King, in our name, if the Queen our mother was not permitted to come to us, to send some one to ac-

quaint us with the crime for which we were kept in
confinement.

M. de Combaut, who was at the head of the young
counsellors, was accordingly sent to us; and he, with
a great deal of gravity, informed us that he came
from the King to inquire what it was we wished to
communicate to his Majesty. We answered that we
wished to speak to some one near the King's person,
in order to our being informed what we were kept
in confinement for, as we were unable to assign any
reason for it ourselves. He answered, with great
solemnity, that we ought not to ask of God or the
King reasons for what they did; as all their actions
emanated from wisdom and justice. We replied
that we were not persons to be treated like those
shut up in the Inquisition, who are left to guess at
the cause of their being there.

We could obtain from him, after all we said, no
other satisfaction than his promise to interest himself
in our behalf, and to do us all the service in his
power. At this my brother broke out into a fit of
laughter; but I confess I was too much alarmed to
treat his message with such indifference, and could
scarcely refrain from talking to this messenger as he
deserved.

Whilst he was making his report to the King, the
Queen my mother kept her chamber, being under
great concern, as may well be supposed, to witness
such proceedings. She plainly foresaw, in her prudence, that these excesses would end fatally, should
the mildness of my brother's disposition, and his regard for the welfare of the State, be once wearied
out with submitting to such repeated acts of injustice. She therefore sent for the senior members of
the Council, the chancellor, princes, nobles, and marshals of France, who all were greatly scandalised at

the bad counsel which had been given to the King, and told the Queen my mother that she ought to remonstrate with the King upon the injustice of his proceedings. They observed that what had been done could not now be recalled, but matters might yet be set upon a right footing. The Queen my mother hereupon went to the King, followed by these counsellors, and represented to him the ill consequences which might proceed from the steps he had taken.

The King's eyes were by this time opened, and he saw that he had been ill advised. He therefore begged the Queen my mother to set things to rights, and to prevail on my brother to forget all that had happened, and to bear no resentment against these young men, but to make up the breach betwixt Bussi and Quélus.

Things being thus set to rights again, the guard which had been placed over my brother was dismissed, and the Queen my mother, coming to his apartment, told him he ought to return thanks to God for his deliverance, for that there had been a moment when even she herself despaired of saving his life; that since he must now have discovered that the King's temper of mind was such that he took the alarm at the very imagination of danger, and that, when once he was resolved upon a measure, no advice that she or any other could give would prevent him from putting it into execution, she would recommend it to him to submit himself to the King's pleasure in everything, in order to prevent the like in future; and, for the present, to take the earliest opportunity of seeing the King, and to appear as if he thought no more about the past.

We replied that we were both of us sensible of God's great mercy in delivering us from the injustice of our enemies, and that, next to God, our greatest obligation was to her; but that my brother's rank did not admit of his being put in confinement without cause, and released from it again without the formality of an acknowledgment. Upon this, the Queen observed that it was not in the power even of God himself to undo what had been done; that what could be effected to save his honour, and give him satisfaction for the irregularity of the arrest, should have place. My brother, therefore, she observed, ought to strive to mollify the King by addressing him with expressions of regard to his person and attachment to his service; and, in the meantime, use his influence over Bussi to reconcile him to Quélus, and to end all disputes betwixt them. She then declared that the principal motive for putting my brother and his servants under arrest was to prevent the combat for which old Bussi, the brave father of a brave son, had solicited the King's leave, wherein he proposed to be his son's second, whilst the father of Quélus was to be his. These four had agreed in this way to determine the matter in dispute, and give the Court no further disturbance.

My brother now engaged himself to the Queen that, as Bussi would see he could not be permitted to decide his quarrel by combat, he should, in order to deliver himself from his arrest, do as she had commanded.

The Queen my mother, going down to the King, prevailed with him to restore my brother to liberty with every honour. In order to which the King came to her apartment, followed by the princes, noblemen, and other members of the Council, and sent for us by M. de Villequier. As we went along we found all the rooms crowded with people, who, with tears in their eyes, blessed God for our deliverance. Coming into the apartments of the Queen my mother, we found the King attended as I before related. The King desired my brother not to take anything ill that had been done, as the motive for it was his concern for the good of his kingdom, and not any bad intention towards himself. My brother replied that he had, as he ought, devoted his life to his service, and, therefore, was governed by his pleasure; but that he most humbly begged him to consider that his fidelity and attachment did not merit the return he had met with; that, notwithstanding, he should impute it entirely to his own ill-fortune, and should be perfectly satisfied if the King acknowledged his innocence. Hereupon the King said that he entertained not the least doubt of his innocence, and only desired him to believe he held the same place in his esteem he ever had. The Queen my mother then, taking both of them by the hand, made them embrace each other.

Afterwards the King commanded Bussi to be brought forth, to make a reconciliation betwixt him and Quélus, giving orders, at the same time, for the release of Simier and M. de la Chastre. Bussi coming into the room with his usual grace, the King told him he must be reconciled with Quélus, and forbade him to say a word more concerning their quarrel. He then commanded them to embrace. " Sire," said Bussi, " if it is your pleasure that we kiss and are friends again, I am ready to obey your command;" then, putting himself in the attitude of Pantaloon, he went up to Quélus and gave him a hug, which set all present in a titter, notwithstanding they had been seriously affected by the scene which had passed just before.

Many persons of discretion thought what had been done was too slight a reparation for the injuries my brother had received. When all was over, the King and the Queen my mother, coming up to me, said it

would be incumbent on me to use my utmost endeavours to prevent my brother from calling to mind anything past which should make him swerve from the
duty and affection he owed the King. I replied that
my brother was so prudent, and so strongly attached
to the King's service, that he needed no admonition
on that head from me or any one else; and that, with
respect to myself, I had never given him any other
advice than to conform himself to the King's pleasure and the duty he owed him.

## LETTER XIX

IT was now three o'clock in the afternoon, and no one present had yet dined. The Queen my mother was desirous that we should eat together, and, after dinner, she ordered my brother and me to change our dress (as the clothes we had on were suitable only to our late melancholy situation) and come to the King's supper and ball. We complied with her orders as far as a change of dress, but our countenances still retained the impressions of grief and resentment which we inwardly felt.

I must inform you that when the tragi-comedy I have given you an account of was over, the Queen my mother turned round to the Chevalier de Seurre, whom she recommended to my brother to sleep in his bedchamber, and in whose conversation she some-times took delight because he was a man of some humour, but rather inclined to be cynical.

"Well," said she, "M. de Seurre, what do you think of all this?"

"Madame, I think there is too much of it for earnest, and not enough for jest."

Then addressing himself to me, he said, but not loud enough for the Queen to hear him: "I do not believe all is over yet; I am very much mistaken if this young man" (meaning my brother) "rests satisfied with this."

This day having passed in the manner before related, the wound being only skinned over and far from healed, the young men about the King's person set themselves to operate in order to break it out afresh.

These persons, judging of my brother by themselves, and not having sufficient experience to know the power of duty over the minds of personages of exalted rank and high birth, persuaded the King, still connecting his case with their own, that it was impossible my brother should ever forgive the affront he had received, and not seek to avenge himself with the first opportunity. The King, forgetting the ill-judged steps these young men had so lately induced him to take, hereupon receives this new impression, and gives orders to the officers of the guard to keep strict watch at the gates that his brother go not out, and that his people be made to leave the Louvre every evening, except such of them as usually slept in his bedchamber or wardrobe.

My brother, seeing himself thus exposed to the caprices of these headstrong young fellows, who led the King according to their own fancies, and fearing something worse might happen than what he had yet experienced, at the end of three days, during which time he laboured under apprehensions of this kind, came to a determination to leave the Court, and never more return to it, but retire to his principality and make preparations with all haste for his expedition to Flanders.

He communicated his design to me, and I approved of it, as I considered he had no other view in it than providing for his own safety, and that neither the King nor his government were likely to sustain any injury by it.

When we consulted upon the means of its accomplishment, we could find no other than his descending from my window, which was on the second story and opened to the ditch, for the gates were so closely watched that it was impossible to pass them, the face of every one going out of the Louvre being curiously examined. He begged of me, therefore, to procure for him a rope of sufficient strength and long enough for the purpose. This I set about immediately, for, having the sacking of a bed that wanted mending, I sent it out of the palace by a lad whom I could trust, with orders to bring it back repaired, and to wrap up the proper length of rope inside.

When all was prepared, one evening, at supper time, I went to the Queen my mother, who supped alone in her own apartment, it being fast-day and the King eating no supper. My brother, who on most occasions was patient and discreet, spurred on by the indignities he had received, and anxious to extricate himself from danger and regain his liberty, came to me as I was rising from table, and whispered to me to make haste and come to him in my own apartment. M. de Matignon, at that time a marshal, a sly, cunning Norman, and one who had no love for my brother, whether he had some knowledge of his design from some one who could not keep a secret, or only guessed at it, observed to the Queen my mother as she left the room (which I overheard, being near her, and circumspectly watching every word and motion, as may well be imagined, situated as I was betwixt fear and hope, and involved in perplexity) that my brother had undoubtedly an intention of withdrawing himself, and would not be there the next day; adding that he was assured of it, and she might take her measures accordingly.

I observed that she was much disconcerted by this observation, and I had my fears lest we should be discovered. When we came into her closet, she drew me aside and asked if I heard what Matignon had said.

I replied: "I did not hear it, Madame, but I observe that it has given you uneasiness."

"Yes," said she, "a great deal of uneasiness, for you know I have pledged myself to the King that your brother shall not depart hence, and Matignon has declared that he knows very well he will not be here to-morrow."

I now found myself under a great embarrassment; I was in danger either of proving unfaithful to my brother, and thereby bringing his life into jeopardy, or of being obliged to declare that to be truth which I knew to be false, and this I would have died rather than be guilty of.

In this extremity, if I had not been aided by God, my countenance, without speaking, would plainly have discovered what I wished to conceal. But God, who assists those who mean well, and whose divine goodness was discoverable in my brother's escape, enabled me to compose my looks and suggested to me such a reply as gave her to understand no more than I wished her to know, and cleared my conscience from making any declaration contrary to the truth. I answered her in these words:

"You cannot, Madame, but be sensible that M. de Matignon is not one of my brother's friends, and that he is, besides, a busy, meddling kind of man, who is sorry to find a reconciliation has taken place with us; and, as to my brother, I will answer for him with my life in case he goes hence, of which, if he had any design, I should, as I am well assured, not be ignorant, he never having yet concealed anything he meant to do from me."

All this was said by me with the assurance that, after my brother's escape, they would not dare to do me any injury; and in case of the worst, and when we should be discovered, I had much rather pledge my life than hazard my soul by a false declaration, and endanger my brother's life. Without scrutinising the import of my speech, she replied: "Remember what you now say,—you will be bound for him on the penalty of your life."

I smiled and answered that such was my intention. Then, wishing her a good night, I retired to my own bedchamber, where, undressing myself in haste and getting into bed, in order to dismiss the ladies and maids of honour, and there then remaining only my chamber-women, my brother came in, accompanied by Simier and Cangé. Rising from my bed, we made the cord fast, and having looked out at the window to discover if any one was in the ditch, with the assistance of three of my women, who slept in my room, and the lad who had brought in the rope, we let down my brother, who laughed and joked upon the occasion without the least apprehension, notwithstanding the height was considerable. We next lowered Simier into the ditch, who was in such a fright that he had scarcely strength to hold the rope fast; and lastly descended my brother's *valet de chambre*, Cangé.

Through God's providence my brother got off undiscovered, and going to Ste. Geneviève, he found Bussi waiting there for him. By consent of the abbot, a hole had been made in the city wall, through which they passed, and horses being provided and in waiting, they mounted, and reached Angers without the least accident.

Whilst we were lowering down Cangé, who, as I mentioned before, was the last, we observed a man rising out of the ditch, who ran towards the lodge adjoining to the tennis-court, in the direct way leading to the guard-house. I had no apprehensions on my own account, all my fears being absorbed by those

I entertained for my brother; and now I was almost dead with alarm, supposing this might be a spy placed there by M. de Matignon, and that my brother would be taken. Whilst I was in this cruel state of anxiety, which can be judged of only by those who have experienced a similar situation, my women took a precaution for my safety and their own, which did not suggest itself to me. This was to burn the rope, that it might not appear to our conviction in case the man in question had been placed there to watch us. This rope occasioned so great a flame in burning, that it set fire to the chimney, which, being seen from without, alarmed the guard, who ran to us, knocking violently at the door, calling for it to be opened.

I now concluded that my brother was stopped, and that we were both undone. However, as, by the blessing of God and through his divine mercy alone, I have, amidst every danger with which I have been repeatedly surrounded, constantly preserved a presence of mind which directed what was best to be done, and observing that the rope was not more than half consumed, I told my women to go to the door, and speaking softly, as if I was asleep, to ask the men what they wanted. They did so, and the archers replied that the chimney was on fire, and they came to extinguish it. My women answered it was of no consequence, and they could put it out themselves, begging them not to awake me. This alarm thus passed off quietly, and they went away; but, in two hours afterward, M. de Cossé came for me to go to the King and the Queen my mother, to give an account of my brother's escape, of which they had received intelligence by the Abbot of Ste. Geneviève.

It seems it had been concerted betwixt my brother and the abbot, in order to prevent the latter from falling under disgrace, that, when my brother might be supposed to have reached a sufficient distance, the abbot should go to Court, and say that he had been put into confinement whilst the hole was being made, and that he came to inform the King as soon as he had released himself.

I was in bed, for it was yet night; and rising hastily, I put on my night-clothes. One of my women was indiscreet enough to hold me round the waist, and exclaim aloud, shedding a flood of tears, that she should never see me more. M. de Cossé, pushing her away, said to me: "If I were not a person thoroughly devoted to your service, this woman has said enough to bring you into trouble. But," continued he, "fear nothing. God be praised, by this time the Prince your brother is out of danger."

These words were very necessary, in the present state of my mind, to fortify it against the reproaches and threats I had reason to expect from the King. I found him sitting at the foot of the Queen my mother's bed, in such a violent rage that I am inclined to believe I should have felt the effects of it, had he not been restrained by the absence of my brother and my mother's presence. They both told me that I had assured them my brother would not leave the Court, and that I pledged myself for his stay. I replied that it was true that he had deceived me, as he had them; however, I was ready still to pledge my life that his departure would not operate to the prejudice of the King's service, and that it would appear he was only gone to his own principality to give orders and forward his expedition to Flanders.

The King appeared to be somewhat mollified by this declaration, and now gave me permission to return to my own apartments. Soon afterwards he received letters from my brother, containing assurances of his attachment, in the terms I had before expressed. This caused a cessation of complaints, but by no means removed the King's dissatisfaction, who made a show of affording assistance to his expedition, but was secretly using every means to frustrate and defeat it.

# LETTER XX

I NOW renewed my application for leave to go to the King my husband, which I continued to press on every opportunity. The King, perceiving that he could not refuse my leave any longer, was willing I should depart satisfied. He had this further view in complying with my wishes, that by this means he should withdraw me from my attachment to my brother. He therefore strove to oblige me in every way he could think of, and, to fulfil the promise made by the Queen my mother at the Peace of Sens, he gave me an assignment of my portion in territory, with the power of nomination to all vacant benefices and all offices; and, over and above the customary pension to the daughters of France, he gave another out of his privy purse.

He daily paid me a visit in my apartment, in which he took occasion to represent to me how useful his friendship would be to me; whereas that of my brother could be only injurious,—with arguments of the like kind.

However, all he could say was insufficient to prevail on me to swerve from the fidelity I had vowed to observe to my brother. The King was able to draw from me no other declaration than this: that it ever was, and should be, my earnest wish to see my brother firmly established in his gracious favour, which he had never appeared to me to have forfeited; that I was well assured he would exert himself to the utmost to regain it by every act of duty and meritorious service; that, with respect to myself, I thought

I was so much obliged to him for the great honour he did me by repeated acts of generosity, that he might be assured, when I was with the King my husband I should consider myself bound in duty to obey all such commands as he should be pleased to give me; and that it would be my whole study to maintain the King my husband in a submission to his pleasure.

My brother was now on the point of leaving Alençon to go to Flanders; the Queen my mother was desirous to see him before his departure. I begged the King to permit me to take the opportunity of accompanying her to take leave of my brother, which he granted; but, as it seemed, with great unwillingness. When we returned from Alençon, I solicited the King to permit me to take leave of himself, as I had everything prepared for my journey. The Queen my mother being desirous to go to Gascony, where her presence was necessary for the King's service, was unwilling that I should depart without her. When we left Paris, the King accompanied us on the way as far as his palace of Dolinville. There we stayed with him a few days, and there we took our leave, and in a little time reached Guienne, which belonging to, and being under the government of the King my husband, I was everywhere received as Queen. My husband gave the Queen my mother a meeting at Réolle, which was held by the Huguenots as a cautionary town; and the country not being sufficiently quieted, she was permitted to go no further.

It was the intention of the Queen my mother to make but a short stay; but so many accidents arose from disputes betwixt the Huguenots and Catholics, that she was under the necessity of stopping there eighteen months. As this was very much against her inclination, she was sometimes inclined to think there was a design to keep her, in order to have the company of her maids of honour. For my husband had been greatly smitten with Dayelle, and M. de Thurène was in love with La Vergne. However, I received every mark of honour and attention from the King that I could expect or desire. He related to me, as soon as we met, the artifices which had been put in practice whilst he remained at Court to create a misunderstanding betwixt him and me; all this, he said, he knew was with a design to cause a rupture betwixt my brother and him, and thereby ruin us all three, as there was an exceeding great jealousy entertained of the friendship which existed betwixt us.

We remained in the disagreeable situation I have before described all the time the Queen my mother stayed in Gascony; but, as soon as she could re-establish peace, she, by desire of the King my husband, removed the King's lieutenant, the Marquis de Villars, putting in his place the Maréchal de Biron. She then departed for Languedoc, and we conducted her to Castelnaudary; where, taking our leave, we returned to Pau, in Béarn; in which place, the Catholic religion not being tolerated, I was only allowed to have mass celebrated in a chapel of about three or four feet in length, and so narrow that it could scarcely hold seven or eight persons. During the celebration of mass, the bridge of the castle was drawn up to prevent the Catholics of the town and country from coming to assist at it; who having been, for some years, deprived of the benefit of following their own mode of worship, would have gladly been present. Actuated by so holy and laudable a desire, some of the inhabitants of Pau, on Whit-sunday, found means to get into the castle before the bridge was drawn up, and were present at the cele-

bration of mass, not being discovered until it was
nearly over.  At length the Huguenots espied them,
and ran to acquaint Le Pin, secretary to the King my
husband, who was greatly in his favour, and who
conducted the whole business relating to the new
religion.  Upon receiving this intelligence, Le Pin
ordered the guard to arrest these poor people, who
were severely beaten in my presence, and afterwards
locked up in prison, whence they were not released
without paying a considerable fine.

This indignity gave me great offence, as I never
expected anything of the kind.  Accordingly, I complained of it to the King my husband, begging him
to give orders for the release of these poor Catholics,
who did not deserve to be punished for coming to my
chapel to hear mass, a celebration of which they had
been so long deprived of the benefit.  Le Pin, with
the greatest disrespect to his master, took upon him
to reply, without waiting to hear what the King had
to say.  He told me that I ought not to trouble the
King my husband about such matters; that what
had been done was very right and proper; that those
people had justly merited the treatment they met
with, and all I could say would go for nothing, for it
must be so; and that I ought to rest satisfied with
being permitted to have mass said to me and my
servants.  This insolent speech from a person of his
inferior condition incensed me greatly, and I entreated the King my husband, if I had the least share
in his good graces, to do me justice, and avenge the
insult offered me by this low man.

The King my husband, perceiving that I was
offended, as I had reason to be, with this gross
indignity, ordered Le Pin to quit our presence immediately; and, expressing his concern at his secretary's behaviour, who, he said, was overzealous in

the cause of religion, he promised that he would make an example of him.  As to the Catholic prisoners, he said he would advise with his parliament what ought to be done for my satisfaction.

Having said this, he went to his closet, where he found Le Pin, who, by dint of persuasion, made him change his resolution; insomuch that, fearing I should insist upon his dismissing his secretary, he avoided meeting me.  At last, finding that I was firmly resolved to leave him, unless he dismissed Le Pin, he took advice of some persons, who, having themselves a dislike to the secretary, represented that he ought not to give me cause of displeasure for the sake of a man of his small importance,—especially one who, like him, had given me just reason to be offended; that, when it became known to the King my brother and the Queen my mother, they would certainly take it ill that he had not only not resented it, but, on the contrary, still kept him near his person.

This counsel prevailed with him, and he at length discarded his secretary.  The King, however, continued to behave to me with great coolness, being influenced, as he afterwards confessed, by the counsel of M. de Pibrac, who acted the part of a double dealer, telling me that I ought not to pardon an affront offered by such a mean fellow, but insist upon his being dismissed; whilst he persuaded the King my husband that there was no reason for parting with a man so useful to him, for such a trivial cause.  This was done by M. de Pibrac, thinking I might be induced, from such mortifications, to return to France, where he enjoyed the offices of president and King's counsellor.

I now met with a fresh cause for disquietude in my present situation, for, Dayelle being gone, the King my husband placed his affections on Rebours. She was an artful young person, and had no regard for me; accordingly, she did me all the ill offices in her power with him. In the midst of these trials, I put my trust in God, and he, moved with pity by my tears, gave permission for our leaving Pau, that "little Geneva;" and, fortunately for me, Rebours was taken ill and stayed behind. The King my husband no sooner lost sight of her than he forgot her; he now turned his eyes and attention towards Fosseuse. She was much handsomer than the other, and was at that time young, and really a very amiable person.

Pursuing the road to Montauban, we stopped at a little town called Eause, where, in the night, the King my husband was attacked with a high fever, accompanied with most violent pains in his head. This fever lasted for seventeen days, during which time he had no rest night or day, but was continually removed from one bed to another. I nursed him the whole time, never stirring from his bedside, and never putting off my clothes. He took notice of my extraordinary tenderness, and spoke of it to several persons, and particularly to my cousin M——, who, acting the part of an affectionate relation, restored me to his favour, insomuch that I never stood so highly in it before. This happiness I had the good fortune to enjoy during the four or five years that I remained with him in Gascony.

Our residence, for the most part of the time I have mentioned, was at Nérac, where our Court was so brilliant that we had no cause to regret our absence from the Court of France. We had with us the Princesse de Navarre, my husband's sister, since married to the Duc de Bar; there were besides a number of ladies belonging to myself. The King my husband was attended by a numerous body of lords and gentlemen, all as gallant persons as I have seen in any Court; and we had only to lament that they were Huguenots. This difference of religion, however, caused no dispute among us; the King my husband and the Princess his sister heard a sermon, whilst I and my servants heard mass. I had a chapel in the park for the purpose, and, as soon as the service of both religions was over, we joined company in a beautiful garden, ornamented with long walks shaded with laurel and cypress trees. Sometimes we took a walk in the park on the banks of the river, bordered by an avenue of trees three thousand yards in length. The rest of the day was passed in innocent amusements; and in the afternoon, or at night, we commonly had a ball.

The King was very assiduous with Fosseuse, who, being dependent on me, kept herself within the strict bounds of honour and virtue. Had she always done so, she had not brought upon herself a misfortune which has proved of such fatal consequence to myself as well as to her.

But our happiness was too great to be of long continuance, and fresh troubles broke out betwixt the King my husband and the Catholics, and gave rise to a new war. The King my husband and the Maréchal de Biron, who was the King's lieutenant in Guienne, had a difference, which was aggravated by the Huguenots. This breach became in a short time so wide that all my efforts to close it were useless. They made their separate complaints to the King. The King my husband insisted on the removal of the Maréchal de Biron, and the Marshal charged the King my husband, and the rest of those who were of the pretended reformed religion, with designs contrary to peace. I saw, with great concern, that affairs were likely soon to come to an open rupture; and I had no power to prevent it.

The Marshal advised the King to come to Guienne himself, saying that in his presence matters might be settled. The Huguenots, hearing of this proposal, supposed the King would take possession of their towns, and, thereupon, came to a resolution to take up arms. This was what I feared; I was become a sharer in the King my husband's fortune, and was now to be in opposition to the King my brother and the religion I had been bred up in. I gave my opinion upon this war to the King my husband and his Council, and strove to dissuade them from engaging in it. I represented to them the hazards of carrying on a war when they were to be opposed against so able a general as the Maréchal de Biron, who would not spare them, as other generals had done, he being their private enemy. I begged them to consider that, if the King brought his whole force against them, with intention to exterminate their religion, it would not be in their power to oppose or prevent it. But they were so headstrong, and so blinded with the hope of succeeding in the surprise of certain towns in Languedoc and Gascony, that, though the King did me the honour, upon all occasions, to listen to my advice, as did most of the Huguenots, yet I could not prevail on them to follow it in the present situation of affairs, until it was too late, and after they had found, to their cost, that my counsel was good. The torrent was now burst forth, and there was no possibility of stopping its course until it had spent its utmost strength.

Before that period arrived, foreseeing the consequences, I had often written to the King and the Queen my mother, to offer something to the King my husband by way of accommodating matters. But

they were bent against it, and seemed to be pleased
that matters had taken such a turn, being assured
by Maréchal de Biron that he had it in his power
to crush the Huguenots whenever he pleased. In this
crisis my advice was not attended to, the dissensions
increased, and recourse was had to arms.

The Huguenots had reckoned upon a force more
considerable than they were able to collect together,
and the King my husband found himself outnumbered
by Maréchal de Biron. In consequence, those of the
pretended reformed religion failed in all their plans,
except their attack upon Cahors, which they took with
petards, after having lost a great number of men,—
M. de Vezins, who commanded in the town, disputing
their entrance for two or three days, from street to
street, and even from house to house. The King my
husband displayed great valour and conduct upon the
occasion, and showed himself to be a gallant and
brave general. Though the Huguenots succeeded
in this attempt, their loss was so great that they
gained nothing from it. Maréchal de Biron kept
the field, and took every place that declared for
the Huguenots, putting all that opposed him to the
sword.

From the commencement of this war, the King my
husband doing me the honour to love me, and commanding me not to leave him, I had resolved to share
his fortune, not without extreme regret, in observing
that this war was of such a nature that I could not,
in conscience, wish success to either side; for if the
Huguenots got the upper hand, the religion which I
cherished as much as my life was lost, and if the
Catholics prevailed, the King my husband was undone. But, being thus attached to my husband, by
the duty I owed him, and obliged by the attentions
he was pleased to show me, I could only acquaint the

King and the Queen my mother with the situation to which I was reduced, occasioned by my advice to them not having been attended to. I, therefore, prayed them, if they could not extinguish the flames of war in the midst of which I was placed, at least to give orders to Maréchal de Biron to consider the town I resided in, and three leagues round it, as neutral ground, and that I would get the King my husband to do the same. This the King granted me for Nérac, provided my husband was not there; but if he should enter it, the neutrality was to cease, and so to remain as long as he continued there. This convention was observed, on both sides, with all the exactness I could desire. However, the King my husband was not to be prevented from often visiting Nérac, which was the residence of his sister and me. He was fond of the society of ladies, and, moreover, was at that time greatly enamoured with Fosseuse, who held the place in his affections which Rebours had lately occupied. Fosseuse did me no ill offices, so that the King my husband and I continued to live on very good terms, especially as he perceived me unwilling to oppose his inclinations.

Led by such inducements, he came to Nérac, once, with a body of troops, and stayed three days, not being able to leave the agreeable company he found there. Maréchal de Biron, who wished for nothing so much as such an opportunity, was apprised of it, and, under pretence of joining M. de Cornusson, the seneschal of Toulouse, who was expected with a reinforcement for his army, he began his march; but, instead of pursuing the road, according to the orders he had issued, he suddenly ordered his troops to file off towards Nérac, and, before nine in the morning, his whole force was drawn up within sight of the town, and within cannon-shot of it.

The King my husband had received intelligence, the
evening before, of the expected arrival of M. de
Cornusson, and was desirous of preventing the junc-
tion, for which purpose he resolved to attack him and
the Marshal separately.  As he had been lately joined
by M. de La Rochefoucauld, with a corps of cavalry
consisting of eight hundred men, formed from the
nobility of Saintonge, he found himself sufficiently
strong to undertake such a plan.  He, therefore, set
out before break of day to make his attack as they
crossed the river.  But his intelligence did not prove
to be correct, for De Cornusson passed it the evening
before.  My husband, being thus disappointed in his
design, returned to Nérac, and entered at one gate just
as Maréchal de Biron drew up his troops before the
other.  There fell so heavy a rain at that moment
that the musketry was of no use.  The King my husband, however, threw a body of his troops into a
vineyard to stop the Marshal's progress, not being able
to do more on account of the unfavourableness of the
weather.

In the meantime, the Marshal continued with his
troops drawn up in order of battle, permitting only
two or three of his men to advance, who challenged
a like number to break lances in honour of their mistresses.  The rest of the army kept their ground, to
mask their artillery, which, being ready to play, they
opened to the right and left, and fired seven or eight
shots upon the town, one of which struck the palace.
The Marshal, having done this, marched off, despatch-
ing a trumpeter to me with his excuse.  He acquainted me that, had I been alone, he would on no
account have fired on the town; but the terms of
neutrality for the town, agreed upon by the King,
were, as I well knew, in case the King my husband
should not be found in it, and, if otherwise, they were

void. Besides which, his orders were to attack the King my husband wherever he should find him.

I must acknowledge on every other occasion the Marshal showed me the greatest respect, and appeared to be much my friend. During the war my letters have frequently fallen into his hands, when he as constantly forwarded them to me unopened. And whenever my people have happened to be taken prisoners by his army, they were always well treated as soon as they mentioned to whom they belonged.

I answered his message by the trumpeter, saying that I well knew what he had done was strictly agreeable to the convention made and the orders he had received, but that a gallant officer like him would know how to do his duty without giving his friends cause of offence; that he might have permitted me the enjoyment of the King my husband's company in Nérac for three days. adding, that he could not attack him, in my presence, without attacking me; and concluding that, certainly, I was greatly offended by his conduct, and would take the first opportunity of making my complaint to the King my brother.

## LETTER XXI

THE war lasted some time longer, but with disadvantage to the Huguenots. The King my husband at length became desirous to make a peace. I wrote on the subject to the King and the Queen my mother; but so elated were they both with Maréchal de Biron's success that they would not agree to any terms.

About the time this war broke out, Cambray, which had been delivered up to my brother by M. d'Ainsi, according to his engagement with me, as I have before related, was besieged by the forces of Spain. My brother received the news of this siege at his castle of Plessis-les-Tours, whither he had retired after his return from Flanders, where, by the assistance of the Comte de Lalain, he had been invested with the government of Mons, Valenciennes, and their dependencies.

My brother, being anxious to relieve Cambray, set about raising an army with all the expedition possible; but, finding it could not be accomplished very speedily, he sent forward a reinforcement under the command of M. de Balagny, to succour the place until he arrived himself with a sufficient force to raise the siege. Whilst he was in the midst of these preparations this Huguenot war broke out, and the men he had raised left him to incorporate themselves with the King's army, which had reached Gascony.

My brother was now without hope of raising the siege, and to lose Cambray would be attended with the loss of the other countries he had just obtained. Besides, what he should regret more, such losses would reduce to great straits M. de Balagny and the gallant troops so nobly defending the place.

His grief on this occasion was poignant, and, as his excellent judgment furnished him with expedients under all his difficulties, he resolved to endeavour to bring about a peace. Accordingly he despatched a gentleman to the King with his advice to accede to terms, offering to undertake the treaty himself. His design in offering himself as negotiator was to prevent the treaty being drawn out to too great a length, as might be the case if confided to others. It was necessary that he should speedily relieve Cambray, for M. de Balagny, who had thrown himself into the city as I have before mentioned, had written to him that he should be able to defend the place for six months; but, if he received no succours within that time, his provisions would be all expended, and he should be obliged to give way to the clamours of the inhabitants, and surrender the town.

By God's favour, the King was induced to listen to my brother's proposal of undertaking a negotiation for a peace. The King hoped thereby to disappoint him in his expectations in Flanders, which he never had approved. Accordingly he sent word back to my brother that he should accept his proffer of negotiating a peace, and would send him for his coadjutors, M. de Villeroy and M. de Bellièvre. The commission my brother was charged with succeeded, and, after a stay of seven months in Gascony, he settled a peace and left us, his thoughts being employed during the whole time on the means of relieving Cambray, which the satisfaction he found in being with us could not altogether abate.

The peace my brother made, as I have just mentioned, was so judiciously framed that it gave equal satisfaction to the King and the Catholics, and to the King my husband and the Huguenots, and obtained him the affections of both parties. He likewise acquired from it the assistance of that able general, Maréchal de Biron, who undertook the command of the army destined to raise the siege of Cambray. The King my husband was equally gratified in the Marshal's removal from Gascony and having Maréchal de Matignon in his place.

Before my brother set off he was desirous to bring about a reconciliation betwixt the King my husband and Maréchal de Biron, provided the latter should make his apologies to me for his conduct at Nérac. My brother had desired me to treat him with all disdain, but I used this hasty advice with discretion, considering that my brother might one day or other repent having given it, as he had everything to hope, in his present situation, from the bravery of this officer.

My brother returned to France accompanied by Maréchal de Biron. By his negotiation of a peace he had acquired to himself great credit with both parties, and secured a powerful force for the purpose of raising the siege of Cambray. But honours and success are followed by envy. The King beheld this accession of glory to his brother with great dissatisfaction. He had been for seven months, while my brother and I were together in Gascony, brooding over his malice, and produced the strangest invention that can be imagined. He pretended to believe (what the King my husband can easily prove to be false) that I instigated him to go to war that I might procure for my brother the credit of making peace. This is not at all probable when it is considered the prejudice my brother's affairs in Flanders sustained by the war.

But envy and malice are self-deceivers, and pretend to discover what no one else can perceive. On this frail foundation the King raised an altar of hatred, on which he swore never to cease till he had accomplished my brother's ruin and mine. He had never forgiven me for the attachment I had discovered for my brother's interest during the time he was in Poland and since.

Fortune chose to favour the King's animosity; for, during the seven months that my brother stayed in Gascony, he conceived a passion for Fosseuse, who was become the doting piece of the King my husband, as I have already mentioned, since he had quitted Rebours. This new passion in my brother had induced the King my husband to treat me with coldness, supposing that I countenanced my brother's addresses. I no sooner discovered this than I remonstrated with my brother, as I knew he would make every sacrifice for my repose. I begged him to give over his pursuit, and not to speak to her again. I succeeded this way to defeat the malice of my ill-fortune; but there was still behind another secret ambush, and that of a more fatal nature; for Fosseuse, who was passionately fond of the King my husband, but had hitherto granted no favours inconsistent with prudence and modesty, piqued by his jealousy of my brother, gave herself up suddenly to his will, and unfortunately became pregnant. She no sooner made this discovery, than she altered her conduct towards me entirely from what it was before. She now shunned my presence as much as she had been accustomed to seek it, and whereas before she strove to do me every good office with the King my husband, she now endeavoured to make all the mischief she was able betwixt us. For his part, he avoided me; he grew cold and indifferent, and since

Fosseuse ceased to conduct herself with discretion, the happy moments that we experienced during the four or five years we were together in Gascony were no more.

Peace being restored, and my brother departed for France, as I have already related, the King my husband and I returned to Nérac. We were no sooner there than Fosseuse persuaded the King my husband to make a journey to the waters of Aigues-Caudes, in Béarn, perhaps with a design to rid herself of her burden there. I begged the King my husband to excuse my accompanying him, as, since the affront that I had received at Pau, I had made a vow never to set foot in Béarn until the Catholic religion was reëstablished there. He pressed me much to go with him, and grew angry at my persisting to refuse his request. He told me that his *little girl* (for so he affected to call Fosseuse) was desirous to go there on account of a colic, which she felt frequent returns of. I answered that I had no objection to his taking her with him. He then said that she could not go unless I went; that it would occasion scandal, which might as well be avoided. He continued to press me to accompany him, but at length I prevailed with him to consent to go without me, and to take her with him, and, with her, two of her companions, Rebours and Ville-Savin, together with the governess. They set out accordingly, and I waited their return at Bavière.

I had every day news from Rebours, informing me how matters went. This Rebours I have mentioned before to have been the object of my husband's passion, but she was now cast off, and, consequently, was no friend to Fosseuse, who had gained that place in his affection she had before held. She, therefore, strove all she could to circumvent her; and, indeed, she was fully qualified for such a purpose, as she was a cunning, deceitful young person. She gave me to understand that Fosseuse laboured to do me every ill office in her power; that she spoke of me with the greatest disrespect on all occasions, and expressed her expectations of marrying the King herself, in case she should be delivered of a son, when I was to be divorced. She had said, further, that when the King my husband returned to Bavière, he had resolved to go to Pau, and that I should go with him, whether I would or not.

This intelligence was far from being agreeable to me, and I knew not what to think of it. I trusted in the goodness of God, and I had a reliance on the generosity of the King my husband; yet I passed the time I waited for his return but uncomfortably, and often thought I shed more tears than they drank water. The Catholic nobility of the neighbourhood of Bavière used their utmost endeavours to divert my chagrin, for the month or five weeks that the King my husband and Fosseuse stayed at Aigues-Caudes.

On his return, a certain nobleman acquainted the King my husband with the concern I was under lest he should go to Pau, whereupon he did not press me on the subject, but only said he should have been glad if I had consented to go with him. Perceiving, by my tears and the expressions I made use of, that I should prefer even death to such a journey, he altered his intentions and we returned to Nérac.

The pregnancy of Fosseuse was now no longer a secret. The whole Court talked of it, and not only the Court, but all the country. I was willing to prevent the scandal from spreading, and accordingly resolved to talk to her on the subject. With this resolution, I took her into my closet, and spoke to her thus: "Though you have for some time estranged yourself from me, and, as it has been reported to me, striven to do me many ill offices with the King my husband, yet the regard I once had for you, and the esteem which I still entertain for those honourable persons to whose family you belong, do not admit of my neglecting to afford you all the assistance in my power in your present unhappy situation. I beg you, therefore, not to conceal the truth, it being both for your interest and mine, under whose protection you are, to declare it. Tell me the truth, and I will act towards you as a mother. You know that a contagious disorder has broken out in the place, and, under pretence of avoiding it, I will go to Mas-d'Agenois, which is a house belonging to the King my husband, in a very retired situation. I will take you with me, and such other persons as you shall name. Whilst we are there, the King will take the diversion of hunting in some other part of the country, and I shall not stir thence before your delivery. By this means we shall put a stop to the scandalous reports which are now current, and which concern you more than myself."

So far from showing any contrition, or returning thanks for my kindness, she replied, with the utmost arrogance, that she would prove all those to be liars who had reported such things of her; that, for my part, I had ceased for a long time to show her any marks of regard, and she saw that I was determined upon her ruin. These words she delivered in as loud a tone as mine had been mildly expressed; and, leaving me abruptly, she flew in a rage to the King my husband, to relate to him what I had said to her. He was very angry upon the occasion, and declared he would make them all liars who had laid such things to her charge. From that moment until the hour of her delivery, which was a few months after, he never spoke to me.

She found the pains of labour come upon her about daybreak, whilst she was in bed in the chamber where the maids of honour slept. She sent for my physician, and begged him to go and acquaint the King my husband that she was taken ill. We slept in separate beds in the same chamber, and had done so for some time.

The physician delivered the message as he was directed, which greatly embarrassed my husband. What to do he did not know. On the one hand, he was fearful of a discovery; on the other, he foresaw that, without proper assistance, there was danger of losing one he so much loved. In this dilemma, he resolved to apply to me, confess all, and implore my aid and advice, well knowing that, notwithstanding what had passed, I should be ready to do him a pleasure. Having come to this resolution, he withdrew my curtains, and spoke to me thus: " My dear, I have concealed a matter from you which I now confess. I beg you to forgive me, and to think no more about what I have said to you on the subject. Will you oblige me so far as to rise and go to Fosseuse, who is taken very ill? I am well assured that, in her present situation, you will forget everything and resent nothing. You know how dearly I love her, and I hope you will comply with my request." I answered that I had too great a respect for him to be offended at anything he should do, and that I would go to her immediately, and do as much for her as if she were a child of my own. I advised him, in the meantime, to go out and hunt, by which means he would draw away all his people, and prevent tattling.

I removed Fosseuse, with all convenient haste, from the chamber in which the maids of honours were, to

one in a more retired part of the palace, got a physician and some women about her, and saw that she
wanted for nothing that was proper in her situation.
It pleased God that she should bring forth a daughter,
since dead. As soon as she was delivered I ordered
her to be taken back to the chamber from which she
had been brought. Notwithstanding these precau-
tions, it was not possible to prevent the story from
circulating through the palace. When the King my
husband returned from hunting he paid her a visit,
according to custom. She begged that I might come
and see her, as was usual with me when any one of
my maids of honour was taken ill. By this means
she expected to put a stop to stories to her prejudice.
The King my husband came from her into my bedchamber, and found me in bed, as I was fatigued and
required rest, after having been called up so early.
He begged me to get up and pay her a visit. I told
him I went according to his desire before, when she
stood in need of assistance, but now she wanted no
help; that to visit her at this time would be only
exposing her more, and cause myself to be pointed at
by all the world. He seemed to be greatly displeased
at what I said, which vexed me the more as I thought
I did not deserve such treatment after what I had
done at his request in the morning; she likewise
contributed all in her power to aggravate matters
betwixt him and me.

In the meantime, the King my brother, always well
informed of what is passing in the families of the
nobility of his kingdom, was not ignorant of the transactions of our Court. He was particularly curious
to learn everything that happened with us, and knew
every minute circumstance that I have now related.
Thinking this a favourable occasion to wreak his
vengeance on me for having been the means of my

brother acquiring so much reputation by the peace he had brought about, he made use of the accident that happened in our Court to withdraw me from the King my husband, and thereby reduce me to the state of misery he wished to plunge me in. To this purpose he prevailed on the Queen my mother to write to me, and express her anxious desire to see me after an absence of five or six years. She added that a journey of this sort to Court would be serviceable to the affairs of the King my husband as well as my own; that the King my brother himself was desirous of seeing me, and that if I wanted money for the journey he would send it me. The King wrote to the same purpose, and despatched Manique, the steward of his household, with instructions to use every persuasion with me to undertake the journey. The length of time I had been absent in Gascony, and the unkind usage I received on account of Fosseuse, contributed to induce me to listen to the proposal made me.

The King and the Queen both wrote to me. I received three letters, in quick succession; and, that I might have no pretence for staying, I had the sum of fifteen hundred crowns paid me to defray the expenses of my journey. The Queen my mother wrote that she would give me the meeting in Saintonge, and that, if the King my husband would accompany me so far, she would treat with him there, and give him every satisfaction with respect to the King. But the King and she were desirous to have him at their Court, as he had been before with my brother; and the Maréchal de Matignon had pressed the matter with the King, that he might have no one to interfere with him in Gascony. I had had too long experience of what was to be expected at their Court to hope much from all the fine promises that were made to me. I had resolved, however, to avail myself of the opportunity of an absence of a few months, thinking it might prove the means of setting matters to rights. Besides which, I thought that, as I should take Fosseuse with me, it was possible that the King's passion for her might cool when she was no longer in his sight, or he might attach himself to some other that was less inclined to do me mischief.

It was with some difficulty that the King my husband would consent to a removal, so unwilling was he to leave his Fosseuse. He paid more attention to me, in hopes that I should refuse to set out on this journey to France; but, as I had given my word in my letters to the King and the Queen my mother that I would go, and as I had even received money for the purpose, I could not do otherwise.

And herein my ill-fortune prevailed over the reluctance I had to leave the King my husband, after the instances of renewed love and regard which he had begun to show me.

# THE MEMOIRS OF LOUIS XV.

### AND OF

# MADAME DE POMPADOUR

## ON MADAME DE POMPADOUR

"Madame de Pompadour was not merely a grisette, as her enemies attempted to say, and as Voltaire repeated in one of his malicious days. She was the prettiest woman in Paris, spirituelle, elegant, adorned with a thousand gifts and a thousand talents, but with a sort of sentiment which had not the grandeur of an aristocratic ambition. She loved the king for himself, as the finest man in the kingdom, as the person who appeared to her the most admirable. She loved him sincerely, with a degree of sentimentalism, if not with a profound passion. Her ideal had been on arriving at the court to fascinate him, to keep him amused by a thousand diversions suggested by art or intellect, to make him happy and contented in a circle of ever-changing enchantments and pleasures. A Watteau-like country, plays, comedies, pastorals in the shade, a continual embarking for Cytherea, that would have been the setting she preferred. But once she had set foot on the shifting soil of the court, she could only realize her ideal imperfectly. Naturally obliging and good-hearted, she had to face enmity open and concealed, and to take the offensive to avoid her downfall. Necessity drove her into politics, and to become a minister of state. Madame de Pompadour can be considered as the last king's mistress, deserving of the name. The race of the royal mistresses can then be said, if not ended, to have been at least greatly broken. And Madame de Pompadour remains in our eyes the last in our history, and the most brilliant."

SAINTE-BEUVE.

# INTRODUCTION

It is one of the oldest of truisms that truth is stranger than fiction. The present volume is but another striking example in point. The legend of King Cophetua and the Beggar Maid palls before the historic story of a certain Jeanne Poisson, an obscure French girl who won a king's favor and wielded his sceptre for twenty years. We do not hear anything further from the Beggar Maid, after she became queen; but the famous Pompadour became the most powerful figure of her day in all France, not excepting the king himself.

These veritable *Memoirs* of her reign are ascribed to her attendant, Madame du Hausset, a woman of good family and, above all, of good memory, who has here given us a faithful account of her remarkable subject. Her opportunities for exact knowledge may be gathered from her mistress's own words: "The king and I trust you so completely that we look upon you as we might a cat or a dog, and talk ahead with as much freedom as though you were not there." And the critic, Sainte-Beuve, adds: "When the destiny of a nation is in a woman's bedroom, the best place for the historian is in the ante-chamber. Madame du Hausset seemed created for this rôle of a Suetonius by her position and her character. . . . A good woman, furthermore, incapable of lying, and remaining on the whole quite respectable."

After the death of Madame de Pompadour, the journal of this waiting-woman fell into the hands of M. de Marigny, brother of the favorite, with whom it remained in manuscript form for some years. It was finally published, in 1802, ostensibly as "Drawn from the Portfolio of the Maréchale D—— by Soulavie"; but the French editors, MM. Vitrac and Galopin, assert that Soulavie only lent his name to the work. They also call attention to the fact that a *History of Madame de Pompadour*, by Mlle. Fouqué, was published in London, as early as 1759. But no such general history, or biography, could possibly have the intimate value of a document written at the closest range of its subject. "These *Memoirs*," say the French editors, "give a faithful portrait of Madame de Pompadour. . . . They are clearly hostile, as are nearly all documents preserved about her; for it was one of the evil fortunes of Madame de Pompadour to be made known to us chiefly through her enemies, D'Argenson, the Duc de Luynes, and Richelieu."

The above opinion sums up neatly the consensus of historical opinion concerning this famous woman. She has, indeed, been in the hands of her enemies, ever since the day of her death, in 1764. But this fact is not surprising. The mistress of a weak monarch, she made use of her large influence over him to further her own ends and appoint her own ministers to power. She was, in fact, "the King." Michelet, the historian, asserts in so many words that she "reigned twenty years," and he admits that "although of mean birth, she had some patriotic ideas." However, leaving the question of her political career aside, for the moment, the reader will be interested to make the acquaintance of this remarkable woman, herself. Who was she? What was the secret of her long continued hold upon the King? Louis XV. was a notoriously fickle monarch, whose many amours have become a part of history. But none exercised the influence over him—and over all France, through him—

as did this person of " mean birth." Even her enemies
have had to admit her wonderful executive ability, in
addition to her womanly charms. These *Memoirs,*
though rambling and without strict sequence, answer
our many questions interestingly. They have been
written, very evidently, by an inmate of the household. They give, in addition, much of the secret history of the Court at this important period, and point
out, to the discerning reader, a few of the chief causes
which were to make possible the French Revolution, at
the century's close.

Madame de Pompadour's elevation to power was
the result neither of chance nor of romance. It was
brought about by a carefully laid plan, on the part
of her parents and certain scheming politicians, to
make use of a beautiful girl to advance their own
interests. Jeanne Poisson was born in 1722, and at
an early age gave evidence of such unusual qualities,
that her mother and her guardian, M. Le Normant de
Tournehem (who also is believed to be her father),
devoted their energies to making her worthy of a
place at court. She had a fine natural talent for music,
drawing, and engraving—some excellent examples of
her work in the latter field still being preserved—and
she united with these a rare physical beauty. M.
Leroy, Keeper of the Park of Versailles, thus describes
her at the time of her meeting with the King: " She
was taller than the average, graceful, supple, and elegant. Her features comported well with her stature,
a perfect oval face, framed by beautiful hair of a light
shade, large eyes marked by eyebrows of the same hue,
a perfect nose, a charming mouth, teeth of exceptional
beauty displayed in a delicious smile, the rarest of
complexions," etc., etc. He continues his superlative
adjectives, indicating that the King was not the only
susceptible person in the Park, finally adding: " The

features of the Marquise were lighted by the play of
infinite variety, but never could one perceive any dis-
cordance.  All was harmony and grace."  Truly, a
worthy portrait of a famous beauty!

At the age of nineteen, Mlle. Poisson gave her
hand to a kinsman of her guardian, M. Le Normant
d'Etoiles.  The marriage seems to have been the result
of a sincere passion on his part, but was looked upon
merely as a matter of convenience by everybody else;
for not long thereafter we find her luring the King
with her " delicious smile," while he was hunting in
the forest of Senart; and in 1745 she was formally installed at Court, under the title of the Marquise de
Pompadour.  This story, unadorned, may sound pal-
try, even commercial, but we should not fall into the
error of judging it by twentieth century standards.
The morals of the French Court, never austere, were
especially lax in the reign of Louis XV., and *galan-
teries* were the fashion, rather than the exception;
while for the post of King's favorite there was a
continual rivalry among high-born dames.

Once in this coveted position, the Marquise devoted
her energies to two things, and these she kept ever
before her,—the pleasing of her royal master, and the
furthering of her party's interests.  How well she succeeded, this book shows.  She entertained and amused
the King by elaborate pageants, in the various châ-
teaux which she built, or remodelled. Bellevue, Choisy,
the Hermitage at Versailles, Menars, La Celle, Montre-
tout,—these are among the monuments of her lavish
career, and in these palaces she accumulated costly art
objects, such as the Saxe porcelains, the Boulle mar-
bles, and the sumptuous hangings and fittings which
have later been known as " Pompadour."  Herself an
artist and connoisseur, she " set the pace " during a
period of unbridled luxury.  She was patroness of the

famous Sèvres ware. She drew around her such painters and littérateurs as Bouchardon, Carle Van Loo, Marmontel, Bernis, Crébillon, and Duclos. To her Voltaire dedicated his *Tancrède*.

This was her brilliant side; but upon the deplorable side must be reckoned her extravagance and her meddling in statecraft. Ambitious for power, she surrounded the doting monarch with her " creatures "—Rouillé, Saint Florentin, Puisieux, Machault. With the exception of the Duc de Choiseul, her appointees were notoriously weak—and this at a time when the War of the Austrian Succession and the Seven Years' War called for strong government. Won over by the cajoleries of Maria Theresa, who called her " cousin," she induced the King to accept the Austrian Alliance; and again, in 1758, despite Bernis and other ministers, she prevailed upon him to maintain it throughout the disastrous war which was only ended by the Treaty of Paris. In addition to this, she became embroiled with the Church party, being especially bitter against the Jesuits. It is no wonder, therefore, that she left her memory in the hands of her enemies. It is no wonder that the seeds of her folly and extravagance, as well as those of her successor, Du Barry, resulted in the bloody harvest of the Revolution. " Après nous le déluge! " (" After us the deluge ") was her sinister motto, now famous in history, and it carried with it the weight of prophecy.

To the end she remained, exteriorly, in full power. In 1752 the Marquise was made Duchesse de Pompadour; and four years later " Dame d'Honneur " to the Queen, a title of charmingly unconscious irony! The day of her demise (1764) was stormy, and the King is said to have been genuinely grieved over the loss, remarking: " Madame la Marquise has ill weather for her journey."

But to the last she herself was charming, débon-naire, masterful. She had smiled her way into power, and she smiled even in the face of death. " She felt it a duty to maintain to the end the pose of elegance which she had established for herself," say her French critics. " For the last time she applied the touch of rouge to her cheeks, by which she had hidden, for several years, the slow ravages of decay; set her lips in a final smile; and with the air of a coquette uttered to the priest, who extended to her the last rites of reli-gion, this laughing quip (mot d'élégance) : " Attendez-moi, monsieur le curé, nous partirons ensemble" ("Wait a moment, monsieur, and we will set forth together ").

# THE MEMOIRS OF LOUIS XV.

AND OF

# MADAME DE POMPADOUR

### SECTION I

AN early friend of mine, who married well at Paris, and who has the reputation of being a very clever woman, has often asked me to write down what daily passed under my notice; to please her, I made little notes, of three or four lines each, to recall to my memory the most singular or interesting facts; as, for instance—*attempt to assassinate the King; he orders Madame de Pompadour to leave the Court; M. de Machault's ingratitude, etc.* I always promised my friend that I would, some time or other, reduce all these materials into the form of a regular narrative. She mentioned the " Recollections of Madame de Caylus," which were, however, not then printed; and pressed me so much to produce a similar work, that I have taken advantage of a few leisure moments to write this, which I intend to give her, in order that she may arrange it and correct the style. I was for a long time about the person of Madame de Pompadour, and my birth procured for me respectful treatment from herself, and from some distinguished persons who conceived a regard for me. I soon became the intimate friend of Doctor Quesnay, who frequently came to pass two or three hours with me.

His house was frequented by people of all parties, but the number was small, and restricted to those who were on terms of greatest intimacy with him. All subjects were handled with the utmost freedom, and it is infinitely to his honour and theirs that nothing was ever repeated.

The Countess D—— also visited me. She was a frank and lively woman, and much liked by Madame de Pompadour. The Baschi family paid me great attention. M. de Marigny had received some little services from me, in the course of the frequent quarrels between him and his sister, and he had a great friendship for me. The King was in the constant habit of seeing me; and an accident, which I shall have occasion to relate, rendered him very familiar with me. He talked without any constraint when I was in the room. During Madame de Pompadour's illness I scarcely ever left her chamber, and passed the night there. Sometimes, though rarely, I accompanied her in her carriage with Doctor Quesnay, to whom she scarcely spoke a word, though he was a man of great talents. When I was alone with her, she talked of many affairs which nearly concerned her, and she once said to me, " The King and I have such implicit confidence in you, that we look upon you as a cat, or a dog, and go on talking as if you were not there." There was a little nook, adjoining her chamber, which has since been altered, where she knew I usually sat when I was alone, and where I heard everything that was said in the room, unless it was spoken in a low voice. But when the King wanted to speak to her in private, or in the presence of any of his Ministers, he went with her into a closet, by the side of the chamber, whither she also retired when she had secret business with the Ministers, or with other important persons; as, for instance, the Lieutenant of Police, the Postmaster-General, etc.    All these circumstances brought to my knowledge a great many things which probity will neither allow me to tell or to record.    I generally wrote without order of time, so that a fact may be related before others which preceded it.    Madame de Pompadour had a great friendship for three Ministers; the first was M. de Machault, to whom she was indebted for the regulation of her income, and the payment of her debts.    She gave him the seals, and he retained the first place in her regard till the attempt to assassinate the King.    Many people said that his conduct on that occasion was not attributable to bad intentions; that he thought it his duty to obey the King without making himself in any way a party to the affair, and that his cold manners gave him the appearance of an indifference which he did not feel. Madame de Pompadour regarded him in the light of a faithless friend; and, perhaps, there was some justice on both sides.    But for the Abbé de Bernis, M. de Machault might, probably, have retained his place.

The second Minister, whom Madame de Pompadour liked, was the Abbé de Bernis.    She was soon disgusted with him when she saw the absurdity of his conduct.    He gave a singular specimen of this on the very day of his dismissal.    He had invited a great many people of distinction to a splendid entertainment, which was to have taken place on the very day when he received his order of banishment, and had written in the notes of invitation—*M. Le Comte de Lusace will be there.*    This Count was the brother of the Dauphine, and this mention of him was deservedly thought impertinent.    The King said, wittily enough, *" Lambert and Molière will be there."*    She scarcely ever spoke of the Cardinal de Bernis after his dismissal from the Court.

He was extremely ridiculous, but he was a good
sort of man. Madame, the Infanta, died a little time
before, and, by the way, of such a complication of
putrid and malignant diseases, that the Capuchins
who bore the body, and the men who committed it
to the grave, were overcome by the effluvia. Her
papers appeared no less impure in the eyes of the
King. He discovered that the Abbé de Bernis had
been intriguing with her, and that they had deceived
him, and had obtained the Cardinal's hat by making
use of his name. The King was so indignant that he
was very near refusing him the *barrette*. He did
grant it—but just as he would have thrown a bone to
a dog. The Abbé had always the air of a protégé
when he was in the company of Madame de Pompadour. She had known him in positive distress. The
Duc de Choiseul was very differently situated; his
birth, his air, his manners, gave him claims to consideration, and he far exceeded every other man in
the art of ingratiating himself with Madame de Pompadour. She looked upon him as one of the most
illustrious nobles of the Court, as the most able
Minister, and the most agreeable man. M. de Choiseul had a sister and a wife, whom he had introduced
to her, and who sedulously cultivated her favourable
sentiments towards him. From the time he was
Minister, she saw only with his eyes; he had the
talent of amusing her, and his manners to women,
generally, were extremely agreeable.

Two persons—the Lieutenant of Police and the
Postmaster-General—were very much in Madame
de Pompadour's confidence; the latter, however, became less necessary to her from the time that the
King communicated to M. de Choiseul the secret of
the post-office, that is to say, the system of opening
letters and extracting matter from them: this had

never been imparted to M. d'Argenson, in spite of the high favour he enjoyed. I have heard that M. de Choiseul abused the confidence reposed in him, and related to his friends the ludicrous stories, and the love affairs contained in the letters which were broken open. The plan they pursued, as I have heard, was very simple. Six or seven clerks of the post-office picked out the letters they were ordered to break open, and took the impression of the seals with a ball of quicksilver. Then they put each letter, with the seal downwards, over a glass of hot water, which melted the wax without injuring the paper. It was then opened, the desired matter extracted, and it was sealed again, by means of the impression. This is the account of the matter I have heard. The Postmaster-General carried the extracts to the King on Sundays. He was seen coming and going on this noble errand as openly as the Ministers. Doctor Quesnay often, in my presence, flew in such a rage about that *infamous* Minister, as he called him, that he foamed at the mouth. " I would as soon dine with the hangman as with the Postmaster-General," said the Doctor. It must be acknowledged that this was astonishing language to be uttered in the apartments of the King's mistress; yet it went on for twenty years without being talked of. " It was probity speaking with earnestness," said M. de Marigny, " and not a mere burst of spite or malignity."

The Duc de Gontaut was the brother-in-law and friend of M. de Choiseul, and was assiduous in his attendance on Madame de Pompadour. The sister of M. de Choiseul, Madame de Grammont, and his wife were equally constant in their attentions. This will sufficiently account for the ascendency of M. de Choiseul, whom nobody would have ventured to

attack.    Chance, however, discovered to me a secret
correspondence of the King, with a man in a very
obscure station.    This man, who had a place in the
Farmers General, of from two to three hundred a
year, was related to one of the young ladies of the
Parc-aux-cerfs, by whom he was recommended to the
King.  He was also connected in some way with M.
de Broglie, in whom the King placed great confidence.    Wearied with finding that this correspondence procured him no advancement, he took the
resolution of writing to me, and requesting an interview, which I granted, after acquainting Madame de
Pompadour with the circumstance.    After a great
deal of preamble and of flattery, he said to me, " Can
you give me your word of hour, and that of
Madame de Pompadour, that no mention whatever
of what I am going to tell you will be made to the
King?"    "I think I can assure you that, if you
require such a promise from Madame de Pompadour,
and if it can produce no ill consequence to the King's
service, she will give it you."  He gave me his word
that what he requested would have no bad effect;
upon which I listened to what he had to say.  He
shewed me several memorials, containing accusations
of M. de Choiseul, and revealed some curious circumstances relative to the secret functions of the Comte
de Broglie.    These, however, led rather to conjectures than to certainty, as to the nature of the
services he rendered to the King.    Lastly, he shewed
me several letters in the King's handwriting.  " I
request," said he, " that the Marquise de Pompadour
will procure for me the place of Receiver-General of
Finances; I will give her information of whatever
I send the King; I will write according to her
instructions, and I will send her his answers."  As I
did not choose to take liberties with the King's

papers, I only undertook to deliver the memorials. Madame de Pompadour having given me her word according to the conditions on which I had received the communication, I revealed to her everything I had heard.    She sent the memorials to M. de Choiseul, who thought them very maliciously and very cleverly written.    Madame de Pompadour and he had a long conference as to the reply that was to be given to the person by whom those disclosures were made.    What I was commissioned to say was this: that the place of Receiver-General was at present too important, and would occasion too much surprise and speculation; that it would not do to go beyond a place worth fifteen thousand to twenty thousand francs a year; that they had no desire to pry into the King's secrets; and that his correspondence ought not to be communicated to any one; that this did not apply to papers like those of which I was the bearer, which might fall into his hands; that he would confer an obligation by communicating them, in order that blows aimed in the dark, and directed by malignity and imposture, might be parried.   The answer was respectful and proper, in what related to the King; it was, however, calculated to counteract the schemes of the Comte de Broglie, by making M. de Choiseul acquainted with his attacks, and with the nature of the weapons he employed.    It was from the Count that he received statements relating to the war and to the navy; but he had no communication with him concerning foreign affairs, which the Count, as it was said, transacted immediately with the King.   The Duc de Choiseul got the man who spoke to me recommended to the Controller-General, without his appearing in the business; he had the place which was agreed upon, and the hope of a still better, and he entrusted to me the King's corre-

spondence, which I told him I should not mention to
Madame de Pompadour, according to her injunctions.
He sent several memorials to M. de Choiseul, con-
taining accusations of him, addressed to the King.
This timely information enabled him to refute them
triumphantly.

The King was very fond of having little private
correspondences, very often unknown to Madame de
Pompadour: she knew, however, of the existence of
some, for he passed part of his mornings in writing
to his family, to the King of Spain, to Cardinal
Tencin, to the Abbé de Broglie, and also to some
obscure persons. "It is, doubtless, from such people
as these," said she to me, one day, "that the King
learns expressions which perfectly surprise me. For
instance, he said to me yesterday, when he saw a man
pass with an old coat on, '*il y a là un habit bien exa-
miné.*' He once said to me, when he meant to express
that a thing was probable, '*il y a gros*'; I am told
this is a saying of the common people, meaning, *il y a
gros à parier.*" I took the liberty to say, "But is it
not more likely from his young ladies at the Parc,
that he learns these elegant expressions?" She
laughed, and said, "You are right; *il y a gros.*" The
King, however, used these expressions designedly, and
with a laugh.

The King knew a great many anecdotes, and there
were people enough who furnished him with such as
were likely to mortify the self-love of others. One
day, at Choisy, he went into a room where some
people were employed about embroidered furniture,
to see how they were going on; and looking out of
the window, he saw at the end of a long avenue two
men in the Choisy uniform. "Who are those two
noblemen?" said he. Madame de Pompadour took
up her glass, and said, "They are the Duc d'Aumont,

and ———." "Ah!" said the King; "the Duc
d'Aumont's grandfather would be greatly astonished
if he could see his grandson arm in arm with the
grandson of his *valet de Chambre*, L——, in a dress
which may be called a patent of nobility!" He went
on to tell Madame de Pompadour a long history, to
prove the truth of what he said. The King went out
to accompany her into the garden; and, soon after,
Quesnay and M. de Marigny came in. I spoke with
contempt of some one who was very fond of money.
At this the Doctor laughed, and said, "I had a curious dream last night: I was in the country of the
ancient Germans; I had a large house, stacks of corn,
herds of cattle, a great number of horses, and huge
barrels of ale; but I suffered dreadfully from rheu-
matism, and knew not how to manage to go to a
fountain, at fifty leagues' distance, the waters of
which would cure me. I was to go among a strange
people. An enchanter appeared before me, and said
to me, 'I pity your distress; here, I will give you a
little packet of the powder of *prelinpinpin;* whoever
receives a little of this from you will lodge you, feed
you, and pay you all sorts of civilities.' I took the
powder, and thanked him." "Ah!" said I, "how
I should like to have some powder of *prelinpinpin!*
I wish I had a chest full." "Well," said the Doctor,
"that powder is *money,* for which you have so great
a contempt. Tell me who, of all the men who come
hither, receives the greatest attentions?" "I do not
know," said I. "Why," said he, "it is M. de Mon-
martel, who comes four or five times a year." "Why
does he enjoy so much consideration?" "Because
his coffers are full of the powder of *prelinpinpin.*
Everything in existence," said he, taking a handful
of louis from his pocket, "is contained in these little
pieces of metal, which will convey you commodiously

from one end of the world to the other.   All men
obey those who possess this powder, and eagerly
tender them their services.   To despise money, is to
despise happiness, liberty, in short, enjoyments of
every kind."   A *cordon bleu* passed under the window.
" That nobleman," said I, " is much more delighted
with his *cordon bleu* than he would be with ten thousand of your pieces of metal."   " When I ask the
King for a pension," replied Quesnay, " I say to him,
' Give me the means of having a better dinner, a
warmer coat, a carriage to shelter me from the
weather, and to transport me from place to place
without fatigue.'   But the man who asks him for
that fine blue ribbon would say, if he had the courage
and the honesty to speak as he feels, ' I am vain, and
it will give me great satisfaction to see people look at
me, as I pass, with an eye of stupid admiration, and
make way for me; I wish, when I enter a room, to
produce an effect, and to excite the attention of those
who may, perhaps, laugh at me when I am gone; I
wish to be called *Monseigneur* by the multitude.'   Is
not all this mere empty air?   In scarcely any country will this ribbon be of the slightest use to him; it
will give him no power.   My pieces of metal will give
me the power of assisting the unfortunate everywhere.
Long live the omnipotent powder of *prelinpinpin!* "
At these last words, we heard a burst of laughter
from the adjoining room, which was only separated
by a door from the one we were in.   The door opened,
and in came the King, Madame de Pompadour, and
M. de Gontaut.   " Long live the powder of *prelinpinpin!* " said the King.   " Doctor, can you get me any
of it? "   It happened that, when the King returned
from his walk, he was struck with a fancy to listen
to our conversation.   Madame de Pompadour was
extremely kind to the Doctor, and the King went out

Madame de Pompadour learns of the likelihood of her success in meeting her admirer, the King.

—p. 182

*From the painting by Casanova y Estorach.*

laughing, and talking with great admiration of the powder. I went away, and so did the Doctor. I immediately sat down to commit this conversation to writing. I was afterwards told that M. Quesnay was very learned in certain matters relating to finance, and that he was a great *économiste*. But I do not know very well what that means. What I do know for certain is, that he was very clever, very gay and witty, and a very able physician.

The illness of the little Duke of Burgundy, whose intelligence was much talked of, for a long time occupied the attention of the Court. Great endeavours were made to find out the cause of his malady, and ill-nature went so far as to assert that his nurse, who had an excellent situation at Versailles, had communicated to him a nasty disease. The King shewed Madame de Pompadour the information he had procured from the province she came from, as to her conduct. A silly Bishop thought proper to say she had been very licentious in her youth. The poor nurse was told of this, and begged that he might be made to explain himself. The Bishop replied, that she had been at several balls in the town in which she lived, and that she had gone with her neck uncovered. The poor man actually thought this the height of licentiousness. The King, who had been at first uneasy, when he came to this, called out, *"What a fool!"* After having long been a source of anxiety to the Court, the Duke died. Nothing produces a stronger impression upon Princes, than the spectacle of their equals dying. Everybody is occupied about them while ill—but as soon as they are dead, nobody mentions them. The King frequently talked about death—and about funerals, and places of burial. Nobody could be of a more melancholy temperament. Madame de Pompadour once told me that he experienced a painful sensation whenever he was forced to laugh, and that he had often begged her to break off a droll story. He smiled, and that was all. In general, he had the most gloomy ideas concerning almost all events. When there was a new Minister, he used to say, "*He displays his wares like all the rest, and promises the finest things in the world, not one of which will be fulfilled. He does not know this country—he will see.*" When new projects for reinforcing the navy were laid before him, he said, "This is the twentieth time I have heard this talked of—France never will have a navy, I think." This I heard from M. de Marigny.

I never saw Madame de Pompadour so rejoiced as at the taking of Mahon. The King was very glad, too, but he had no belief in the merit of his courtiers —he looked upon their success as the effect of chance. Maréchal Saxe was, as I have been told, the only man who inspired him with great esteem. But he had scarcely ever seen him in his closet, or playing the courtier.

M. d'Argenson picked a quarrel with M. de Richelieu, after his victory, about his return to Paris. This was intended to prevent his coming to enjoy his triumph. He tried to throw the thing upon Madame de Pompadour, who was enthusiastic about him, and called him by no other name than the "*Minorcan.*" The Chevalier de Montaign was the favourite of the Dauphin, and much beloved by him for his great devotion. He fell ill, and underwent an operation called *l'empième*, which is performed by making an incision between the ribs, in order to let out the pus; it had, to all appearance, a favourable result, but the patient grew worse, and could not breathe. His medical attendants could not conceive what occasioned this accident and retarded his cure. He died almost in the arms of the Dauphin, who went every day to see him. The singularity of his disease determined the surgeons to open the body, and they found, in his chest, part of the leaden syringe with which decoctions had, as was usual, been injected into the part in a state of suppuration. The surgeon, who committed this act of negligence, took care not to boast of his feat, and his patient was the victim. This incident was much talked of by the King, who related it, I believe, not less than thirty times, according to his custom; but what occasioned still more conversation about the Chevalier de Montaign, was a box, found by his bed's side, containing haircloths, and shirts, and whips, stained with blood. This circumstance was spoken of one evening at supper, at Madame de Pompadour's, and not one of the guests seemed at all tempted to imitate the Chevalier. Eight or ten days afterwards, the following tale was sent to the King, to Madame de Pompadour, to the Baschi, and to the Duc d'Ayen. At first nobody could understand to what it referred: at last, the Duc d'Ayen exclaimed. "How stupid we are; this is a joke on the austerities of the Chevalier de Montaign!" This appeared clear enough—so much the more so, as the copies were sent to the Dauphin, the Dauphine, the Abbé de St. Cyr, and to the Duc de V——. The latter had the character of a pretender to devotion, and, in his copy, there was this addition, " You would not be such a fool, my dear Duke, as to be a faquir—confess that you would be very glad to be one of those good monks who lead such a jolly life." The Duc de Richelieu was suspected of having employed one of his wits to write the story. The King was scandalised at it, and ordered the Lieutenant of Police to endeavour to find out the author, but either he could not succeed or he would not betray him.

*Japanese Tale.*

At a distance of three leagues from the capital of Japan, there is a temple celebrated for the concourse of persons, of both sexes, and of all ranks, who crowd thither to worship an idol believed to work miracles. Three hundred men consecrated to the service of religion, and who can give proofs of ancient and illustrious descent, serve this temple, and present to the idol the offerings which are brought from all the provinces of the empire. They inhabit a vast and magnificent edifice, belonging to the temple, and surrounded with gardens where art has combined with nature to produce enchantment. I obtained permission to see the temple, and to walk in the gardens. A monk advanced in years, but still full of vigour and vivacity, accompanied me. I saw several others, of different ages, who were walking there. But what surprised me was to see a great many of them amusing themselves by various agreeable and sportive games with young girls elegantly dressed, listening to their songs, and joining in their dances. The monk, who accompanied me, listened with great civility and kindness to the questions I put to him concerning his order. The following is the sum of his answers to my numerous interrogations. The God Faraki, whom we worship, is so called from a word which signifies the *fabricator*. He made all that we behold—the earth, the stars, the sun, etc. He has endowed men with senses, which are so many sources of pleasure, and we think the only way of shewing our gratitude is to use them. This opinion will, doubtless, appear to you much more rational than that of the faquirs of India, who pass their lives in thwarting nature, and who inflict upon themselves the most melancholy privations and the most severe sufferings.

As soon as the sun rises, we repair to the mountain you see before us, at the foot of which flows a stream of the most limpid water, which meanders in graceful windings through that meadow—enamelled with the loveliest flowers. We gather the most fragrant of them, which we carry and lay upon the altar, together with various fruits, which we receive from the bounty of Faraki. We then sing his praises, and execute dances expressive of our thankfulness, and of all the enjoyments we owe to this beneficent deity. The highest of these is that which love produces, and we testify our ardent gratitude by the manner in which we avail ourselves of this inestimable gift of Faraki. Having left the temple, we go into several shady thickets, where we take a light repast; after which, each of us employs himself in some unoppressive labour. Some embroider, others apply themselves to painting, others cultivate flowers or fruits, others turn little implements for our use. Many of these little works are sold to the people, who purchase them with eagerness. The money arising from this sale forms a considerable part of our revenue. Our morning is thus devoted to the worship of God and to the exercise of the sense of Sight, which begins with the first rays of the sun. The sense of Taste is gratified by our dinner, and we add to it the pleasure of Smell. The most delicious viands are spread for us in apartments strewed with flowers. The table is adorned with them, and the most exquisite wines are handed to us in crystal goblets. When we have glorified God, by the agreeable use of the palate, and the olfactory nerve, we enjoy a delightful sleep of two hours, in bowers of orange trees, roses, and myrtles. Having acquired a fresh store of strength and spirits, we return to our occupations, that we may thus mingle labour with pleasure, which would lose its zest by long continuance.  After our work, we return to the temple, to thank God, and to offer him incense.  From thence we go to the most delightful part of the garden, where we find three hundred young girls, some of whom form lively dances with the younger of our monks; the others execute serious dances, which require neither strength nor agility, and which only keep time to the sound of musical instruments.

We talk and laugh with our companions, who are dressed in a light gauze, and whose tresses are adorned with flowers; we press them to partake of exquisite sherbets, differently prepared.  The hour of supper being arrived, we repair to rooms illuminated with the lustre of a thousand tapers fragrant with amber.  The supper-room is surrounded by three vast galleries, in which are placed musicians, whose various instruments fill the mind with the most pleasurable and the softest emotions.  The young girls are seated at table with us, and, towards the conclusion of the repast, they sing songs, which are hymns in honour of the God who has endowed us with senses which shed such a charm over existence, and which promise us new pleasure from every fresh exercise of them.  After the repast is ended, we return to the dance, and, when the hour of repose arrives, we draw from a kind of lottery, in which every one is sure of a prize that is a sumptuously decorated sleeping room for the night.  These rooms are allotted to each by chance to avoid jealousy, since some rooms are handsomer than others.  Thus ends the day and gives place to a night of exquisite repose in which we enjoy well-earned sleep, that most divine of earthly gifts.

We admire the wisdom and the goodness of Faraki, who has implanted an unconscious mutual attraction between the sexes that constantly draws them towards

each other. It is this mutual love, these invisible
ties, that make the world brighter, cheerier, happier.
It has been truly said that those who selfishly cut
themselves away from these ties, those that lead
narrow, lonely, morbid lives, lose most of life's joys.
What should we say to the favourite of a King
from whom he had received a beautiful house, and
fine estates, and who chose to spoil the house, to
let it fall in ruins, to abandon the cultivation of the
land, and let it become sterile, and covered with
thorns? Such is the conduct of the faquirs of India,
who condemn themselves to the most melancholy
privations, and to the most severe sufferings. Is not
this insulting Faraki? Is it not saying to him, I
despise your gifts? Is it not misrepresenting him
and saying, You are malevolent and cruel, and I
know that I can no otherwise please you than by
offering you the spectacle of my miseries? "I am
told," added he, "that you have, in your country,
faquirs not less insane, not less cruel to themselves."
I thought, with some reason, that he meant the
fathers of La Trappe. The recital of the matter
afforded me much matter for reflection, and I admired
how strange are the systems to which perverted reason gives birth.

The Duc de V—— was a nobleman of high rank
and great wealth. He said to the King one evening
at supper, "Your Majesty does me the favour to treat
me with great kindness: I should be inconsolable if I
had the misfortune to fall under your displeasure.
If such a calamity were to befall me, I should endeavour to divert my grief by improving some beautiful estates of mine in such and such a province;" and
he thereupon gave a description of three or four fine
seats. About a month after, talking of the disgrace

of a Minister, he said, "I hope your Majesty will not withdraw your favour from me; but if I had the misfortune to lose it, I should be more to be pitied than anybody, for I have no asylum in which to hide my head." All those present, who had heard the description of the beautiful country houses, looked at each other and laughed. The King said to Madame de Pompadour, who sat next to him at table, "*People are very right in saying that a liar ought to have a good memory.*"

An event, which made me tremble, as well as Madame, procured me the familiarity of the King. In the middle of the night, Madame came into my chamber, *en chemise,* and in a state of distraction. "Here! Here!" said she, "the King is dying." My alarm may be easily imagined. I put on a petticoat, and found the King in her bed, panting. What was to be done?—it was an indigestion. We threw water upon him, and he came to himself. I made him swallow some Hoffman's drops, and he said to me, "Do not make any noise, but go to Quesnay; say that your mistress is ill; and tell the Doctor's servants to say nothing about it." Quesnay, who lodged close by, came immediately, and was much astonished to see the King in that state. He felt his pulse, and said, "The crisis is over; but, if the King were sixty years old, this might have been serious." He went to seek some drug, and, on his return, set about inundating the King with perfumed water. I forget the name of the medicine he made him take, but the effect was wonderful. I believe it was the *drops of Général Lamotte.* I called up one of the girls of the wardrobe to make tea, as if for myself. The King took three cups, put on his *robe de chambre* and his stockings, and went to his own room, leaning upon the Doctor. What a sight it was to see us all three half naked! Madame put on a robe as soon as possible, and I did the same, and the King changed his clothes behind the curtains, which were very decently closed. He afterwards spoke of this short attack, and expressed his sense of the attentions shown him. An hour after, I felt the greatest possible terror in thinking that the King might have died in our hands. Happily, he quickly recovered himself, and none of the domestics perceived what had taken place. I merely told the girl of the wardrobe to put everything to rights, and she thought it was Madame who had been indisposed. The King, the next morning, gave secretly to Quesnay a little note for Madame, in which he said, *Ma chère amie must have had a great fright, but let her reassure herself—I am now well, which the Doctor will certify to you.* From that moment the King became accustomed to me, and, touched by the interest I had shown for him, he often gave me one of his peculiarly gracious glances, and made me little presents, and, on every New Year's Day, sent me porcelain to the amount of twenty louis d'or. He told Madame that he looked upon me in the apartment as a picture or statue, and never put any constraint upon himself on account of my presence. Doctor Quesnay received a pension of a thousand crowns for his attention and silence, and the promise of a place for his son. The King gave me an order upon the Treasury for four thousand francs, and Madame had presented to her a very handsome chiming-clock and the King's portrait in a snuffbox.

The King was habitually melancholy, and liked everything which recalled the idea of death, in spite of the strongest fears of it. Of this, the following is an instance: Madame de Pompadour was on her way to Crécy, when one of the King's grooms made a sign to her coachman to stop, and told him that the King's carriage had broken down, and that, knowing her to be at no great distance, His Majesty had sent him forward to beg her to wait for him. He soon overtook us, and seated himself in Madame de Pompadour's carriage, in which were, I think, Madame de Château-Rénaud, and Madame de Mirepoix. The lords in attendance placed themselves in some other carriages. I was behind, in a chaise, with Gourbillon, Madame de Pompadour's *valet de chambre.* We were surprised in a short time by the King stopping his carriage. Those which followed, of course stopped also. The King called a groom, and said to him, "You see that little eminence; there are crosses; it must certainly be a buryingground; go and see whether there are any graves newly dug." The groom galloped up to it, returned, and said to the King, "There are three quite freshly made." Madame de Pompadour, as she told me, turned away her head with horror; and the little Maréchale gaily said, "*This is indeed enough to make one's mouth water.*" Madame de Pompadour spoke of it when I was undressing her in the evening. "What a strange pleasure," said she, "to endeavour to fill one's mind with images which one ought to endeavour to banish, especially when one is surrounded by so many sources of happiness! But that is the King's way; he loves to talk about death. He said, some days ago, to M. de Fontanieu, who was seized with a bleeding at the nose, at the levée, 'Take care of yourself; at your age it is a forerunner of apoplexy.' The poor man went home frightened, and absolutely ill."

I never saw the King so agitated as during the illness of the Dauphin. The physicians came incessantly to the apartments of Madame de Pompadour, where the King interrogated them. There was one from Paris, a very odd man, called Pousse, who once said to him, "You are a good papa; I like you for that. But you know we are all your children, and share your distress. Take courage, however; your son will recover." Everybody's eyes were upon the Duc d'Orléans, who knew not how to look. He would have become heir to the crown, the Queen being past the age to have children. Madame de —— said to me, one day, when I was expressing my surprise at the King's grief, " It would annoy him beyond measure to have a Prince of the blood heir apparent. He does not like them, and looks upon their relationship to him as so remote, that he would feel humiliated by it." And, in fact, when his son recovered, he said, " The King of Spain would have had a fine chance." It was thought that he was right in this, and that it would have been agreeable to justice; but that, if the Duc d'Orléans had been supported by a party, he might have supported his pretensions to the crown. It was, doubtless, to remove this impression that he gave a magnificent fête at St. Cloud on the occasion of the Dauphin's recovery. Madame de Pompadour said to Madame de Brancas, speaking of this fête, " He wishes to make us forget the *château en Espagne* he has been dreaming of; in *Spain*, however, they build them of solider materials." The people did not shew so much joy at the Dauphin's recovery. They looked upon him as a devotee, who did nothing but sing psalms. They loved the Duc d'Orléans, who lived in the capital, and had acquired the name of the *King of Paris*. These sentiments were not just; the Dauphin only sang psalms when imitating the tones of one of the choristers of the chapel. The people afterwards acknowledged their error, and did justice to his virtues. The Duc d'Orléans paid the most assiduous court to Madame de Pompadour: the Duchess, on the contrary, detested her. It is possible that words were put into the Duchess's mouth which she never uttered; but she, certainly, often said most cutting things. The King would have sent her into exile, had he listened only to his resentment; but he feared the éclat of such a proceeding, and he knew that she would only be the more malicious. The Duc d'Orléans was, just then, extremely jealous of the Comte de Melfort; and the Lieutenant of Police told the King he had strong reasons for believing that the Duke would stick at nothing to rid himself of this gallant, and that he thought it his duty to give the Count notice, that he ought to be upon his guard. The King said, "He would not dare to attempt any such violence as you seem to apprehend; but there is a better way: let him try to surprise them, and he will find me very well inclined to have his cursed wife shut up; but if he got rid of this lover, she would have another to-morrow. Nay, she has others at this moment; for instance, the Chevalier de Colbert, and the Comte de l'Aigle." Madame de Pompadour, however, told me these two last affairs were not certain.

An adventure happened about the same time, which the Lieutenant of Police reported to the King. The Duchesse d'Orléans had amused herself one evening, about eight o'clock, with ogling a handsome young Dutchman, whom she took a fancy to, from a window of the Palais Royal. The young man, taking her for a woman of the town, wanted to make short work, at which she was very much shocked. She called a Swiss, and made herself known. The stranger was arrested; but he defended himself by affirming that she had talked very loosely to him.

He was dismissed, and the Duc d'Orléans gave his wife a severe reprimand.

The King (who hated her so much that he spoke of her without the slightest restraint) one day said to Madame de Pompadour, in my presence, "Her mother knew what she was, for, before her marriage, she never suffered her to say more than yes and no. Do you know her joke on the nomination of Moras? She sent to congratulate him upon it: two minutes after, she called back the messenger she had sent, and said, before everybody present, 'Before you speak to him, ask the Swiss if he still has the place.'" Madame de Pompadour was not vindictive, and, in spite of the malicious speeches of the Duchesse d'Orléans, she tried to excuse her conduct. "Almost all women," she said, "have lovers; she has not all that are imputed to her: but her free manners, and her conversation, which is beyond all bounds, have brought her into general disrepute."

My companion came into my room the other day, quite delighted. She had been with M. de Chenevières, first Clerk in the War-office, and a constant correspondent of Voltaire, whom she looks upon as a god. She was, by the bye, put into a great rage one day, lately, by a print-seller in the street, who was crying, "Here is Voltaire, the famous Prussian; here you see him, with a great bear-skin cap, to keep him from the cold! Here is the famous Prussian, for six sous!" "What a profanation!" said she. To return to my story: M. de Chenevières had shewn her some letters from Voltaire, and M. Marmontel had read an *Epistle to his Library*.

M. Quesnay came in for a moment; she told him all this: and, as he did not appear to take any great interest in it, she asked him if he did not admire great poets. "Oh, yes; just as I admire great bilboquet players," said he, in that tone of his, which rendered everything he said diverting. " I have written some verses, however," said he, " and I will repeat them to you; they are upon a certain M. Rodot, an Intendant of the Marine, who was very fond of abusing medicine and medical men. I made these verses to revenge Æsculapius and Hippocrates.

> Antoine se medicina
>   En decriant la medicine,
> Et de ses propres mains mina
>   Les fondemens de sa machine:
> Très rarement il opina
>   Sans humeur bizarre ou chagrine,
> Et, l'esprit qui le domina
>   Etait affiché sur sa mine.

" What do you say to them? " said the Doctor. My companion thought them very pretty, and the Doctor gave me them in his handwriting, begging me, at the same time, not to give any copies.

Madame de Pompadour joked my companion about her *bel-esprit*, but sometimes she reposed confidence in her. Knowing that she was often writing, she said to her, " You are writing a novel, which will appear some day or other; or, perhaps, the age of Louis XV.: I beg you to treat me well." I have no reason to complain of her. It signifies very little to me that she can talk more learnedly than I can about prose and verse.

She never told me her real name; but one day I was malicious enough to say to her, " Some one was maintaining, yesterday, that the family of Madame de Mar—— was of more importance than many of good extraction. They say it is the first in Cadiz. She had very honourable alliances, and yet she has thought it no degradation to be governess to Madame de Pompadour's daughter. One day you will see her sons or her nephews Farmers General, and her granddaughters

married to Dukes." I had remarked that Madame de
Pompadour for some days had taken chocolate, *à
triple vanille et ambré*, at her breakfast; and that she
ate truffles and celery soup: finding her in a very
heated state, I one day remonstrated with her about
her diet, to which she paid no attention.   I then
thought it right to speak to her friend, the Duchesse
de Brancas.   "I had remarked the same thing," said
she, "and I will speak to her about it before you."
After she was dressed, Madame de Brancas, accordingly, told her she was uneasy about her health.   "I
have just been talking to her about it," said the
Duchess, pointing to me, "and she is of my opinion."
Madame de Pompadour seemed a little displeased; at
last, she burst into tears.   I immediately went out,
shut the door, and returned to my place to listen.
"My dear friend," she said to Madame de Brancas,
"I am agitated by the fear of losing the King's heart
by ceasing to be attractive to him.   Men, you know,
set great value on certain things, and I have the misfortune to be of a very cold temperament.   I, therefore, determined to adopt a heating diet, in order to
remedy this defect, and for two days this elixir has
been of great service to me, or, at least, I have
thought I felt its good effects."   The Duchesse de
Brancas took the phial which was upon the toilet,
and after having smelt at it, "Fie!" said she, and
threw it into the fire.   Madame de Pompadour scolded
her, and said, "I don't like to be treated like a child."
She wept again, and said, "You don't know what
happened to me a week ago.   The King, under pretext of the heat of the weather, lay down upon my
sofa, and passed half the night there.   He will take
a disgust to me and have another mistress."   "You
will not avoid that," replied the Duchess, "by following your new diet, and that diet will kill you; render

your company more and more precious to the King by your gentleness: do not repulse him in his fond moments, and let time do the rest; the chains of habit will bind him to you for ever." They then embraced; Madame de Pompadour recommended secrecy to Madame de Brancas, and the diet was abandoned.

A little while after, she said to me, "Our master is better pleased with me. This is since I spoke to Quesnay, without, however, telling him all. He told me, that to accomplish my end, I must try to be in good health, to digest well, and, for that purpose, take exercise. I think the Doctor is right. I feel quite a different creature. I adore that man (the King), I wish so earnestly to be agreeable to him! But, alas! sometimes he says I am a *macreuse* (a cold-blooded aquatic bird). I would give my life to please him."

One day, the King came in very much heated. I withdrew to my post, where I listened. "What is the matter?" said Madame de Pompadour. "The long robes and the clergy," replied he, "are always at drawn daggers, they distract me by their quarrels. But I detest the long robes the most. My clergy, on the whole, is attached and faithful to me; the others want to keep me in a state of tutelage." "Firmness," said Madame de Pompadour, "is the only thing that can subdue them." "Robert Saint Vincent is an incendiary, whom I wish I could banish, but that would make a terrible tumult. On the other hand, the Archbishop is an iron-hearted fellow, who tries to pick quarrels. Happily, there are some in the Parliament upon whom I can rely, and who affect to be very violent, but can be softened upon occasion. It costs me a few abbeys, and a few secret pensions, to accomplish this. There is a certain V—— who serves me very well, while he appears to be furious on the other side." " I can

tell you some news of him, Sire," said Madame de
Pompadour. " He wrote to me yesterday, pretending
that he is related to me, and begging for an interview." " Well," said the King, " let him come. See
him; and if he behaves well, we shall have a pretext
for giving him something." M. de Gontaut came in,
and seeing that they were talking seriously, said
nothing. The King walked about in an agitated
manner, and suddenly exclaimed, " The Regent was
very wrong in restoring to them the right of remonstrating; they will end in ruining the State." " Ah,
Sire," said M. de Gontaut, " it is too strong to be
shaken by a set of petty justices." " You don't know
what they do, nor what they think. They are an assembly of republicans; however, here is enough of
the subject. Things will last as they are as long as I
shall. Talk about this on Sunday, Madame, with
M. Berrier." Madame d'Amblimont and Madame
d'Esparbès came in. " Ah! here come my kittens,"
said Madame de Pompadour; " all that we are about
is Greek to them; but their gaiety restores my tranquillity, and enables me to attend again to serious
affairs. You, Sire, have the chase to divert you—
they answer the same purpose to me." The King
then began to talk about his morning's sport, and
Lansmatte. It was necessary to let the King go on
upon these subjects, and even, sometimes, to hear the
same story three or four times over, if new persons
came into the room. Madame de Pompadour never
betrayed the least ennui. She even sometimes persuaded him to begin his story anew.

I one day said to her, " It appears to me, Madame,
that you are fonder than ever of the Comtesse d'Amblimont." " I have reason to be so," said she. " She
is unique, I think, for her fidelity to her friends, and
for her honour. Listen, but tell nobody—four days

ago, the King, passing her to go to supper, approached her, under the pretence of tickling her, and tried to slip a note into her hand. D'Amblimont, in her madcap way, put her hands behind her back, and the King was obliged to pick up the note, which had fallen on the ground. Gontaut was the only person who saw all this, and after supper, he went up to the little lady, and said, 'You are an excellent friend.' 'I did my duty,' said she, and immediately put her finger on her lips to enjoin him to be silent. He, however, informed me of this act of friendship of the little heroine, who had not told me of it herself." I admired the Countess's virtue, and Madame de Pompadour said, " She is giddy and headlong; but she has more sense and more feeling than a thousand prudes and devotees. D'Esparbès would not do as much— most likely she would meet him more than half-way. The King appeared disconcerted, but he still pays her great attentions." " You will, doubtless, Madame," said I, " show your sense of such admirable conduct." "You need not doubt it," said she, " but I don't wish her to think that I am informed of it." The King, prompted either by the remains of his liking, or from the suggestions of Madame de Pompadour, one morning went to call on Madame d'Amblimont, at Choisy, and threw round her neck a collar of diamonds and emeralds, worth between fifty thousand and seventy-five thousand francs. This happened a long time after the circumstance I have just related.

There was a large sofa in a little room adjoining Madame de Pompadour's, upon which I often reposed.

One evening, towards midnight, a bat flew into the apartment where the Court was; the King immediately cried out, " Where is General Crillon? " (He had just left the room.) " He is the General to command against the bats." This set everybody calling

out, " *Où étais-tu, Crillon?* "   M. de Crillon soon after
came in, and was told where the enemy was.   He
immediately threw off his coat, drew his sword, and
commenced an attack upon the bat, which flew into
the closet where I was fast asleep.   I started out of
sleep at the noise, and saw the King and all the company around me.   This furnished amusement for the
rest of the evening.   M. de Crillon was a very excellent and agreeable man, but he had the fault of
indulging in buffooneries of this kind, which, however, were the result of his natural gaiety, and not of
any subserviency of character.   Such, however, was
not the case with another exalted nobleman, a Knight
of the Golden Fleece, whom Madame saw one day
shaking hands with her *valet de chambre*.   As he
was one of the vainest men at Court, Madame could
not refrain from telling the circumstance to the King;
and, as he had no employment at Court, the King
scarcely ever after named him on the Supper List.

I had a cousin at Saint Cyr, who was married.
She was greatly distressed at having a relation waiting woman to Madame de Pompadour, and often
treated me in the most mortifying manner.   Madame
knew this from Colin, her steward, and spoke of it
to the King.   "I am not surprised at it," said he;
" this is a specimen of the silly women of Saint Cyr.
Madame de Maintenon had excellent intentions, but
she made a great mistake.   These girls are brought
up in such a manner, that, unless they are all made
ladies of the palace, they are unhappy and impertinent."

Some time after, this relation of mine was at my
house.   Colin, who knew her, though she did not
know him, came in.   He said to me, "Do you know
that the Prince de Chimay has made a violent
attack upon the Chevalier d'Henin for being equerry

to the Marquise." At these words, my cousin looked very much astonished, and said, "Was he not right?" "I don't mean to enter into that question," said Colin—"but only to repeat his words, which were these: 'If you were only a man of moderately good family and poor, I should not blame you, knowing, as I do, that there are hundreds such, who would quarrel for your place, as young ladies of family would, to be about your mistress. But, recollect, that your relations are princes of the Empire, and that you bear their name.'" "What, sir," said my relation, "the Marquise's equerry of a princely house?" "Of the house of Chimay," said he; "they take the name of Alsace"—witness the Cardinal of that name. Colin went out delighted at what he had said.

"I cannot get over my surprise at what I have heard," said my relation. "It is, nevertheless, very true," replied I; "you may see the Chevalier d'Henin (that is the family name of the Princes de Chimay), with the cloak of Madame upon his arm, and walking alongside her sedan-chair, in order that he may be ready, on her getting in, to cover her shoulders with her cloak, and then remain in the antechamber, if there is no other room, till her return."

From that time, my cousin let me alone; nay, she even applied to me to get a company of horse for her husband, who was very loath to come and thank me. His wife wished him to thank Madame de Pompadour; but the fear he had lest she should tell him, that it was in consideration of his relationship to her waiting-woman that he commanded fifty horse, prevented him. It was, however, a most surprising thing that a man belonging to the house of Chimay should be in the service of any lady whatever; and the commander of Alsace returned from Malta on

purpose to get him out of Madame de Pompadour's
household.　　He got him a pension of a hundred
louis from his family, and the Marquise gave him
a company of horse.　　The Chevalier d'Henin had
been page to the Maréchal de Luxembourg, and one
can hardly imagine how he could have put his relation in such a situation; for, generally speaking, all
great houses keep up the consequence of their members.　M. de Machault, the Keeper of the Seals, had,
at the same time, as equerry, a Knight of St. Louis,
and a man of family—the Chevalier de Peribuse—
who carried his portfolio, and walked by the side of
the chair.

Whether it was from ambition, or from tenderness, Madame de Pompadour had a regard for her
daughter, which seemed to proceed from the bottom
of her heart.　She was brought up like a Princess,
and, like persons of that rank, was called by her
Christian name alone.　　The first persons at Court
had an eye to this alliance, but her mother had,
perhaps, a better project.　The King had a son by
Madame de Vintimille, who resembled him in face,
gesture, and manners.　He was called the Comte du
————.　　Madame de Pompadour had him brought
to Bellevue.　　Colin, her steward, was employed to
find means to persuade his tutor to bring him thither.
They took some refreshment at the house of the
Swiss, and the Marquise, in the course of her
walk, appeared to meet them by accident.　She
asked the name of the child, and admired his beauty.
Her daughter came up at the same moment, and
Madame de Pompadour led them into a part of the
garden where she knew the King would come.　He
did come, and asked the child's name.　He was told,
and looked embarrassed when Madame, pointing to
them, said they would be a beautiful couple.　The

King played with the girl, without appearing to take any notice of the boy, who, while he was eating some figs and cakes which were brought, his attitudes and gestures were so like those of the King, that Madame de Pompadour was in the utmost astonishment. "Ah!" said she, "Sire, look at ———." "At what?" said he. "Nothing," replied Madame, "except that one would think one saw his father."

"I did not know," said the King, smiling, "that you were so intimately acquainted with the Comte du L———." "You ought to embrace him," said she, "he is very handsome." "I will begin, then, with the young lady," said the King, and embraced them in a cold, constrained manner. I was present, having joined Mademoiselle's governess. I remarked to Madame, in the evening, that the King had not appeared very cordial in his caresses. "That is his way," said she; "but do not those children appear made for each other? If it was Louis XIV., he would make a Duc du Maine of the little boy; I do not ask so much; but a place and a dukedom for his son is very little; and it is because he is his son that I prefer him to all the little Dukes of the Court. My grandchildren would blend the resemblance of their grandfather and grandmother; and this combination, which I hope to live to see, would, one day, be my greatest delight." The tears came into her eyes as she spoke. Alas! alas! only six months elapsed, when her darling daughter, the hope of her advanced years, the object of her fondest wishes, died suddenly. Madame de Pompadour was inconsolable, and I must do M. de Marigny the justice to say that he was deeply afflicted. His niece was beautiful as an angel, and destined to the highest fortunes, and I always thought that he had formed the design of marrying her. A dukedom would have given him rank; and that, joined to his place, and to the wealth which she would have had from her mother, would have made him a man of great importance. The difference of age was not sufficient to be a great obstacle. People, as usual, said the young lady was poisoned; for the unexpected death of persons who command a large portion of public attention always gives birth to these rumours. The King shewed great regret, but more for the grief of Madame than on account of the loss itself, though he had often caressed the child, and loaded her with presents. I owe it, also, to justice, to say that M. de Marigny, the heir of all Madame de Pompadour's fortune, after the death of her daughter, evinced the sincerest and deepest regret every time she was seriously ill. She, soon after, began to lay plans for his establishment. Several young ladies of the highest birth were thought of; and, perhaps, he would have been made a Duke, but his turn of mind indisposed him for schemes either of marriage or ambition. Ten times he might have been made Prime Minister, yet he never aspired to it. "That is a man," said Quesnay to me, one day, "who is very little known; nobody talks of his talents or acquirements, nor of his zealous and efficient patronage of the arts: no man, since Colbert, has done so much in his situation: he is, moreover, an extremely honourable man, but people will not see in him anything but the brother of the favourite; and, because he is fat, he is thought dull and heavy." This was all perfectly true. M. de Marigny had travelled in Italy with very able artists, and had acquired taste, and much more information than any of his predecessors had possessed. As for the heaviness of his air, it only came upon him when he grew fat; before that, he had a delightful face. He was then as handsome as his sister. He paid court to nobody, had no vanity, and confined himself to the society of persons with whom he was at his ease. He went rather more into company at Court after the King had taken him to ride with him in his carriage, thinking it then his duty to shew himself among the courtiers.

Madame called me, one day, into her closet, where the King was walking up and down in a very serious mood. "You must," said she, "pass some days in a house in the Avenue de St. Cloud, whither I shall send you. You will there find a young lady about to lie in." The King said nothing, and I was mute from astonishment. "You will be mistress of the house, and preside, like one of the fabulous goddesses, at the accouchement. Your presence is necessary, in order that everything may pass secretly, and according to the King's wish. You will be present at the baptism, and name the father and mother." The King began to laugh, and said, "The father is a very honest man;" Madame added, "beloved by every one, and adored by those who know him." Madame then took from a little cupboard a small box, and drew from it an aigrette of diamonds, at the same time saying to the King, "I have my reasons for it not being handsomer." "It is but too much so," said the King; "how kind you are;" and he then embraced Madame, who wept with emotion, and, putting her hand upon the King's heart, said, "This is what I wish to secure." The King's eyes then filled with tears, and I also began weeping, without knowing why. Afterwards, the King said, "Guimard will call upon you every day, to assist you with his advice, and at the critical moment you will send for him. You will say that you expect the sponsors, and a moment after you will pretend to have received a letter, stating that they cannot come. You will, of course, affect to be very much embarrassed; and

Guimard will then say that there is nothing for it
but to take the first comers.  You will then appoint
as godfather and godmother some beggar, or chair-
man, and the servant girl of the house, and to whom
you will give but twelve francs, in order not to
attract attention."  "A louis," added Madame, "to
obviate anything singular, on the other hand."  "It is
you who make me economical, under certain circumstances," said the King.  "Do you remember the
driver of the *fiacre?*  I wanted to give him a louis,
and Duc d'Ayen said, 'You will be known;' so that I
gave him a crown."  He was going to tell the whole
story.  Madame made a sign to him to be silent,
which he obeyed, not without considerable reluctance.
She afterwards told me that at the time of the fêtes
given on occasion of the Dauphin's marriage, the
King came to see her at her mother's house in a
hackney-coach.  The coachman would not go on, and
the King would have given him a louis.  "The police
will hear of it, if you do," said the Duc d'Ayen, "and
its spies will make inquiries, which will, perhaps, lead
to a discovery."

"Guimard," continued the King, "will tell you the
names of the father and mother; he will be present
at the ceremony, and make the usual presents.  It is
but fair that you also should receive yours;" and, as
he said this, he gave me fifty louis, with that gracious
air that he could so well assume upon certain occasions, and which no person in the kingdom had but
himself.  I kissed his hand and wept.  "You will
take care of the *accouchée,* will you not?  She is a
good creature, who has not invented gunpowder, and
I confide her entirely to your direction; my chancellor will tell you the rest," he said, turning t
Madame, and then quitted the room.  "Well, wh
think you of the part I am playing?" ask

"It is that of a superior woman, and an excellent friend," I replied. "It is his heart I wish to secure," said she; "and all those young girls who have no education will not run away with it from me. I should not be equally confident were I to see some fine woman belonging to the Court, or the city, attempt his conquest."

I asked Madame, if the young lady knew that the King was the father of her child? "I do not think she does," replied she; "but, as he appeared fond of her, there is some reason to fear that those about her might be too ready to tell her; otherwise," said she, shrugging her shoulders, "she, and all the others, are told that he is a Polish nobleman, a relation of the Queen, who has apartments in the castle." This story was contrived on account of the *cordon bleu*, which the King has not always time to lay aside, because, to do that, he must change his coat, and in order to account for his having a lodging in the castle so near the King. There were two little rooms by the side of the chapel, whither the King retired from his apartment, without being seen by anybody but a sentinel, who had his orders, and who did not know who passed through those rooms. The King sometimes went to the Parc-aux-cerfs, or received those young ladies in the apartments I have mentioned.

I must here interrupt my narrative, to relate a singular adventure, which is only known to six or seven persons, masters or valets. At the time of the attempt to assassinate the King, a young girl, whom he had seen several times, and for whom he had manifested more tenderness than for most, was distracted at this horrible event. The Mother-Abbess of the Parc-aux-cerfs perceived her extraordinary grief, and managed so as to make her confess that she knew the Polish Count was the King of France. She confessed that she had taken from his pocket two letters, one of which was from the King of Spain, the other from the Abbé de Broglie. This was discovered afterwards, for neither she nor the Mother-Abbess knew the names of the writers. The girl was scolded, and M. Lebel, first *valet de chambre,* who had the management of all these affairs, was called; he took the letters, and carried them to the King, who was very much embarrassed in what manner to meet a person so well informed of his condition. The girl in question, having perceived that the King came secretly to see her companion, while she was neglected, watched his arrival, and, at the moment he entered with the Abbess, who was about to withdraw, she rushed distractedly into the room where her rival was. She immediately threw herself at the King's feet. " Yes," said she, " you are King of all France; but that would be nothing to me if you were not also monarch of my heart: do not forsake me, my beloved sovereign; I was nearly mad when your life was attempted!" The Mother-Abbess cried out, " You are mad now." The King embraced her, which appeared to restore her to tranquillity. They succeeded in getting her out of the room, and a few days afterwards the unhappy girl was taken to a madhouse, where she was treated as if she had been insane, for some days. But she knew well enough that she was not so, and that the King had really been her lover. This lamentable affair was related to me by the Mother-Abbess, when I had some acquaintance with her at the time of the accouchement I have spoken of, which I never had before, nor since.

To return to my history: Madame de Pompadour said to me, " Be constantly with the *accouchée,* to prevent any stranger, or even the people of the house, from speaking to her. You will always say that he

is a very rich Polish nobleman, who is obliged to
conceal himself on account of his relationship to the
Queen, who is very devout.    You will find a wet-
nurse in the house, to whom you will deliver the
child. Guimard will manage all the rest. You
will go to church as a witness; everything must be
conducted as if for a substantial citizen.  The young
lady expects to lie in in five or six days; you will
dine with her, and will not leave her till she is in a
state of health to return to the Parc-aux-cerfs, which
she may do in a fortnight, as I imagine, without
running any risk." I went, that same evening, to
the Avenue de Saint Cloud, where I found the
Abbess and Guimard, an attendant belonging to the
castle, but without his blue coat. There were,
besides, a nurse, a wet-nurse, two old men-servants,
and a girl, who was something between a servant
and a waiting-woman. The young lady was extremely pretty, and dressed very elegantly, though
not too remarkably. I supped with her and the
Mother-Abbess, who was called Madame Bertrand.
I had presented the aigrette Madame de Pompadour
gave me before supper, which had greatly delighted
the young lady, and she was in high spirits.
Madame Bertrand had been housekeeper to M. Lebel,
first *valet de chambre* to the King.   He called her
Dominique, and she was entirely in his confidence.
The young lady chatted with us after supper; she
appeared to be very *naïve*. The next day, I talked
to her in private. She said to me, " How is the
Count? " (It was the King whom she called by this
title.) " He will be very sorry not to be with me
now; but he was obliged to set off on a long
journey." I assented to what she said. " He is very
handsome," said she, " and loves me with all his
heart. He promised me an allowance; but I love

him disinterestedly; and, if he would let me, I would
follow him to Poland."   She afterwards talked to
me about her parents, and about M. Lebel, whom she
knew by the name of Durand.   " My mother," said
she, " kept a large grocer's shop, and my father was
a man of some consequence; he belonged to the Six
Corps, and that, as everybody knows, is an excellent
thing.   He was twice very near being head-bailiff."
Her mother had become bankrupt at her father's
death, but *the Count* had come to her assistance, and
settled upon her fifteen hundred francs a year,
besides giving her six thousand francs down.   On
the sixth day, she was brought to bed, and, according
to my instructions, she was told the child was a girl,
though it reality it was a boy; she was soon to be
told that it was dead, in order that no trace of its
existence might remain for a certain time.   It was
eventually to be restored to its mother.   The King
gave each of his children about ten thousand francs
a year.   They inherited after each other as they
died off, and seven or eight were already dead.   I
returned to Madame de Pompadour, to whom I had
written every day by Guimard.   The next day, the
King sent for me into the room; he did not say
a word as to the business I had been employed upon;
but he gave me a large gold snuff-box, containing
two rouleaux of twenty-five louis each.   I curtsied to
him, and retired.   Madame asked me a great many
questions of the young lady, and laughed heartily at
her simplicity, and at all she had said about the
Polish   nobleman.   " He   is   disgusted   with   the
Princess, and, I think, will return to Poland for ever,
in two months."   "And the young lady?" said I.
" She will be married in the country," said she, " with
a portion of forty thousand crowns at the most and a
few diamonds."   This little adventure, which initiated

me into the King's secrets, far from procuring for me increased marks of kindness from him, seemed to produce a coldness towards me; probably because he was ashamed of my knowing his obscure amours. He was also embarrassed by the services Madame de Pompadour had rendered him on this occasion.

Besides the little mistresses of the Parc-aux-cerfs, the King had sometimes intrigues with ladies of the Court, or from Paris, who wrote to him. There was a Madame de L——, who, though married to a young and amiable man, with two hundred thousand francs a year, wished absolutely to become his mistress. She contrived to have a meeting with him: and the King, who knew who she was, was persuaded that she was really madly in love with him. There is no knowing what might have happened, had she not died. Madame was very much alarmed, and was only relieved by her death from inquietude. A circumstance took place at this time which doubled Madame's friendship for me. A rich man, who had a situation in the Revenue Department, called on me one day very secretly, and told me that he had something of importance to communicate to Madame la Marquise, but that he should find himself very much embarrassed in communicating it to her personally, and that he should prefer acquainting me with it. He then told me, what I already knew, that he had a very beautiful wife, of whom he was passionately fond; that having on one occasion perceived her kissing a little *porte-feuille,* he endeavoured to get possession of it, supposing there was some mystery attached to it. One day that she suddenly left the room to go upstairs to see her sister, who had been brought to bed, he took the opportunity of opening the *porte-feuille,* and was very much surprised to find in it a portrait of the King, and a very tender letter written by His Majesty. Of the latter he took a copy, as also of an unfinished letter of his wife, in which she vehemently entreated the King to allow her to have the pleasure of an interview—the means she pointed out. She was to go masked to the public ball at Versailles, where His Majesty could meet her under favour of a mask. I assured M. de ———— that I should acquaint Madame with the affair, who would, no doubt, feel very grateful for the communication. He then added, "Tell Madame la Marquise that my wife is very clever and very intriguing. I adore her, and should run distracted were she to be taken from me." I lost not a moment in acquainting Madame with the affair and gave her the letter. She became serious and pensive, and I since learned that she consulted M. Berrier, Lieutenant of Police, who, by a very simple but ingeniously conceived plan, put an end to the designs of this lady. He demanded an audience of the King, and told him that there was a lady in Paris who was making free with His Majesty's name; that he had been given the copy of a letter, supposed to have been written by His Majesty to the lady in question. The copy he put into the King's hands, who read it in great confusion, and then tore it furiously to pieces. M. Berrier added, that it was rumoured that this lady was to meet His Majesty at the public ball, and, at this very moment, it so happened that a letter was put into the King's hand, which proved to be from the lady, appointing the meeting; at least, M. Berrier judged so, as the King appeared very much surprised on reading it, and said, "It must be allowed, M. le Lieutenant of Police, that you are well informed." M. Berrier added, "I think it my duty to tell Your Majesty that this lady passes for a very intriguing person." "I believe," replied the King, "that it is not without deserving it that she has got that character."

Madame de Pompadour had many vexations in the midst of all her grandeur. She often received anonymous letters, threatening her with poison or assassination: her greatest fear, however, was that of being supplanted by a rival. I never saw her in a greater agitation than, one evening, on her return from the drawing-room at Marly. She threw down her cloak and muff, the instant she came in, with an air of ill-humour, and undressed herself in a hurried manner. Having dismissed her other women, she said to me, " I think I never saw anybody so insolent as Madame de Coaslin. I was seated at the same table with her this evening, at a game of *brelan*, and you cannot imagine what I suffered. The men and women seemed to come in relays to watch us. Madame de Coaslin said two or three times, looking at me, *Va tout*, in the most insulting manner. I thought I should have fainted, when she said, in a triumphant tone, I have the *brelan* of kings. I wish you had seen her courtesy to me on parting." "Did the King," said I, "show her particular attention?" "You don't know him," said she; "if he were going to lodge her this very night in my apartment, he would behave coldly to her before people, and would treat me with the utmost kindness. This is the effect of his education, for he is, by nature, kind-hearted and frank." Madame de Pompadour's alarms lasted for some months, when she, one day, said to me, "That haughty Marquise has missed her aim; she frightened the King by her grand airs, and was incessantly teasing him for money. Now you, perhaps, may not know that the King would sign an order for forty thousand louis without a thought, and would give a hundred out of his little private treasury with the greatest reluctance. Lebel, who likes me better than he would a new mistress in my place, either by chance or design had brought a charming little sultana to the Parc-aux-cerfs, who has cooled the King a little towards the haughty Vashti, by giving him occupation, —— has received a hundred thousand francs, some jewels, and an estate. Jannette has rendered me great service, by showing the King extracts from the letters broken open at the post-office, concerning the report that Madame de Coaslin was coming into favour. The King was much impressed by a letter from an old counsellor of the Parliament, who wrote to one of his friends as follows: " It is quite as reasonable that the King should have a female friend and confidante—as that we, in our several degrees, should so indulge ourselves; but it is desirable that he should keep the one he has; she is gentle, injures nobody, and her fortune is made. The one who is now talked of will be as haughty as high birth can make her. She must have an allowance of a million francs a year, since she is said to be excessively extravagant; her relations must be made Dukes, Governors of provinces, and Marshals, and, in the end, will surround the King, and overawe the Ministers."

Madame de Pompadour had this passage, which had been sent to her by M. Jannette, the Intendant of the Police, who enjoyed the King's entire confidence. He had carefully watched the King's look, while he read the letter, and he saw that the arguments of this counsellor, who was not a disaffected person, made a great impression upon him. Some time afterwards, Madame de Pompadour said to me, " The haughty Marquise behaved like Mademoiselle Deschamps, and she is *turned off*." This was not Madame's only subject of alarm. A relation of

Madame d'Estrades, wife to the Marquis de C——,
had made the most pointed advances to the King,
much more than were necessary for a man who
justly thought himself the handsomest man in
France, and who was, moreover, a King.   He was
perfectly persuaded that every woman would yield to
the slightest desire he might deign to manifest.  He,
therefore, thought it a mere matter of course that
women fell in love with him.   M. de Stainville had
a hand in marring the success of that intrigue; and,
soon afterwards, the Marquise de C——, who was
confined to her apartments at Marly, by her relations, escaped through a closet to a rendezvous, and
was caught with a young man in a corridor.   The
Spanish Ambassador, coming out of his apartments
with flambeaux, was the person who witnessed this
scene.   Madame d'Estrades affected to know nothing
of her cousin's intrigues, and kept up an appearance
of the tenderest attachment to Madame de Pompadour, whom she was habitually betraying.   She
acted as spy for M. d'Argenson, in the cabinets, and
in Madame de Pompadour's apartments; and, when
she could discover nothing, she had recourse to her
invention, in order that she might not lose her
importance with her lover.   This Madame d'Estrades
owed her whole existence to the bounties of Madame,
and yet, ugly as she was, she had tried to get the
King away from her.   One day, when he had got
rather drunk at Choisy (I think, the only time that
ever happened to him), he went on board a beautiful
barge, whither Madame, being ill of an indigestion,
could not accompany him.   Madame d'Estrades
seized this opportunity.   She got into the barge, and,
on their return, as it was dark, she followed the
King into a private closet, where he was believed to
be sleeping on a couch, and there went somewhat

beyond any ordinary advances to him. Her account of the matter to Madame was, that she had gone into the closet upon her own affairs, and that the King had followed her, and had tried to ravish her. She was at full liberty to make what story she pleased, for the King knew neither what he had said, nor what he had done. I shall finish this subject by a short history concerning a young lady. I had been, one day, to the theatre at Compiègne. When I returned, Madame asked me several questions about the play; whether there was much company, and whether I did not see a very beautiful girl. I replied, " That there was, indeed, a girl in a box near mine, who was surrounded by all the young men about the Court." She smiled, and said, " That is Mademoiselle Dorothée; she went, this evening, to see the King sup in public, and to-morrow she is to be taken to the hunt. You are surprised to find me so well informed, but I know a great deal more about her. She was brought here by a Gascon, named Dubarré or Dubarri, who is the greatest scoundrel in France. He founds all his hopes of advancement on Mademoiselle Dorothée's charms, which he thinks the King cannot resist. She is, really, very beautiful. She was pointed out to me in my little garden, whither she was taken to walk on purpose. She is the daughter of a water-carrier, at Strasbourg, and her charming lover demands to be sent Minister to Cologne, as a beginning." " Is it possible, Madame, that you can have been rendered uneasy by such a creature as that?" " Nothing is impossible," replied she; " though I think the King would scarcely dare to give such a scandal. Besides, happily, Lebel, to quiet his conscience, told the King that the beautiful Dorothée's lover is infected with a horrid disease;" and, added he, " Your Majesty would not get rid of

that as you have done of the scrofula." This
was quite enough to keep the young lady at a distance.

"I pity you sincerely, Madame," said I, "while
everybody else envies you." "Ah!" replied she,
"my life is that of the Christian, a perpetual war-
fare. This was not the case with the woman who
enjoyed the favour of Louis XIV. Madame de La
Vallière suffered herself to be deceived by Madame
de Montespan, but it was her own fault, or, rather,
the effect of her extreme good nature. She was
entirely devoid of suspicion at first, because she
could not believe her friend perfidious. Madame
de Montespan's empire was shaken by Madame de
Fontanges, and overthrown by Madame de Maintenon; but her haughtiness, her caprices, had already
alienated the King. He had not, however, such
rivals as mine; it is true, their baseness is my
security. I have, in general, little to fear but casual
infidelities, and the chance that they may not all be
sufficiently transitory for my safety. The King likes
variety, but he is also bound by habit; he fears
éclats, and detests manœuvring women. The little
Maréchale (de Mirepoix) one day said to me, 'It is
your staircase that the King loves; he is accustomed
to go up and down it. But, if he found another
woman to whom he could talk of hunting and business as he does to you, it would be just the same to
him in three days.'"

I write without plan, order, or date, just as things
come into my mind; and I shall now go to the Abbé
de Bernis, whom I liked very much, because he was
good-natured, and treated me kindly. One day, just
as Madame de Pompadour had finished dressing, M.
de Noailles asked to speak to her in private. I, accordingly, retired. The Count looked full of im-

portant business.  I heard their conversation, as there
was only the door between us.

"A circumstance has taken place," said he, "which
I think it my duty to communicate to the King; but
I would not do so without first informing you of it,
since it concerns one of your friends for whom I have
the utmost regard and respect.  The Abbé de Bernis
had a mind to shoot, this morning, and went, with
two or three of his people, armed with guns, into the
little park, where the Dauphin would not venture to
shoot without asking the King's permission.  The
guards, surprised at hearing the report of guns, ran
to the spot, and were greatly astonished at the sight
of M. de Bernis.  They very respectfully asked to see
his permission, when they found, to their astonishment, that he had none.  They begged of him to
desist, telling him that, if they did their duty, they
should arrest him; but they must, at all events, instantly acquaint me with the circumstance, as Ranger
of the Park of Versailles.  They added, that the
King must have heard the firing, and that they begged
of him to retire.  The Abbé apologized, on the score
of ignorance, and assured them that he had my permission.  'The Comte de Noailles,' said they, 'could
only grant permission to shoot in the more remote
parts, and in the great park.'"  The Count made
a great merit of his eagerness to give the earliest
information to Madame.  She told him to leave the
task of communicating it to the King to her, and
begged of him to say nothing about the matter.  M.
de Marigny, who did not like the Abbé, came to see me
in the evening; and I affected to know nothing of
the story, and to hear it for the first time from him.
"He must have been out of his senses," said he, "to
shoot under the King's windows,"—and enlarged
much on the airs he gave himself.  Madame de Pom-

padour gave this affair the best colouring she could:
the King was, nevertheless, greatly disgusted at it,
and twenty times, since the Abbé's disgrace, when he
passed over that part of the park, he said, "This is
where the Abbé took his pleasure." The King never
liked him; and Madame de Pompadour told me one
night, after his disgrace, when I was sitting up with
her in her illness, that she saw, before he had been
Minister a week, that he was not fit for his office.
"If that hypocritical Bishop," said she, speaking of
the Bishop of Mirepoix, "had not prevented the King
from granting him a pension of four hundred louis a
year, which he had promised me, he would never
have been appointed Ambassador. I should, afterwards, have been able to give him an income of eight
hundred louis a year, perhaps the place of master of
the chapel. Thus he would have been happier, and I
should have had nothing to regret." I took the liberty of saying that I did not agree with her. That
he had yet remaining advantages, of which he could
not be deprived; that his exile would terminate; and
that he would then be a Cardinal, with an income of
eight thousand louis a year. "That is true," she
replied; "but I think of the mortifications he has
undergone, and of the ambition which devours him;
and, lastly, I think of myself. I should have still
enjoyed his society, and should have had, in my de-
clining years, an old and amiable friend, if he had
not been Minister." The King sent him away in
anger, and was strongly inclined to refuse him the
hat. M. Quesnay told me, some months afterwards,
that the Abbé wanted to be Prime Minister; that he
had drawn up a memorial, setting forth that in difficult crises the public good required that there should
be a *central point* (that was his expression), towards
which everything should be directed. Madame de

Pompadour would not present the memorial; he insisted, though she said to him, " *You will ruin yourself.*" The King cast his eyes over it, and said "' *central point,*'—that is to say himself, he wants to be Prime Minister." Madame tried to apologize for him, and said, "That expression might refer to the Maréchal de Belle-Isle." " Is he not just about to be made Cardinal?" said the King. "This is a fine manœuvre; he knows well enough that, by means of that dignity, he would compel the Ministers to assemble at his house, and then M. l'Abbé would be the *central point.* Wherever there is a Cardinal in the council, he is sure, in the end, to take the lead. Louis XIV., for this reason, did not choose to admit the Cardinal de Janson into the council, in spite of his great esteem for him. The Cardinal de Fleury told me the same thing. He had some desire that the Cardinal de Tencin should succeed him; but his sister was such an intrigante that Cardinal de Fleury advised me to have nothing to do with the matter, and I behaved so as to destroy all his hopes, and to undeceive others. M. d'Argenson has strongly impressed me with the same opinion, and has succeeded in destroying all my respect for him." This is what the King said, according to my friend Quesnay, who, by the bye, was a great genius, as everybody said, and a very lively, agreeable man. He liked to chat with me about the country. I had been bred up there, and he used to set me a talking about the meadows of Normandy and Poitou, the wealth of the farmers, and the modes of culture. He was the best-natured man in the world, and the farthest removed from petty intrigue. While he lived at Court, he was much more occupied with the best manner of cultivating land than with anything that passed around him. The man whom he esteemed the most was M. de la

Rivière, a Counsellor of Parliament, who was also Intendant of Martinique; he looked upon him as a man of the greatest genius, and thought him the only person fit for the financial department of administration.

The Comtesse d'Estrades, who owed everything to Madame de Pompadour, was incessantly intriguing against her. She was clever enough to destroy all proofs of her manœuvres, but she could not so easily prevent suspicion. Her intimate connection with M. d'Argenson gave offence to Madame, and, for some time, she was more reserved with her. She, afterwards, did a thing which justly irritated the King and Madame. The King, who wrote a great deal, had written to Madame de Pompadour a long letter concerning an assembly of the Chambers of Parliament, and had enclosed a letter of M. Berrier. Madame was ill, and laid those letters on a little table by her bedside. M. de Gontaut came in, and gossipped about trifles, as usual. Madame d'Amblimont also came, and stayed but very little time. Just as I was going to resume a book which I had been reading to Madame, the Comtesse d'Estrades entered, placed herself near Madame's bed, and talked to her for some time. As soon as she was gone, Madame called me, asked what was o'clock, and said, " Order my door to be shut, the King will soon be here." I gave the order, and returned; and Madame told me to give her the King's letter, which was on the table with some other papers. I gave her the papers, and told her there was nothing else. She was very uneasy at not finding the letter, and, after enumerating the persons who had been in the room, she said, " It cannot be the little Countess, nor Gontaut, who has taken this letter. It can only be the Comtesse d'Estrades; —and that is too bad." The King came, and was extremely angry, as Madame told me. Two days afterwards, he sent Madame d'Estrades into exile. There was no doubt that she took the letter; the King's handwriting had probably awakened her curiosity. This occurrence gave great pain to M. d'Argenson, who was bound to her, as Madame de Pompadour said, by his love of intrigue. This redoubled his hatred of Madame, and she accused him of favouring the publication of a libel, in which she was represented as a worn-out mistress, reduced to the vile occupation of providing new objects to please her lover's appetite. She was characterised as superintendent of the Parc-aux-cerfs, which was said to cost hundreds of thousands of louis a year. Madame de Pompadour did, indeed, try to conceal some of the King's weaknesses, but she never knew one of the sultanas of that seraglio. There were, however, scarcely ever more than two at once, and often only one. When they married, they received some jewels, and four thousand louis. The Parc-aux-cerfs was sometimes vacant for five or six months. I was surprised, some time after, at seeing the Duchesse de Luynes, Lady of Honour to the Queen, come privately to see Madame de Pompadour. She afterwards came openly. One evening, after Madame was in bed, she called me, and said, " My dear, you will be delighted; the Queen has given me the place of Lady of the Palace; to-morrow I am to be presented to her: you must make me look well." I knew that the King was not so well pleased at this as she was; he was afraid that it would give rise to scandal, and that it might be thought he had forced this nomination upon the Queen. He had, however, done no such thing. It had been represented to the Queen that it was an act of heroism on her part to forget the past; that all scandal would be obliterated when Madame de Pom-

padour was seen to belong to the Court in an honourable manner; and that it would be the best proof that
nothing more than friendship now subsisted between
the King and the favourite.  The Queen received her
very graciously.    The devotees flattered themselves
they should be protected by Madame, and, for some
time, were full of her praises.  Several of the Dauphin's friends came in private to see her, and some
obtained promotion.  The Chevalier du Muy, however, refused to come.  The King had the greatest
possible contempt for them, and granted them nothing with a good grace.  He, one day, said of a man
of great family, who wished to be made Captain of the
Guards, " He is a double spy, who wants to be paid on
both sides."  This was the moment at which Madame
de Pompadour seemed to me to enjoy the most complete satisfaction.  The devotees came to visit her
without scruple, and did not forget to make use of
every opportunity of serving themselves.  Madame
de Lu—— had set them the example.  The Doctor
laughed at this change in affairs, and was very merry
at the expense of the saints.   " You must allow, however, that they are consistent," said I, " and may be
sincere."  " Yes," said he; " but then they should
not ask for anything."

One day, I was at Doctor Quesnay's, whilst
Madame de Pompadour was at the theatre.   The
Marquis de Mirabeau came in, and the conversation
was, for some time, extremely tedious to me, running entirely on *net produce;* at length, they talked of
other things.

Mirabeau said, " I think the King looks ill, he
grows old."  " So much the worse, a thousand times
so much the worse," said Quesnay; " it would be the
greatest possible loss to France if he died;" and
he raised his hands, and sighed deeply.  " I do not

doubt that you are attached to the King, and with reason," said Mirabeau; "I am attached to him too; but I never saw you so much moved." "Ah!" said Quesnay, "I think of what would follow." "Well, the Dauphin is virtuous." "Yes; and full of good intentions; nor is he deficient in understanding; but canting hypocrites would possess an absolute empire over a Prince who regards them as oracles. The Jesuits would govern the kingdom, as they did at the end of Louis XIV.'s reign: and you would see the fanatical Bishop of Verdun Prime Minister, and La Vauguyon all-powerful under some other title. The Parliaments must then mind how they behave; they will not be better treated than my friends the philosophers." "But they go too far," said Mirabeau; "why openly attack religion?" "I allow that," replied the Doctor; "but how is it possible not to be rendered indignant by the fanaticism of others, and by recollecting all the blood that has flowed during the last two hundred years? You must not then again irritate them, and revive in France the time of Mary in England. But what is done is done, and I often exhort them to be moderate; I wish they would follow the example of our friend Duclos." "You are right," replied Mirabeau; "he said to me a few days ago, 'These philosophers are going on at such a rate that they will force me to go to vespers and high mass;' but, in fine, the Dauphin is virtuous, well-informed, and intellectual." "It is the commencement of his reign, I fear," said Quesnay, "when the imprudent proceedings of our friends will be represented to him in the most unfavourable point of view; when the Jansenists and Molinists will make common cause, and be strongly supported by the Dauphine. I thought that M. de Muy was moderate, and that he would temper the headlong fury of the others; but I heard him say that Voltaire merited condign punishment.  Be assured, sir, that the times of John Huss and Jerome of Prague will return; but I hope not to live to see it.  I approve of Voltaire having hunted down the Pompignans: were it not for the ridicule with which he covered them, that *bourgeois* Marquis would have been preceptor to the young Princes, and, aided by his brother, would have succeeded in again lighting the faggots of persecution." "What ought to give you confidence in the Dauphin," said Mirabeau, "is, that, notwithstanding the devotion of Pompignan, he turns him into ridicule.   A short time back, seeing him strutting about with an air of inflated pride, he said to a person, who told it to me, 'Our friend Pompignan thinks that he is something.'"  On returning home, I wrote down this conversation.

I, one day, found Quesnay in great distress.  "Mirabeau," said he, "is sent to Vincennes, for his work on taxation.  The Farmers General have denounced him, and procured his arrest; his wife is going to throw herself at the feet of Madame de Pompadour to-day."  A few minutes afterwards, I went into Madame's apartment, to assist at her toilet, and the Doctor came in.  Madame said to him, "You must be much concerned at the disgrace of your friend Mirabeau.   I am sorry for it too, for I like his brother."  Quesnay replied, "I am very far from believing him to be actuated by bad intentions, Madame; he loves the King and the people."   "Yes," said she; "his *Ami des Hommes* did him great honour." At this moment the Lieutenant of Police entered, and Madame said to him, "Have you seen M. de Mirabeau's book?"  "Yes, Madame; but it was not I who denounced it?"   "What do you think of it?" "I think he might have said almost all it contains with impunity, if he had been more circumspect as to the manner; there is, among other objectionable passages, this, which occurs at the beginning: *Your Majesty has about twenty millions of subjects; it is only by means of money that you can obtain their services, and there is no money."* " What, is there really that, Doctor?" said Madame. " It is true, they are the first lines in the book, and I confess that they are imprudent; but, in reading the work, it is clear that he laments that patriotism is extinct in the hearts of his fellow-citizens, and that he desires to rekindle it." The King entered: we went out, and I wrote down on Quesnay's table what I had just heard. I then returned to finish dressing Madame de Pompadour: she said to me, " The King is extremely angry with Mirabeau; but I tried to soften him, and so did the Lieutenant of Police. This will increase Quesnay's fears. Do you know what he said to me to-day? The King had been talking to him in my room, and the Doctor appeared timid and agitated. After the King was gone, I said to him, ' You always seem so embarrassed in the King's presence, and yet he is so good-natured.' ' Madame,' said he, ' I left my native village at the age of forty, and I have very little experience of the world, nor can I accustom myself to its usages without great difficulty. When I am in a room with the King, I say to myself, ' This is a man who can order my head to be cut off; and that idea embarrasses me.' ' But do not the King's justice and kindness set you at ease?' ' That is very true in reasoning,' said he; ' but the sentiment is more prompt, and inspires me with fear before I have time to say to myself all that is calculated to allay it.' "

I got her to repeat this conversation, and wrote it down immediately, that I might not forget it.

An anonymous letter was addressed to the King and Madame de Pompadour; and, as the author was very anxious that it should not miscarry, he sent copies to the Lieutenant of Police, sealed and directed *to the King, to Madame de Pompadour, and to M. de Marigny.* This letter produced a strong impression on Madame, and on the King, and still more, I believe, on the Duc de Choiseul, who had received a similar one. I went on my knees to M. de Marigny, to prevail on him to allow me to copy it, that I might show it to the Doctor. It is as follows:

" Sire—It is a zealous servant who writes to Your Majesty. Truth is always better, particularly to Kings; habituated to flattery, they see objects only under those colours most likely to please them. I have reflected, and read much; and here is what my meditations have suggested to me to lay before Your Majesty. They have accustomed you to be invisible, and inspired you with a timidity which prevents you from speaking; thus all direct communication is cut off between the master and his subjects. Shut up in the interior of your palace, you are becoming every day like the Emperors of the East; but see, Sire, their fate! 'I have troops,' Your Majesty will say; such, also, is their support: but, when the only security of a King rests upon his troops; when he is only, as one may say, a King of the soldiers, these latter feel their own strength, and abuse it. Your finances are in the greatest disorder, and the great majority of states have perished through this cause. A patriotic spirit sustained the ancient states, and united all classes for the safety of their country. In the present times, money has taken the place of this spirit; it has become the universal lever, and you are in want of it. A spirit of finance affects every department of the state; it reigns triumphant at Court; all have become

venal; and all distinction of rank is broken up.  Your
Ministers are without genius and capacity since the
dismissal of MM. d'Argenson and de Machault. You
alone cannot judge of their incapacity, because they
lay before you what has been prepared by skilful
clerks, but which they pass as their own.  They provide only for the necessity of the day, but there is no
spirit of government in their acts.   The military
changes that have taken place disgust the troops, and
cause the most deserving officers to resign; a sedi-
tious flame has sprung up in the very bosom of the
Parliaments; you seek to corrupt them, and the remedy is worse than the disease.  It is introducing vice
into the sanctuary of justice, and gangrene into the
vital parts of the commonwealth.  Would a corrupted
Parliament have braved the fury of the League, in
order to preserve the crown for the legitimate sovereign?  Forgetting the maxims of Louis XIV., who
well understood the danger of confiding the administration to noblemen, you have chosen M. de Choiseul,
and even given him three departments; which is a
much heavier burden than that which he would have
to support as Prime Minister, because the latter has
only to oversee the details executed by the Secretaries
of State.  The public fully appreciate this dazzling
Minister.  He is nothing more than a *petit-maître*,
without talents or information, who has a little phos-
phorus in his mind.  There is a thing well worthy of
remark, Sire; that is, the open war carried on against
religion.  Henceforward there can spring up no new
sects, because the general belief has been shaken, that
no one feels inclined to occupy himself with difference
of sentiment upon some of the articles.  The Encyclo-
pedists, under pretence of enlightening mankind, are
sapping the foundations of religion.  All the different
kinds of liberty are connected; the Philosophers and

the Protestants tend towards republicanism, as well
as the Jansenists. The Philosophers strike at the
root, the others lop the branches; and their efforts,
without being concerted, will one day lay the tree
low.     Add to these the Economists, whose object is
political liberty, as that of the others is liberty of
worship, and the Government may find itself, in
twenty or thirty years, undermined in every direction,
and will then fall with a crash.   If Your Majesty,
struck by this picture, but too true, should ask me for
a remedy, I should say, that it is necessary to bring
back the Government to its principles, and, above
all, to lose no time in restoring order to the state of
the finances, because the embarrassments incident to
a country in a state of debt necessitate fresh taxes,
which, after grinding the people, induce them towards
revolt.   It is my opinion that Your Majesty would
do well to appear more among your people; to shew
your approbation of useful services, and your displeasure of errors and prevarications, and neglect of
duty: in a word, to let it be seen that rewards and
punishments, appointments and dismissals, proceed
from yourself.    You will then inspire gratitude by
your favours, and fear by your reproaches; you will
then be the object of immediate and personal attachment, instead of which, everything is now referred
to your Ministers.  The confidence in the King, which
is habitual to your people, is shewn by the exclamation, so common among them, ' Ah! if the King
knew it.'    They love to believe that the King would
remedy all their evils, if he knew of them.   But, on
the other hand, what sort of ideas must they form of
Kings, whose duty it is to be informed of everything,
and to superintend everything, that concerns the public, but who are, nevertheless, ignorant of everything
which the discharge of their functions requires them

to know?  *Rex, roi, regere, régir, conduire*—to rule,
to conduct—these words sufficiently denote their duties.  What would be said of a father who got rid
of the charge of his children as of a burthen?

"A time will come, Sire, when the people shall be
enlightened—and that time is probably approaching.
Resume the reins of government, hold them with a
firm hand, and act, so that it cannot be said of you,
*Fœminas et scorta volvit animo et hæc principatûs
præmia putat:*—Sire, if I see that my sincere advice
should have produced any change, I shall continue
it, and enter into more details; if not, I shall remain
silent."

Now that I am upon the subject of anonymous
letters to the King, I must just mention that it is
impossible to conceive how frequent they were.  People were extremely assiduous in telling either un-
pleasant truths, or alarming lies, with a view to injure others.  As an instance, I shall transcribe one
concerning Voltaire, who paid great court to Madame
de Pompadour when he was in France.  This letter
was written long after the former.

"Madame—M. de Voltaire has just dedicated his
tragedy of *Tancred* to you; this ought to be an offering of respect and gratitude; but it is, in fact, an
insult, and you will form the same opinion of it as the
public has done if you read it with attention.  You
will see that this distinguished writer appears to betray a consciousness that the subject of his encomiums
is not worthy of them, and to endeavour to excuse
himself for them to the public.  These are his words:
'I have seen your graces and talents unfold themselves from your infancy.  At all periods of your
life I have received proofs of your uniform and un-
changing kindness.  If any critic be found to censure
the homage I pay you, he must have a heart formed

for ingratitude. I am under great obligations to you,
Madame, and these obligations it is my duty to pro-
claim.'

"What do these words really signify, unless that
Voltaire feels it may be thought extraordinary that
he should dedicate his work to a woman who possesses
but a small share of the public esteem, and that the
sentiment of gratitude must plead his excuse? Why
should he suppose that the homage he pays you will
be censured, whilst we daily see dedications addressed
to silly gossips who have neither rank nor celebrity,
or to women of exceptional conduct, without any censure being attracted by it?"

M. de Marigny, and Colin, Madame de Pompadour's
steward, were of the same opinion as Quesnay, that
the author of this letter was extremely malicious;
that he insulted Madame, and tried to injure Voltaire; but that he was, in fact, right. Voltaire, from
that moment, was entirely out of favour with Madame,
and with the King, and he certainly never discovered
the cause.

The King, who admired everything of the age of
Louis XIV., and recollected that the Boileaus and
Racines had been protected by that monarch, who
was indebted to them, in part, for the lustre of his
reign, was flattered at having such a man as Voltaire
among his subjects. But still he feared him, and
had but little esteem for him. He could not help
saying, "Moreover, I have treated him as well as
Louis XIV. treated Racine and Boileau. I have
given him, as Louis XIV. gave to Racine, some pensions, and a place of gentleman in ordinary. It is
not my fault if he has committed absurdities, and
has had the pretension to become a chamberlain, to
wear an order, and sup with a King. It is not the
fashion in France; and, as there are here a few more

men of wit and noblemen than in Prussia, it would require that I should have a very large table to assemble them all at it." And then he reckoned upon his fingers, Maupertuis, Fontenelle, La Mothe, Voltaire, Piron, Destouches, Montesquieu, the Cardinal Polignac. "Your Majesty forgets," said some one, "D'Alembert and Clairaut." "And Crébillon," said he. "And la Chaussée, and the younger Crébillon," said some one. "He ought to be more agreeable than his father." "And there are also the Abbés Prévôt and d'Olivet." "Pretty well," said the King; "and for the last twenty years *all that* (*tout cela*) would have dined and supped at my table."

Madame de Pompadour repeated to me this conversation, which I wrote down the same evening. M. de Marigny, also, talked to me about it. "Voltaire," said he, "has always had a fancy for being Ambassador, and he did all he could to make the people believe that he was charged with some political mission, the first time he visited Prussia."

The people heard of the attempt on the King's life with transports of fury, and with the greatest distress. Their cries were heard under the windows of Madame de Pompadour's apartment. Mobs were collected, and Madame feared the fate of Madame de Châteauroux. Her friends came in, every minute, to give her intelligence. Her room was, at all times, like a church; everybody seemed to claim a right to go in and out when he chose. Some came, under pretence of sympathising, to observe her countenance and manner. She did nothing but weep and faint away. Doctor Quesnay never left her, nor did I. M. de St. Florentin came to see her several times, so did the Comptroller-General, and M. Rouillé; but M. de Machault did not come. The Duchesse de Brancas came very frequently. The Abbé de Bernis never

left us, except to go to enquire for the King. The
tears came in his eyes whenever he looked at Madame.
Doctor Quesnay saw the King five or six times a
day. "There is nothing to fear," said he to Madame.
"If it were anybody else, he might go to a ball,"
My son went the next day, as he had done the day
the event occurred, to see what was going on at the
Castle. He told us, on his return, that the Keeper
of the Seals was with the King. I sent him back,
to see what course he took on leaving the King. He
came running back in half an hour, to tell me that
the Keeper of the Seals had gone to his own house,
followed by a crowd of people. When I told this to
Madame, she burst into tears, and said, "*Is that a
friend?*" The Abbé de Bernis said, "You must not
judge him hastily, in such a moment as this." I returned into the drawing-room about an hour after,
when the Keeper of the Seals entered. He passed
me, with his usual cold and severe look. "How is
Madame de Pompadour?" said he. "Alas!" replied I, "as you may imagine!" He passed on to
her closet. Everybody retired, and he remained for
half an hour. The Abbé returned and Madame rang.
I went into her room, the Abbé following me. She
was in tears. "I must go, my dear Abbé," said she.
I made her take some orange-flower water, in a silver goblet, for her teeth chattered. She then told
me to call her equerry. He came in, and she calmly
gave him her orders, to have everything prepared at
her hotel, in Paris; to tell all her people to get
ready to go; and to desire her coachman not to be
out of the way. She then shut herself up, to confer
with the Abbé de Bernis, who left her, to go to the
Council. Her door was then shut, except to the
ladies with whom she was particularly intimate, M.
de Soubise, M. de Gontaut, the Ministers, and some

others. Several ladies, in the greatest distress, came
to talk to me in my room: they compared the conduct of M. de Machault with that of M. de Richelieu,
at Metz. Madame had related to them the circumstances extremely to the honour of the Duke, and, by
contrast, the severest satire on the Keeper of the
Seals. "He thinks, or pretends to think," said she,
"that the priests will be clamorous for my dismissal;
but Quesnay and all the physicians declare that there
is not the slightest danger." Madame having sent for
me, I saw the Maréchale de Mirepoix coming in.
While she was at the door, she cried out, "What are
all those trunks, Madame? Your people tell me you
are going." "Alas! my dear friend, such is our
Master's desire, as M. de Machault tells me." "And
what does he advise?" said the Maréchale. "That
I should go without delay." During this conversation, I was undressing Madame, who wished to be at
her ease on her chaise-longue. "Your Keeper of
the Seals wants to get the power into his own hands,
and betrays you; he who quits the field loses it." I
went out. M. de Soubise entered, then the Abbé
and M. de Marigny. The latter, who was very kind
to me, came into my room an hour afterwards. I
was alone. "She will remain," said he; "but, hush!
—she will make an appearance of going, in order not
to set her enemies at work. It is the little Maréchale
who prevailed upon her to stay: her keeper (so she
called M. de Machault) will pay for it." Quesnay
came in, and, having heard what was said, with his
monkey airs, began to relate a fable of a fox, who,
being at dinner with other beasts, persuaded one of
them that his enemies were seeking him, in order that
he might get possession of his share in his absence.
I did not see Madame again till very late, at her going to bed. She was more calm. Things improved,

from day to day, and de Machault, the faithless friend, was dismissed. The King returned to Madame de Pompadour, as usual. I learnt, by M. de Marigny, that the Abbé had been, one day, with M. d'Argenson, to endeavour to persuade him to live on friendly terms with Madame, and that he had been very coldly received. "He is the more arrogant," said he, "on account of Machault's dismissal, which leaves the field clear for him, who has more experience, and more talent; and I fear that he will, therefore, be disposed to declare *war till death*." The next day, Madame having ordered her chaise, I was curious to know where she was going, for she went out but little, except to church, and to the houses of the Ministers. I was told that she was gone to visit M. d'Argenson. She returned in an hour, at farthest, and seemed very much out of spirits. She leaned on the chimney-piece, with her eyes fixed on the border of it. M. de Bernis entered. I waited for her to take off her cloak and gloves. She had her hands in her muff. The Abbé stood looking at her for some minutes; at last he said, "You look like a sheep in a reflecting mood." She awoke from her reverie, and, throwing her muff on the easy-chair, replied, "It is a wolf who makes the sheep reflect." I went out: the King entered shortly after, and I heard Madame de Pompadour sobbing. The Abbé came into my room, and told me to bring some Hoffman's drops: the King himself mixed the draught with sugar, and presented it to her in the kindest manner possible. She smiled, and kissed the King's hands. I left the room. Two days after, very early in the morning, I heard of M. d'Argenson's exile. It was her doing, and was, indeed, the strongest proof of her influence that could be given. The King was much attached to M. d'Argenson, and the war, then carrying on, both by sea and land, rendered the dismissal of two such Ministers extremely imprudent. This was the universal opinion at the time.

Many people talk of the letter of the Comte d'Argenson to Madame d'Esparbès. I give it, according to the most correct version: " The doubtful is, at length, decided. The Keeper of the Seals is dismissed. You will be recalled, my dear Countess, and we shall be masters of the field."

It is much less generally known that Arboulin, whom Madame calls Bou-bou, was supposed to be the person who, on the very day of the dismissal of the Keeper of the Seals, bribed the Count's confidential courier, who gave him this letter. Is this report founded on truth? I cannot swear that it is; but it is asserted that the letter is written in the Count's style. Besides, who could so immediately have invented it? It, however, appeared certain, from the extreme displeasure of the King, that he had some other subject of complaint against M. d'Argenson, besides his refusing to be reconciled with Madame. Nobody dares to show the slightest attachment to the disgraced Minister. I asked the ladies who were most intimate with Madame de Pompadour, as well as my own friends, what they knew of the matter; but they knew nothing. I can understand why Madame did not let them into her confidence at that moment. She will be less reserved in time. I care very little about it, since I see that she is well, and appears happy.

The King said a thing, which did him honour, to a person whose name Madame withheld from me. A nobleman, who had been a most assiduous courtier of the Count, said, rubbing his hands with an air of great joy, " I have just seen the Comte d'Argenson's baggage set out." When the King heard him, he went up to Madame, shrugged his shoulders, and said, "And immediately the cock crew."

I believe this is taken from Scripture, where Peter denies Our Lord. I confess, this circumstance gave me great pleasure. It showed that the King is not the dupe of those around him, and that he hates treachery and ingratitude.

Madame sent for me yesterday evening, at seven o'clock, to read something to her; the ladies who were intimate with her were at Paris, and M. de Gontaut ill. "The King," said she, "will stay late at the Council this evening; they are occupied with the affairs of the Parliament again." She bade me leave off reading, and I was going to quit the room, but she called out, "Stop." She rose; a letter was brought in for her, and she took it with an air of impatience and ill-humour. After a considerable time she began to talk openly, which only happened when she was extremely vexed; and, as none of her confidential friends were at hand, she said to me, "This is from my brother. It is what he would not have dared to say to me, so he writes. I had arranged a marriage for him with the daughter of a man of title; he appeared to be well inclined to it, and I, therefore, pledged my word. He now tells me that he has made inquiries; that the parents are people of insupportable hauteur; that the daughter is very badly educated; and that he knows, from authority not to be doubted, that when she heard this marriage discussed, she spoke of the connection with the most supreme contempt; that he is certain of this fact; and that I was still more contemptuously spoken of than himself. In a word, he begs me to break off the treaty. But he has let me go too far; and now he will make these people my irreconcilable enemies. This has been put in his head by some of his flatterers; they do not wish him to change his way of living; and very few of them would be received by his wife." I tried to soften Madame, and, though I did not venture to tell her so, I thought her brother right. She persisted in saying these were lies, and, on the following Sunday, treated her brother very coldly. He said nothing to me at that time; if he had, he would have embarrassed me greatly. Madame atoned for everything by procuring favours, which were the means of facilitating the young lady's marriage with a gentleman of the Court. Her conduct, two months after marriage, compelled Madame to confess that her brother had been perfectly right.

I saw my friend, Madame du Chiron. "Why," said she, " is the Marquise so violent an enemy to the Jesuits? I assure you she is wrong. All-powerful as she is, she may find herself the worse for their enmity." I replied that I knew nothing about the matter. " It is, however, unquestionably a fact; and she does not feel that a word more or less might decide her fate." " How do you mean? " said I. " Well, I will explain myself fully," said she. " You know what took place at the time the King was stabbed: an attempt was made to get her out of the Castle instantly. The Jesuits have no other object than the salvation of their penitents; but they are men, and hatred may, without their being aware of it, influence their minds, and inspire them with a greater degree of severity than circumstances absolutely demand. Favour and partiality may, on the other hand, induce the confessor to make great concessions; and the shortest interval may suffice to save a favourite, especially if any decent pretext can be found for prolonging her stay at Court." I agreed with her in all she said, but I told her that I dared not touch that string. On reflecting on this conversation after-

wards, I was forcibly struck with this fresh proof of
the intrigues of the Jesuits, which, indeed, I knew well
already.  I thought that, in spite of what I had replied to Madame du Chiron, I ought to communicate
this to Madame de Pompadour, for the ease of my
conscience; but that I would abstain from making any
reflection upon it.  "Your friend, Madame du
Chiron," said she, "is, I perceive, affiliated to the
Jesuits, and what she says does not originate with
herself.  She is commissioned by some reverend
father, and I will know by whom."  Spies were, accordingly, set to watch her movements, and they discovered that one Father de Saci, and, still more particularly, one Father Frey, guided this lady's conduct,
"What a pity," said Madame to me, "that the Abbé
Chauvelin cannot know this."  He was the most formidable enemy of the reverend fathers.  Madame
du Chiron always looked upon me as a Jansenist, because I would not espouse the interests of the good
fathers with as much warmth as she did.

Madame is completely absorbed in the Abbé de
Bernis, whom she thinks capable of anything; she
talks of him incessantly.  Apropos of this Abbé, I
must relate an anecdote, which almost makes one believe in conjurors.  A year, or fifteen months, before
her disgrace, Madame de Pompadour, being at Fontainebleau, sat down to write at a desk, over which
hung a portrait of the King.   While she was shut-
ting the desk, after she had finished writing, the
picture fell, and struck her violently on the head.
The persons who saw the accident were alarmed, and
sent for Dr. Quesnay.  He asked the circumstances
of the case, and ordered bleeding and anodynes.  Just
as she had been bled, Madame de Brancas entered,
and saw us all in confusion and agitation, and
Madame lying on her chaise-longue.  She asked what

was the matter, and was told. After having expressed her regret, and having consoled her, she said, " I ask it as a favour of Madame, and of the King (who had just come in), that they will instantly send a courier to the Abbé de Bernis, and that the Marquise will have the goodness to write a letter, merely requesting him to inform her what his fortune-tellers told him, and to withhold nothing from the fear of making her uneasy." The thing was done as she desired, and she then told us that La Bontemps had predicted, from the dregs in the coffee-cup, in which she read everything, that the head of her best friend was in danger, but that no fatal consequences would ensue.

The next day, the Abbé wrote word that Madame Bontemps also said to him, " You came into the world almost black," and that this was the fact. This colour, which lasted for some time, was attributed to a picture which hung at the foot of his mother's bed, and which she often looked at. It represented a Moor bringing to Cleopatra a basket of flowers, containing the asp by whose bite she destroyed herself. He said that she also told him, " You have a great deal of money about you, but it does not belong to you;" and that he had actually in his pocket two hundred louis for the Duc de La Vallière. Lastly, he informed us that she said, looking in the cup, " I see one of your friends—the best—a distinguished lady, threatened with an accident;" that he confessed that, in spite of all his philosophy, he turned pale; that she remarked this, looked again into the cup, and continued, " Her head will be slightly in danger, but of this no appearance will remain half an hour afterwards." It was impossible to doubt the facts. They appeared so surprising to the King, that he desired some inquiry to be made concerning the fortune-teller. Madame, however, protected her from the pursuit of the Police.

A man, who was quite as astonishing as this fortune-teller, often visited Madame de Pompadour. This was the Comte de St. Germain, who wished to have it believed that he had lived several centuries. One day, at her toilet, Madame said to him, in my presence, " What was the personal appearance of Francis I.? He was a King I should have liked." " He was, indeed, very captivating," said St. Germain; and he proceeded to describe his face and person as one does that of a man one has accurately observed. " It is a pity he was too ardent. I could have given him some good advice, which would have saved him from all his misfortunes; but he would not have followed it; for it seems as if a fatality attended Princes, forcing them to shut their ears, those of the mind, at least, to the best advice, and especially in the most critical moments." " And the Constable," said Madame, " what do you say of him?" " I cannot say much good or much harm of him," replied he. " Was the Court of Francis I. very brilliant?" " Very brilliant; but those of his grandsons infinitely surpassed it. In the time of Mary Stuart and Margaret of Valois it was a land of enchantment—a temple, sacred to pleasures of every kind; those of the mind were not neglected. The two Queens were learned, wrote verses, and spoke with captivating grace and eloquence." Madame said, laughing, " You seem to have seen all this." " I have an excellent memory," said he, " and have read the history of France with great care. I sometimes amuse myself, not by *making*, but by *letting* it be believed that I lived in old times." " You do not tell me your age, however, and you give yourself out for very old. The Comtesse de Gergy, who was Ambassadress to Venice,

I think, fifty years ago, says she knew you there exactly what you are now." "It is true, Madame, that I have known Madame de Gergy a long time." "But, according to what she says, you would be more than a hundred." "That is not impossible," said he, laughing; "but it is, I allow, still more possible that Madame de Gergy, for whom I have the greatest respect, may be in her dotage." "You have given her an elixir, the effect of which is surprising. She declares that for a long time she has felt as if she was only four-and-twenty years of age; why don't you give some to the King?" "Ah! Madame," said he, with a sort of terror, "I must be mad to think of giving the King an unknown drug." I went into my room to write down this conversation.

Some days afterwards, the King, Madame de Pompadour, some Lords of the Court, and the Comte de St. Germain, were talking about his secret for causing the spots in diamonds to disappear. The King ordered a diamond of middling size, which had a spot, to be brought. It was weighed; and the King said to the Count, "It is valued at two hundred and forty louis; but it would be worth four hundred if it had no spot. Will you try to put a hundred and sixty louis into my pocket?" He examined it carefully, and said, "It may be done; and I will bring it you again in a month." At the time appointed, the Count brought back the diamond without a spot, and gave it to the King. It was wrapped in a cloth of amianthus, which he took off. The King had it weighed, and found it but very little diminished. The King sent it to his jeweller by M. de Gontaut, without telling him anything of what had passed. The jeweller gave three hundred and eighty louis for it. The King, however, sent for it back again, and kept it as a curiosity. He could not overcome his surprise, and said that M. de St. Germain must be worth millions, especially if he had also the secret of making large diamonds out of a number of small ones. He neither said that he had, nor that he had not; but he positively asserted that he could make pearls grow, and give them the finest water. The King paid him great attention, and so did Madame de Pompadour. It was from her I learnt what I have just related. M. Quesnay said, talking of the pearls, " They are produced by a disease in the oyster. It is possible to know the cause of it; but, be that as it may, he is not the less a quack, since he pretends to have the *elixir vitæ*, and to have lived several centuries. Our master is, however, infatuated by him, and sometimes talks of him as if his descent were illustrious."

I have seen him frequently: he appeared to be about fifty; he was neither fat nor thin; he had an acute, intelligent look, dressed very simply, but in good taste; he wore very fine diamonds in his rings, watch, and snuff-box. He came, one day, to visit Madame de Pompadour, at a time when the Court was in full splendour, with knee and shoe-buckles of diamonds so fine and brilliant that Madame said she did not believe the King had any equal to them. He went into the antechamber to take them off, and brought them to be examined; they were compared with others in the room, and the Duc de Gontaut, who was present, said they were both at least eight thousand louis. He wore, at the same time, a snuff-box of inestimable value, and ruby sleeve-buttons, which were perfectly dazzling. Nobody could find out by what means this man became so rich and so remarkable; but the King would not suffer him to be spoken of with ridicule or contempt. He was said to be a bastard son of the King of Portugal.

I learnt, from M. de Marigny, that the relations of the good little Maréchale (de Mirepoix) had been extremely severe upon her, for what they called the baseness of her conduct, with regard to Madame de Pompadour. They said she held the stones of the cherries which Madame ate in her carriage, in her beautiful little hands, and that she sate in the front of the carriage, while Madame occupied the whole seat in the inside. The truth was, that, in going to Crécy, on an insupportably hot day, they both wished to sit alone, that they might be cooler; and as to the matter of the cherries, the villagers having brought them some, they ate them to refresh themselves, while the horses were changed; and the Maréchale emptied her pocket-handkerchief, into which they had both thrown the cherry-stones, out of the carriage window. The people who were changing the horses had given their own version of the affair.

I had, as you know, a very pretty room at Madame's hotel, whither I generally went privately. I had, one day, had visits from two or three Paris representatives, who told me news; and Madame, having sent for me, I went to her, and found her with M. de Gontaut. I could not help instantly saying to her, " You must be much pleased, Madame, at the noble action of the Marquis de ——." Madame replied, drily, " Hold your tongue, and listen to what I have to say to you." I returned to my little room, where I found the Comtesse d'Amblimont, to whom I mentioned Madame's reception of me. " I know what is the matter," said she; " it has no relation to you. I will explain it to you. The Marquis de —— has told all Paris, that, some days ago, going home at night, alone, and on foot, he heard cries in a street called Férou, which is dark, and, in great part, arched over; that he drew his sword, and went down the street, in which he saw, by the light of a lamp, a very handsome woman, to whom some ruffians were offering violence; that he approached, and that the woman cried out, ' Save me! save me!' that he rushed upon the wretches, two of whom fought him, sword in hand, whilst a third held the woman, and tried to stop her mouth; that he wounded one in the arm; and that the ruffians, hearing people pass at the end of the street, and fearing they might come to his assistance, fled; that he went up to the lady, who told him that they were not robbers, but villains, one of whom was desperately in love with her; and that the lady knew not how to express her gratitude; that she had begged him not to follow her, after he had conducted her to a *fiacre;* that she would not tell him her name, but that she insisted on his accepting a little ring, as a token of remembrance; and that she promised to see him again, and to tell him her whole history, if he gave her his address; that he complied with this request of the lady, whom he represented as a charming person, and who, in the overflowing of her gratitude, embraced him several times. This is all very fine, so far," said Madame d'Amblimont, " but hear the rest. The Marquis de —— exhibited himself everywhere the next day, with a black ribbon bound round his arm, near the wrist, in which part he said he had received the wound. He related his story to everybody, and everybody commented upon it after his own fashion. He went to dine with the Dauphin, who spoke to him of his bravery, and of his fair unknown, and told him that he had already complimented the Duc de C—— on the affair. I forgot to tell you," continued Madame d'Amblimont, " that, on the very night of the adventure, he called on Madame d'Estillac, an old gambler, whose house is open till four in the morning; that everybody there was sur-

Madame de Pompadour.

*From the original painting by Nattier in the Royal Gallery in Scotland.*

prised at the disordered state in which he appeared; that his bagwig had fallen off, one skirt of his coat was cut, and his right hand bleeding. That they instantly bound it up, and gave him some Rota wine. Four days ago, the Duc de C—— supped with the King, and sat near M. de St. Florentin. He talked to him of his relation's adventure, and asked him if he had made any inquiries concerning the lady. M. de St. Florentin coldly answered, 'No;' and M. de C—— remarked, on asking him some further questions, that he kept his eyes fixed on his plate, looking embarrassed, and answered in monosyllables. He asked him the reason of this, upon which M. de Florentin told him that it was extremely distressing to him to see him under such a mistake. 'How can you know that, supposing it to be the fact?' said M. de ——. 'Nothing is more easy to prove,' replied M. de St. Florentin. 'You may imagine that, as soon as I was informed of the Marquis de ——'s adventure, I set on foot inquiries, the result of which was, that, on the night when this affair was said to have taken place, a party of the watch was set in ambuscade in this very street, for the purpose of catching a thief who was coming out of the gaming house; that this party was there four hours, and heard not the slightest noise.' M. de C—— was greatly incensed at this recital, which M. de St. Florentin ought, indeed, to have communicated to the King. He has ordered, or will order, his relation to retire to his province.

"After this, you will judge, my dear, whether you were very likely to be graciously received when you went open-mouthed with your compliment to the Marquise. This adventure," continued she, "reminded the King of one which occurred about fifteen years ago. The Comte d'E——, who was what is called

*enfant d'honneur* to the Dauphin, and about fourteen
years of age, came into the Dauphin's apartments, one
evening, with his bag-wig snatched off, and his ruffles
torn, and said that, having walked rather late near
the piece of water *des Suisses,* he had been attacked
by two robbers; that he had refused to give them
anything, drawn his sword, and put himself in an
attitude of defence; that one of the robbers was armed
with a sword, the other with a large stick, from which
he had received several blows, but that he had
wounded one in the arm, and that, hearing a noise
at that moment, they had fled. But unluckily for the
little Count, it was known that people were on the
spot at the precise time he mentioned, and had heard
nothing. The Count was pardoned, on account of his
youth. The Dauphin made him confess the truth,
and it was looked upon as a childish freak to set people talking about him."

The King disliked the King of Prussia because he
knew that the latter was in the habit of jesting upon
his mistress, and the kind of life he led. It was
Frederick's fault, as I have heard it said, that the
King was not his most steadfast ally and friend, as
much as sovereigns can be towards each other; but
the jestings of Frederick had stung him, and made
him conclude the treaty of Versailles. One day, he
entered Madame's apartment with a paper in his hand,
and said, "The King of Prussia is certainly a great
man; he loves men of talent, and, like Louis XIV., he
wishes to make Europe ring with his favours towards
foreign *savans.* There is a letter from him, addressed to Milord Marshal, ordering him to acquaint
a *supérieur* man of my kingdom (D'Alembert) that
he has granted him a pension;" and, looking at the
letter, he read the following words: "You must know
that there is in Paris a man of the greatest merit,

whose fortune is not proportionate to his talents and character. I may serve as eyes to the blind goddess, and repair in some measure the injustice, and I beg you to offer on that account. I flatter myself that he will accept this pension because of the pleasure I shall feel in obliging a man who joins beauty of character to the most sublime intellectual talents." The King here stopped, on seeing MM. d'Ayen and de Gontaut enter, and then recommenced reading the letter to them, and added, " It was given me by the Minister for Foreign Affairs, to whom it was confided by Milord Marshal, for the purpose of obtaining my permission for this *sublime genius* to accept the favour. But," said the King, " what do you think is the amount?" Some said six, eight, ten thousand livres. " You have not guessed," said the King; " it is twelve hundred livres." " For sublime talents," said the Duc d'Ayen, " it is not much. But the philosophers will make Europe resound with this letter, and the King of Prussia will have the pleasure of making a great noise at little expense."

The Chevalier de Courten, who had been in Prussia, came in, and, hearing this story told, said, " I have seen what is much better than that: passing through a village in Prussia, I got out at the posthouse, while I was waiting for horses; and the postmaster, who was a captain in the Prussian service, showed me several letters in Frederick's handwriting, addressed to his uncle, who was a man of rank, promising him to provide for his nephews; the provision he made for this, the eldest of these nephews, who was dreadfully wounded, was the postmastership which he then held." M. de Marigny related this story at Quesnay's, and added, that the man of genius above mentioned was D'Alembert, and that the King had permitted him to accept the pension. He added, that his sister had suggested to the King that he had better give D'Alembert a pension of twice the value, and forbid him to take the King of Prussia's. This advice he would not take, because he looked upon D'Alembert as an infidel. M. de Marigny took a copy of the letter, which he lent me.

A certain nobleman, at one time, affected to cast tender glances on Madame Adélaïde. She was wholly unconscious of it; but, as there are Arguses at Court, the King was, of course, told of it, and, indeed, he thought he had perceived it himself. I know that he came into Madame de Pompadour's room one day, in a great passion, and said, " Would you believe that there is a man in my Court insolent enough to dare to raise his eyes to one of my daughters?" Madame had never seen him so exasperated, and this illustrious nobleman was advised to feign a necessity for visiting his estates. He remained there two months. Madame told me, long after, that she thought that there were no tortures to which the King would not have condemned any man who had seduced one of his daughters. Madame Adélaïde, at the time in question, was a charming person, and united infinite grace, and much talent, to a most agreeable face.

A courier brought Madame de Pompadour a letter, on reading which she burst into tears. It contained the intelligence of the battle of Rosbach, which M. de Soubise sent her, with all the details. I heard her say to the Maréchal de Belle-Isle, wiping her eyes, " M. de Soubise is inconsolable; he does not try to excuse his conduct, he sees nothing but the disastrous fortune which pursues him." " M. de Soubise must, however, have many things to urge in his own behalf," said M. de Belle-Isle, " and so I told the King." " It is very noble in you, Marshal, not to suffer

an unfortunate man to be overwhelmed; the public
are furious against him, and what has he done to
deserve it?" "There is not a more honourable nor
a kinder man in the world. I only fulfil my duty in
doing justice to the truth, and to a man for whom I
have the most profound esteem. The King will explain to you, Madame, how M. de Soubise was forced
to give battle by the Prince of Saxe-Hildbourgshau-
sen, whose troops fled first, and carried along the
French troops." Madame would have embraced the
old Marshal if she had dared, she was so delighted
with him.

M. de Soubise, having gained a battle, was made
Marshal of France: Madame was enchanted with her
friend's success. But, either it was unimportant, or
the public were offended at his promotion; nobody
talked of it but Madame's friends. This unpopularity
was concealed from her, and she said to Colin, her
steward, at her toilet, "Are you not delighted at
the victory M. de Soubise has gained? What does
the public say of it? He has taken his revenge well."
Colin was embarrassed, and knew not what to answer. As she pressed him further, he replied that
he had been ill, and had seen nobody for a week.

M. de Marigny came to see me one day, very much
out of humour. I asked him the cause. "I have,"
said he, "just been intreating my sister not to make
M. le Normand-de-Mezi Minister of the Marine. I
told her that she was heaping coals of fire upon her
own head. A favourite ought not to multiply the
points of attack upon herself." The Doctor entered.
"You," said the Doctor, "are worth your weight
in gold, for the good sense and capacity you have
shewn in your office, and for your moderation, but
you will never be appreciated as you deserve; your
advice is excellent; there will never be a ship taken

but Madame will be held responsible for it to the public, and you are very wise not to think of being in the Ministry yourself."

One day, when I was at Paris, I went to dine with the Doctor, who happened to be there at the same time; there were, contrary to his usual custom, a good many people, and, among others, a handsome young Master of the Requests, who took a title from some place, the name of which I have forgotten, but who was a son of M. Turgot, the *prévôt des marchands*. They talked a great deal about administration, which was not very amusing to me; they then fell upon the subject of the love Frenchmen bear to their Kings. M. Turgot here joined in the conversation, and said, " This is not a blind attachment; it is a deeply rooted sentiment, arising from an indistinct recollection of great benefits. The French nation—I may go farther—Europe, and all mankind, owe to a King of France " (I have forgotten his name) "whatever liberty they enjoy. He established *communes*, and conferred on an immense number of men a civil existence. I am aware that it may be said, with justice, that he served his own interests by granting these franchises; that the cities paid him taxes, and that his design was to use them as instruments of weakening the power of great nobles; but what does that prove, but that this measure was at once useful, politic, and humane? " From Kings in general the conversation turned upon Louis XV., and M. Turgot remarked that his reign would be always celebrated for the advancement of the sciences, the progress of knowledge, and of philosophy. He added that Louis XV. was deficient in the quality which Louis XIV. possessed to excess; that is to say, in a good opinion of himself; that he was well-informed; that nobody was more perfectly master of the topography of France; that his opinion in the Council was always the most judicious; and that it was much to be lamented that he had not more confidence in himself, or that he did not rely upon some Minister who enjoyed the confidence of the nation. Everybody agreed with him. I begged M. Quesnay to write down what young Turgot had said, and showed it to Madame. She praised this Master of the Requests greatly, and spoke of him to the King. "It is a good breed," said he.

One day, I went out to walk, and saw, on my return, a great many people going and coming, and speaking to each other privately: it was evident that something extraordinary had happened. I asked a person of my acquaintance what was the matter. "Alas!" said he, with tears in his eyes, "some assassins, who had formed the project of murdering the King, have inflicted several wounds on a garde-du-corps, who overheard them in a dark corridor; he is carried to the hospital: and as he has described the colour of these men's coats, the Police are in quest of them in all directions, and some people, dressed in clothes of that colour, are already arrested." I saw Madame with M. de Gontaut, and I hastened home. She found her door besieged by a multitude of people, and was alarmed: when she got in, she found the Comte de Noailles. "What is all this, Count?" said she. He said he was come expressly to speak to her, and they retired to her closet together. The conference was not long. I had remained in the drawing-room, with Madame's equerry, the Chevalier de Sosent, Gourbillon, her *valet de chambre*, and some strangers. A great many details were related; but, the wounds being little more than scratches, and the garde-du-corps having let fall some contradictions, it was thought that he was an impostor, who had invented all this story to bring himself into favour. Before the night was over, this was proved to be the fact, and, I believe, from his own confession. The King came, that evening, to see Madame de Pompadour; he spoke of this occurrence with great *sang froid,* and said, " The gentleman who wanted to kill me was a wicked madman; this is a low scoundrel."

When he spoke of Damiens, which was only while his trial lasted, he never called him anything but *that gentleman.*

I have heard it said that he proposed having him shut up in a dungeon for life; but that the horrible nature of the crime made the judges insist upon his suffering all the tortures inflicted upon like occasions. Great numbers, many of them women, had a barbarous curiosity to witness the execution; amongst others, Madame de P——, a very beautiful woman, and the wife of a Farmer General. She hired two places at a window for twelve louis, and played a game of cards in the room whilst waiting for the execution to begin. On this being told to the King, he covered his eyes with his hands and exclaimed, *" Fi, la Vilaine! "* I have been told that she, and others, thought to pay their court in this way, and signalise their attachment to the King's person.

Two things were related to me by M. Duclos at the time of the attempt on the King's life.

The first, relative to the Comte de Sponheim, who was the Duc de Deux-Ponts, and next in succession to the Palatinate and Electorate of Bavaria. He was thought to be a great friend to the King, and had made several long sojourns in France. He came frequently to see Madame. M. Duclos told us that the Duc de Deux-Ponts, having learned, at Deux-Ponts, the attempt on the King's life, immediately set out in a carriage for Versailles: "But remark," said he, "the spirit of *courtisanerie* of a Prince, who may be Elector of Bavaria and the Palatinate to-morrow. This was not enough. When he arrived within ten leagues of Paris, he put on an enormous pair of jack-boots, mounted a post-horse, and arrived in the court of the palace cracking his whip. If this had been real impatience, and not charlatanism, he would have taken horse twenty leagues from Paris." "I don't agree with you," said a gentleman whom I did not know; "impatience sometimes seizes one towards the end of an undertaking, and one employs the readiest means then in one's power. Besides, the Duc de Deux-Ponts might wish, by showing himself thus on horseback, to serve the King, to whom he is attached, by proving to Frenchmen how greatly he is beloved and honoured in other countries." Duclos resumed: "Well," said he, "do you know the story of M. de C——? The first day the King saw company, after the attempt of Damiens, M. de C—— pushed so vigorously through the crowd that he was one of the first to come into the King's presence, but he had on so shabby a black coat that it caught the King's attention, who burst out laughing, and said, 'Look at C——, he has had the skirt of his coat torn off.' M. de C—— looked as if he was only then first conscious of his loss, and said, 'Sire, there is such a multitude hurrying to see Your Majesty, that I was obliged to fight my way through them, and, in the effort, my coat has been torn.' 'Fortunately it was not worth much,' said the Marquis de Souvré, 'and you could not have chosen a worse one to sacrifice on the occasion.'"

Madame de Pompadour had been very judiciously advised to get her husband, M. le Normand, sent to Constantinople, as Ambassador. This would have a little diminished the scandal caused by seeing Madame de Pompadour, with the title of Marquise, at Court, and her husband Farmer General at Paris. But he was so attached to a Paris life, and to his opera habits, that he could not be prevailed upon to go. Madame employed a certain M. d'Arboulin, with whom she had been acquainted before she was at Court, to negotiate this affair. He applied to a Mademoiselle Rem, who had been an opera-dancer, and who was M. le Normand's mistress. She made him very fine promises; but she was like him, and preferred a Paris life. She would do nothing in it.

At the time that plays were acted in the little apartments, I obtained a lieutenancy for one of my relations, by a singular means, which proves the value the greatest people set upon the slightest access to the Court. Madame did not like to ask anything of M. d'Argenson, and, being pressed by my family, who could not imagine that, situated as I was, it could be difficult for me to obtain a command for a good soldier, I determined to go and ask the Comte d'Argenson. I made my request, and presented my memorial. He received me coldly, and gave me vague answers. I went out, and the Marquis de V——, who was in his closet, followed me. "You wish to obtain a command," said he; "there is one vacant, which is promised me for one of my protégés; but if you will do me a favour in return, or obtain one for me, I will give it to you. I want to be a *police officer*, and you have it in your power to get me a place." I told him I did not understand the purport of his jest. "I will tell you," said he; "*Tartuffe* is going to be acted in the cabinets, and there is the part of a police officer, which only consists of a few lines. Prevail upon Madame de Pompadour to assign me that part, and the command is yours." I promised nothing, but I re-

lated the history to Madame, who said she would arrange it for me. The thing was done, and I obtained
the command, and the Marquis de V—— thanked
Madame as if she had made him a Duke.

The King was often annoyed by the Parliaments,
and said a very remarkable thing concerning them,
which M. de Gontaut repeated to Doctor Quesnay in
my presence. "Yesterday," said he, "the King
walked up and down the room with an anxious air.
Madame de Pompadour asked him if he was uneasy
about his health, as he had been, for some time,
rather unwell. 'No,' replied he; 'but I am greatly
annoyed by all these remonstrances.' 'What can
come of them,' said she, 'that need seriously disquiet
Your Majesty? Are you not master of the Parliaments, as well as of all the rest of the kingdom?' 'That is true,' said the King; 'but, if it had
not been for these counsellors and presidents, I should
never have been stabbed by *that gentleman*' (he always called Damiens so). 'Ah! Sire,' cried Madame
de Pompadour. 'Read the trial,' said he. 'It was
the language of those gentlemen he names which
turned his head.' 'But,' said Madame, 'I have often
thought that, if the Archbishop could be sent to
Rome—' 'Find anybody who will accomplish that
business, and I will give him whatever he pleases.'"
Quesnay said the King was right in all he had uttered. The Archbishop was exiled shortly after, and
the King was seriously afflicted at being driven to
take such a step. "What a pity," he often said, "that
so excellent a man should be so obstinate." "And so
shallow," said somebody, one day. "Hold your
tongue," replied the King, somewhat sternly. The
Archbishop was very charitable, and liberal to excess,
but he often granted pensions without discernment.
He granted one of an hundred louis to a pretty

woman, who was very poor, and who assumed an illustrious name, to which she had no right. The fear lest she should be plunged into vice led him to bestow such excessive bounty upon her; and the woman was an admirable dissembler. She went to the Archbishop's, covered with a great hood, and, when she left him, she amused herself with a variety of lovers.

Great people have the bad habit of talking very indiscreetly before their servants. M. de Gontaut once said these words covertly, as he thought, to the Duc de ——, " That measures had been taken which would, probably, have the effect of determining the Archbishop to go to Rome, with a Cardinal's hat; and that, if he desired it, he was to have a coadjutor."

A very plausible pretext had been found for making this proposition, and for rendering it flattering to the Archbishop, and agreeable to his sentiments. The affair had been very adroitly begun, and success appeared certain. The King had the air, towards the Archbishop, of entire unconsciousness of what was going on. The negotiator acted as if he were only following the suggestions of his own mind, for the general good. He was a friend of the Archbishop, and was very sure of a liberal reward. A valet of the Duc de Gontaut, a very handsome young fellow, had perfectly caught the sense of what was spoken in a mysterious manner. He was one of the lovers of the lady of the hundred louis a year, and had heard her talk of the Archbishop, whose relation she pretended to be. He thought he should secure her good graces by informing her that great efforts were being made to induce her patron to reside at Rome, with a view to get him away from Paris. The lady instantly told the Archbishop, as she was afraid of losing her pension if he went. The information squared so well with the negotiation then on foot, that the Archbishop had no doubt of its truth. He cooled, by degrees, in his conversations with the negotiator, whom he regarded as a traitor, and ended by breaking with him. These details were not known till long afterwards. The lover of the lady having been sent to the Bicêtre, some letters were found among his papers, which gave a scent of the affair, and he was made to confess the rest.

In order not to compromise the Duc de Gontaut, the King was told that the valet had come to a knowledge of the business from a letter which he had found in his master's clothes. The King took his revenge by humiliating the Archbishop, which he was enabled to do by means of the information he had obtained concerning the conduct of the lady, his protégée. She was found guilty of swindling, in concert with her beloved valet; but, before her punishment was inflicted, the Lieutenant of Police was ordered to lay before Monseigneur a full account of the conduct of his relation and pensioner. The Archbishop had nothing to object to in the proofs which were submitted to him; he said, with perfect calmness, that she was not his relation; and, raising his hands to heaven, "She is an unhappy wretch," said he, "who has robbed me of the money which was destined for the poor. But God knows that, in giving her so large a pension, I did not act lightly. I had, at the time, before my eyes the example of a young woman who once asked me to grant her seventy louis a year, promising me that she would always live very virtuously, as she had hitherto done. I refused her, and she said, on leaving me, 'I must turn to the left, Monseigneur, since the way on the right is closed against me.' The unhappy creature has kept her word

but too well. She found means of establishing a
faro-table at her house, which is tolerated; and she
joins to the most profligate conduct in her own person
the infamous trade of a corrupter of youth; her house
is the abode of every vice. Think, sir, after that,
whether it was not an act of prudence, on my part, to
grant the woman in question a pension, suitable to
the rank in which I thought her born, to prevent her
abusing the gifts of youth, beauty, and talents, which
she possessed, to her own perdition, and the destruction of others." The Lieutenant of Police told the
King that he was touched with the candour and the
noble simplicity of the prelate. "I never doubted his
virtues," replied the King, "but I wish he would be
quiet." This same Archbishop gave a pension of fifty
louis a year to the greatest scoundrel in Paris. He is
a poet, who writes abominable verses; this pension
is granted on condition that his poems are never
printed. I learned this fact from M. de Marigny, to
whom he recited some of his horrible verses one evening, when he supped with him, in company with
some people of quality. He chinked the money in his
pocket. "This is my good Archbishop's," said he,
laughing; "I keep my word with him: my poem will
not be printed during my life, but I read it. What
would the good prelate say if he knew that I shared
my last quarter's allowance with a charming little
opera-dancer? 'It is the Archbishop, then, who keeps
me,' said she to me; 'Oh, la! how droll that is!'"
The King heard this, and was much scandalised at
it. "How difficult it is to do good!" said he.

The King came into Madame de Pompadour's
room, one day, as she was finishing dressing. "I
have just had a strange adventure," said he: "would
you believe that, in going out of my wardroom into
my bedroom, I met a gentleman face to face?" "My

God! Sire," cried Madame, terrified. " It was nothing," replied he; " but I confess I was greatly surprised : the man appeared speechless with consterna-
tion. ' What do you do here?' cried I, civilly. He
threw himself on his knees, saying, ' Pardon me, Sire;
and, above all, have me searched.' He instantly
emptied his pockets himself; he pulled off his coat in
the greatest agitation and terror : at last he told me
that he was cook to ———, and a friend of Beccari,
whom he came to visit; that he had mistaken the
staircase, and, finding all the doors open, he had
wandered into the room in which I found him, and
which he would have instantly left : I rang; Guimard
came, and was astonished enough at finding me tête-
à-tête with a man in his shirt. He begged Guimard
to go with him into another room, and to search his
whole person. After this, the poor devil returned,
and put on his coat. Guimard said to me, ' He is
certainly an honest man, and tells the truth; this may,
besides, be easily ascertained.' Another of the servants of the palace came in, and happened to know
him. ' I will answer for this good man,' said he, ' who,
moreover, makes the best *bœuf à l'écarlate* in the
world.' As I saw the man was so agitated that he
could not stand steady, I took fifty louis out of my
bureau, and said, ' Here, sir, are fifty louis, to quiet
your alarms.' He went out, after throwing himself
at my feet." Madame exclaimed on the impropriety
of having the King's bedroom thus accessible to
everybody. He talked with great calmness of this
strange apparition, but it was evident that he con-
trolled himself, and that he had, in fact, been much
frightened, as, indeed, he had reason to be. Madame
highly approved of the gift; and she was the more
right in applauding it, as it was by no means in the
King's usual manner. M. de Marigny said, when I

told him of this adventure, that he would have wagered a thousand louis against the King's making a present of fifty, if anybody but I had told him of the circumstance. "It is a singular fact," continued he, "that all of the race of Valois have been liberal to excess; this is not precisely the case with the Bourbons, who are rather reproached with avarice. Henri IV. was said to be avaricious. He gave to his mistresses, because he could refuse them nothing; but he played with the eagerness of a man whose whole fortune depends on the game. Louis XIV. gave through ostentation. It is most astonishing," added he, "to reflect on what might have happened. The King might actually have been assassinated in his chamber, without anybody knowing anything of the matter and without a possibility of discovering the murderer." For more than a fortnight Madame could not get over this incident.

About that time she had a quarrel with her brother, and both were in the right. Proposals were made to him to marry the daughter of one of the greatest noblemen of the Court, and the King consented to create him a Duke, and even to make the title hereditary. Madame was right in wishing to aggrandise her brother, but he declared that he valued his liberty above all things, and that he would not sacrifice it except for a person he really loved. He was a true Epicurean philosopher, and a man of great capacity, according to the report of those who knew him well, and judged him impartially. It was entirely at his option to have had the reversion of M. de St. Florentin's place, and the place of Minister of Marine, when M. de Machault retired; he said to his sister, at the time, "I spare you many vexations, by depriving you of a slight satisfaction. The people would be unjust to me, however well I might fulfil the duties of my

office.  As to M. de St. Florentin's place, he may live
five-and-twenty years, so that I should not be the
better for it.  Kings' mistresses are hated enough on
their own account; they need not also draw upon
themselves the hatred which is directed against
Ministers."  M. Quesnay repeated this conversation
to me.

The King had another mistress, who gave Madame
de Pompadour some uneasiness.  She was a woman
of quality, and the wife of one of the most assiduous
courtiers.

A man in immediate attendance on the King's person, and who had the care of his clothes, came to
me one day, and told me that, as he was very much
attached to Madame, because she was good and useful
to the King, he wished to inform me that, a letter
having fallen out of the pocket of a coat which His
Majesty had taken off, he had had the curiosity to
read it, and found it to be from the Comtesse de
——, who had already yielded to the King's desires.
In this letter, she required the King to give her fifty
thousand crowns in money, a regiment for one of her
relations, and a bishopric for another, and to dismiss
Madame in the space of fifteen days, etc.  I
acquainted Madame with what this man told me, and
she acted with singular greatness of mind.  She said
to me, " I ought to inform the King of this breach of
trust of his servant, who may, by the same means,
come to the knowledge of, and make a bad use of,
important secrets; but I feel a repugnance to ruin
the man: however, I cannot permit him to remain
near the King's person, and here is what I shall do:
Tell him that there is a place of ten thousand francs
a year vacant in one of the provinces; let him solicit
the Minister of Finance for it, and it shall be granted
to him; but, if he should ever disclose through what

interest he has obtained it, the King shall be made acquainted with his conduct. By this means, I think I shall have done all that my attachment and duty prescribe. I rid the King of a faithless domestic, without ruining the individual." I did as Madame ordered me: her delicacy and address inspired me with admiration. She was not alarmed on account of the lady, seeing what her pretensions were. "She drives too quick," remarked Madame, "and will certainly be overturned on the road." The lady died.

"See what the Court is; all is corruption there, from the highest to the lowest," said I to Madame, one day, when she was speaking to me of some facts that had come to my knowledge. "I could tell you many others," replied Madame; "but the little chamber, where you often remain, must furnish you with a sufficient number." This was a little nook, from whence I could hear a great part of what passed in Madame's apartment. The Lieutenant of Police sometimes came secretly to this apartment, and waited there. Three or four persons, of high consideration, also found their way in, in a mysterious manner, and several devotees, who were, in their hearts, enemies of Madame de Pompadour. But these men had not petty objects in view: one required the government of a province; another, a seat in the Council; a third, a Captaincy of the Guards; and this man would have obtained it if the Maréchale de Mirepoix had not requested it for her brother, the Prince de Beauvan. The Chevalier du Muy was not among these apostates; not even the promise of being High Constable would have tempted him to make up to Madame, still less to betray his master, the Dauphin. The Prince was, to the last degree, weary of the station he held. Sometimes, when teased to death by ambitious people, who pretended to be Catos, or wonderfully devout, he took part against a Minister against whom he was prepossessed; then relapsed into his accustomed state of inactivity and ennui.

The King used to say, " My son is lazy; his temper is Polonese—hasty and changeable; he has no tastes; he cares nothing for hunting, for women, or for good living; perhaps he imagines that if he were in my place he would be happy; at first, he would make great changes, create everything anew, as it were.  In a short time he would be as tired of the rank of King as he now is of his own; he is only fit to live *en philosophe*, with clever people about him."   The King added, " He loves what is right; he is truly virtuous, and does not want understanding."

M. de St. Germain said, one day, to the King, " To think well of mankind, one must be neither a Confessor, nor a Minister, nor a Lieutenant of Police." " Nor a King," said His Majesty.  " Ah! Sire," replied he, " you remember the fog we had a few days ago, when we could not see four steps before us.  Kings are commonly surrounded by still thicker fogs, collected around them by men of intriguing character, and faithless Ministers—all, of every class, unite in endeavouring to make things appear to Kings in any light but the true one."   I heard this from the mouth of the famous Comte de St. Germain, as I was attending upon Madame, who was ill in bed.   The King was there; and the Count, who was a welcome visitor, had been admitted.   There were also present, M. de Gontaut, Madame de Brancas, and the Abbé de Bernis.  I remember that the very same day, after the Count was gone out, the King talked in a style which gave Madame great pain.  Speaking of the King of Prussia, he said, " That is a madman, who will risk all to gain all, and may, perhaps, win the game, though he has neither religion, morals, nor principles. He wants to make a noise in the world, and he will succeed. Julian, the Apostate, did the same." "I never saw the King so animated before," observed Madame, when he was gone out; "and really the comparison with Julian, the Apostate, is not amiss, considering the irreligion of the King of Prussia. If he gets out of his perplexities, surrounded as he is by his enemies, he will be one of the greatest men in history."

M. de Bernis remarked, "Madame is correct in her judgment, for she has no reason to pronounce his praises; nor have I, though I agree with what she says." Madame de Pompadour never enjoyed so much influence as at the time when M. de Choiseul became one of the Ministry. From the time of the Abbé de Bernis she had afforded him her constant support, and he had been employed in foreign affairs, of which he was said to know but little. Madame made the Treaty of Vienna, though the first idea of it was certainly furnished her by the Abbé. I have been informed by several persons that the King often talked to Madame upon this subject; for my own part, I never heard any conversation relative to it, except the high praises bestowed by her on the Empress and the Prince de Kaunitz, whom she had known a good deal of. She said that he had a clear head, the head of a statesman. One day, when she was talking in this strain, some one tried to cast ridicule upon the Prince on account of the style in which he wore his hair, and the four *valets de chambre*, who made the hair-powder fly in all directions, while Kaunitz ran about that he might only catch the superfine part of it. "Aye," said Madame, "just as Alcibiades cut off his dog's tail in order to give the Athenians something to talk about, and to turn their attention from those things he wished to conceal."

Never was the public mind so inflamed against Madame de Pompadour as when news arrived of the battle of Rosbach. Every day she received anonymous letters, full of the grossest abuse; atrocious verses, threats of poison and assassination. She continued long a prey to the most acute sorrow, and could get no sleep but from opiates. All this discontent was excited by her protecting the Prince of Soubise; and the Lieutenant of Police had great difficulty in allaying the ferment of the people. The King affirmed that it was not his fault. M. du Verney was the confidant of Madame in everything relating to war; a subject which he well understood, though not a military man by profession. The old Maréchal de Noailles called him, in derision, the General of the flour, but Maréchal Saxe, one day, told Madame that du Verney knew more of military matters than the old Marshal. Du Verney once paid a visit to Madame de Pompadour, and found her in company with the King, the Minister of War, and two Marshals; he submitted to them the plan of a campaign, which was generally applauded. It was through his influence that M. de Richelieu was appointed to the command of the army, instead of the Maréchal d'Estrées. He came to Quesnay two days after, when I was with him. The Doctor began talking about the art of war, and I remember he said, "Military men make a great mystery of their art; but what is the reason that young Princes have always the most brilliant success? Why, because they are active and daring. When Sovereigns command their troops in person what exploits they perform! Clearly, because they are at liberty to run all risks." These observations made a lasting impression on my mind.

The first physician came, one day, to see Madame:
he was talking of madmen and madness. The King
was present, and everything relating to disease of
any kind interested him. The first physician said
that he could distinguish the symptoms of approaching madness six months beforehand. "Are there any
persons about the Court likely to become mad?" said
the King. "I know one who will be imbecile in less
than three months," replied he. The King pressed
him to tell the name. He excused himself for some
time. At last he said, "It is M. de Séchelles, the
Controller-General." "You have a spite against
him," said Madame, "because he would not grant
what you asked." "That is true," said he, "but
though that might possibly incline me to tell a disagreeable truth, it would not make me invent one.
He is losing his intellects from debility. He affects
gallantry at his age, and I perceive the connection in
his ideas is becoming feeble and irregular." The
King laughed; but three months afterwards he came
to Madame, saying, "Séchelles gives evident proofs
of dotage in the Council. We must appoint a successor to him." Madame de Pompadour told me of
this on the way to Choisy. Some time afterwards,
the first physician came to see Madame, and spoke to
her in private. "You are attached to M. Berryer,
Madame," said he, "and I am sorry to have to warn
you that he will be attacked by madness, or by catalepsy, before long. I saw him this morning at chapel,
sitting on one of those very low little chairs, which
are only meant to kneel upon. His knees touched his
chin. I went to his house after mass; his eyes were
wild, and when his secretary spoke to him, he said,
'Hold your tongue, pen. A pen's business is to write,
and not to speak.'" Madame, who liked the Keeper
of the Seals, was very much concerned, and begged

the first physician not to mention what he had perceived. Four days after this, M. Berryer was seized with catalepsy, after having talked incoherently. This is a disease which I did not know even by name, and got it written down for me. The patient remains in precisely the same position in which the fit seizes him; one leg or arm elevated, the eyes wide open, or just as it may happen. This latter affair was known to all the Court at the death of the Keeper of the Seals.

When the Maréchal de Belle-Isle's son was killed in battle, Madame persuaded the King to pay his father a visit. He was rather reluctant, and Madame said to him, with an air half angry, half playful:

——"Barbare ! dont l'orgueil
Croit le sang d'un sujet trop payé d'un coup d'œil."

The King laughed, and said, "Whose fine verses are those?" "Voltaire's," said Madame ——.
"As barbarous as I am, I gave him the place of gentleman in ordinary, and a pension," said the King.

The King went in state to call on the Marshal, followed by all the Court; and it certainly appeared that this solemn visit consoled the Marshal for the loss of his son, the sole heir to his name.

When the Marshal died, he was carried to his house on a common hand-barrow, covered with a shabby cloth. I met the body. The bearers were laughing and singing. I thought it was some servant, and asked who it was. How great was my surprise at learning that these were the remains of a man abounding in honours and in riches. Such is the Court; the dead are always in fault, and cannot be put out of sight too soon.

The King said, "M. Fouquet is dead, I hear." "He was no longer Fouquet," replied the Duc

d'Ayen; "Your Majesty had permitted him to change
that name, under which, however, he acquired all his
reputation." The King shrugged his shoulders. His
Majesty had, in fact, granted him letters patent, permitting him not to sign Fouquet during his Ministry.
I heard this on the occasion in question. M. de
Choiseul had the war department at his death. He
was every day more and more in favour. Madame
treated him with greater distinction than any previous
Minister, and his manners towards her were the most
agreeable it is possible to conceive, at once respectful
and gallant. He never passed a day without seeing
her. M. de Marigny could not endure M. de Choiseul,
but he never spoke of him, except to his intimate
friends. Calling, one day, at Quesnay's, I found him
there. They were talking of M. de Choiseul. "He
is a mere *petit maître*," said the Doctor, "and, if he
were handsome just fit to be one of Henri the Third's
favourites." The Marquis de Mirabeau and M. de
La Rivière came in. "This kingdom," said Mirabeau, "is in a deplorable state. There is neither na-
tional energy, nor the only substitute for it—money."
"It can only be regenerated," said La Rivière, "by
a conquest, like that of China, or by some great
internal convulsion; but woe to those who live to see
that! The French people do not do things by halves."
These words made me tremble, and I hastened out
of the room. M. de Marigny did the same, though
without appearing at all affected by what had been
said. "You heard De La Rivière," said he,—"but
don't be alarmed, the conversations that pass at the
Doctor's are never repeated; these are honourable
men, though rather chimerical. They know not where
to stop. I think, however, they are in the right way;
only, unfortunately, they go too far." I wrote this
down immediately.

The Comte de St. Germain came to see Madame de Pompadour, who was ill, and lay on the sofa. He shewed her a little box, containing topazes, rubies, and emeralds. He appeared to have enough to furnish a treasury. Madame sent for me to see all these beautiful things. I looked at them with an air of the utmost astonishment, but I made signs to Madame that I thought them all false. The Count felt for something in his pocketbook, about twice as large as a spectacle-case, and, at length, drew out two or three little paper packets, which he unfolded, and exhibited a superb ruby. He threw on the table, with a contemptuous air, a little cross of green and white stones. I looked at it and said, " That is not to be despised." I put it on, and admired it greatly. The Count begged me to accept it. I refused—he urged me to take it. Madame then refused it for me. At length, he pressed it upon me so warmly that Madame, seeing that it could not be worth above forty louis, made me a sign to accept it. I took the cross, much pleased at the Count's politeness and, some days after, Madame presented him with an enamelled box, upon which was the portrait of some Grecian sage (whose name I don't recollect), to whom she compared him. I shewed the cross to a jeweller, who valued it at sixty-five louis. The Count offered to bring Madame some enamel portraits, by Petitot, to look at, and she told him to bring them after dinner, while the King was hunting. He shewed his portraits, after which Madame said to him, " I have heard a great deal of a charming story you told two days ago, at supper, at M. le Premier's, of an occurrence you witnessed fifty or sixty years ago." He smiled and said, " It is rather long." " So much the better," said she, with an air of delight. Madame de Gontaut and the ladies came in, and the door was shut; Madame made a

sign to me to sit down behind the screen.  The Count
made many apologies for the ennui which his story
would, perhaps, occasion.  He said, "Sometimes one
can tell a story pretty well; at other times it is quite
a different thing."

"At the beginning of this century, the Marquis de
St. Gilles was Ambassador from Spain to the Hague.
In his youth he had been particularly intimate with the
Count of Moncade, a grandee of Spain, and one of
the richest nobles of that country.  Some months
after the Marquis's arrival at the Hague, he received
a letter from the Count, entreating him, in the name
of their former friendship, to render him the greatest
possible service.  'You know,' said he, 'my dear Marquis, the mortification I felt that the name of Moncade was likely to expire with me.  At length, it
pleased heaven to hear my prayers, and to grant me
a son: he gave early promise of dispositions worthy
of his birth, but he, some time since, formed an unfortunate and disgraceful attachment to the most celebrated actress of the company of Toledo.  I shut my
eyes to this imprudence on the part of a young man
whose conduct had, till then, caused me unmingled
satisfaction.  But, having learnt that he was so
blinded by passion as to intend to marry this girl, and
that he had even bound himself by a written promise
to that effect, I solicited the King to have her placed
in confinement.  My son, having got information of
the steps I had taken, defeated my intentions by
escaping with the object of his passion.  For more
than six months I have vainly endeavoured to discover where he has concealed himself, but I have now
some reason to think he is at the Hague.'  The Count
earnestly conjured the Marquis to make the most
rigid search, in order to discover his son's retreat, and
to endeavour to prevail upon him to return to his

home. 'It is an act of justice,' continued he, 'to provide for the girl, if she consents to give up the written
promise of marriage which she has received, and I
leave it to your discretion to do what is right for her,
as well as to determine the sum necessary to bring
my son to Madrid in a manner suitable to his condition. I know not,' concluded he, 'whether you are
a father; if you are, you will be able to sympathise
in my anxieties.' The Count subjoined to this letter
an exact description of his son, and the young woman
by whom he was accompanied. On the receipt of this
letter, the Marquis lost not a moment in sending to
all the inns in Amsterdam, Rotterdam, and the
Hague, but in vain—he could find no trace of them.
He began to despair of success, when the idea struck
him that a young French page of his, remarkable for
his quickness and intelligence, might be employed with
advantage. He promised to reward him handsomely
if he succeeded in finding the young woman, who was
the cause of so much anxiety, and gave him the
description of her person. The page visited all the
public places for many days, without success; at
length, one evening, at the play, he saw a young man
and woman, in a box, who attracted his attention.
When he saw that they perceived he was looking at
them, and withdrew to the back of the box to avoid
his observation, he felt confident that they were the
objects of his search. He did not take his eyes from
the box, and watched every movement in it. The
instant the performance ended, he was in the passage
leading from the boxes to the door, and he remarked
that the young man, who, doubtless, observed the
dress he wore, tried to conceal himself, as he passed
him, by putting his handkerchief before his face. He
followed him, at a distance, to the inn called the
*Vicomte de Turenne,* which he saw him and the

woman enter; and, being now certain of success, he ran to inform the Ambassador. The Marquis de St. Gilles immediately repaired to the inn, wrapped in a cloak, and followed by his page and two servants. He desired the landlord to show him to the room of a young man and woman, who had lodged for some time in his house. The landlord, for some time, refused to do so, unless the Marquis would give their name. The page told him to take notice that he was speaking to the Spanish Ambassador, who had strong reasons for wishing to see the persons in question. The innkeeper said they wished not to be known, and that they had absolutely forbidden him to admit anybody into their apartment who did not ask for them by name; but that, since the Ambassador desired it, he would show him their room. He then conducted them up to a dirty, miserable garret. He knocked at the door, and waited for some time; he then knocked again pretty loudly, upon which the door was half-opened. At the sight of the Ambassador and his suite, the person who opened it immediately closed it again, exclaiming that they had made a mistake. The Ambassador pushed hard against him, forced his way in, made a sign to his people to wait outside, and remained in the room. He saw before him a very handsome young man, whose appearance perfectly corresponded with the description, and a young woman, of great beauty, and remarkably fine person, whose countenance, form, colour of the hair, etc., were also precisely those described by the Count of Moncade. The young man spoke first. He complained of the violence used in breaking into the apartment of a stranger, living in a free country, and under the protection of its laws. The Ambassador stepped forward to embrace him, and said, ' It is useless to feign, my dear Count; I know you, and I do not come here to give pain to you or to this lady, whose appearance interests me extremely.' The young man replied that he was totally mistaken; that he was not a Count, but the son of a merchant of Cadiz; that the lady was his wife; and, that they were travelling for pleasure. The Ambassador, casting his eyes round the miserably furnished room, which contained but one bed, and some packages of the shabbiest kind, lying in disorder about the room, ' Is this, my dear child (allow me to address you by a title which is warranted by my tender regard for your father), is this a fit residence for the son of the Count of Moncade?' The young man still protested against the use of any such language, as addressed to him. At length, overcome by the entreaties of the Ambassador, he confessed, weeping, that he was the son of the Count of Moncade, but declared that nothing should induce him to return to his father, if he must abandon a woman he adored. The young woman burst into tears; and threw herself at the feet of the Ambassador, telling him that she would not be the cause of the ruin of the young Count; and that generosity, or rather, love, would enable her to disregard her own happiness, and, for his sake, to separate herself from him. The Ambassador admired her noble disinterestedness. The young man, on the contrary, received her declaration with the most desperate grief. He reproached his mistress, and declared that he would never abandon so estimable a creature, nor suffer the sublime generosity of her heart to be turned against herself. The Ambassador told him that the Count of Moncade was far from wishing to render her miserable, and that he was commissioned to provide her with a sum sufficient to enable her to return into Spain, or to live where she liked. Her noble sentiments, and genuine tenderness, he said, inspired him with the greatest interest for her, and would induce him to go to the utmost limits of his powers, in the sum he was to give her; that he, therefore, promised her ten thousand florins, that is to say, about twelve hundred louis, which would be given her the moment she surrendered the promise of marriage she had received, and the Count of Moncade took up his abode in the Ambassador's house, and promised to return to Spain. The young woman seemed perfectly indifferent to the sum proposed, and wholly absorbed in her lover, and in the grief of leaving him. She seemed insensible to everything but the cruel sacrifice which her reason, and her love itself, demanded. At length, drawing from a little portfolio the promise of marriage, signed by the Count, 'I know his heart too well,' said she, 'to need it.' Then she kissed it again and again, with a sort of transport, and delivered it to the Ambassador, who stood by, astonished at the grandeur of soul he witnessed. He promised her that he would never cease to take the liveliest interest in her fate, and assured the Count of his father's forgiveness. 'He will receive with open arms,' said he, 'the prodigal son, returning to the bosom of his distressed family; the heart of a father is an exhaustless mine of tenderness. How great will be the felicity of my friend on the receipt of these tidings, after his long anxiety and affliction; how happy do I esteem myself, at being the instrument of that felicity!' Such was, in part, the language of the Ambassador, which appeared to produce a strong impression on the young man. But, fearing lest, during the night, love should regain all his power, and should triumph over the generous resolution of the lady, the Marquis pressed the young Count to accompany him to his hotel. The tears, the cries of anguish, which marked this cruel separation, cannot

be described; they deeply touched the heart of the
Ambassador, who promised to watch over the young
lady. The Count's little baggage was not difficult to
remove, and, that very evening, he was installed in
the finest apartment of the Ambassador's house. The
Marquis was overjoyed at having restored to the illustrious house of Moncade the heir of its greatness, and
of its magnificent domains. On the following morning, as soon as the young Count was up, he found
tailors, dealers in cloth, lace, stuffs, etc., out of which
he had only to choose. Two *valets de chambre,* and
three laquais, chosen by the Ambassador for their
intelligence and good conduct, were in waiting in his
antechamber, and presented themselves, to receive his
orders. The Ambassador shewed the young Count
the letter he had just written to his father, in which
he congratulated him on possessing a son whose noble
sentiments and striking qualities were worthy of his
illustrious blood, and announced his speedy return.
The young lady was not forgotten; he confessed that
to her generosity he was partly indebted for the submission of her lover, and expressed his conviction that
the Count would not disapprove the gift he had made
her, of ten thousand florins. That sum was remitted,
on the same day, to this noble and interesting girl,
who left the Hague without delay. The preparations
for the Count's journey were made; a splendid wardrobe and an excellent carriage were embarked at
Rotterdam, in a ship bound for France, on board
which a passage was secured for the Count, who was
to proceed from that country to Spain. A considerable sum of money, and letters of credit on Paris,
were given him at his departure; and the parting
between the Ambassador and the young Count was
most touching. The Marquis de St. Gilles awaited
with impatience the Count's answer, and enjoyed his

friend's delight by anticipation. At the expiration of four months, he received this long-expected letter. It would be utterly impossible to describe his surprise on reading the following words, 'Heaven, my dear Marquis, never granted me the happiness of becoming a father, and, in the midst of abundant wealth and honours, the grief of having no heirs, and seeing an illustrious race end in my person, has shed the greatest bitterness over my whole existence. I see, with extreme regret, that you have been imposed upon by a young adventurer, who has taken advantage of the knowledge he had, by some means, obtained, of our old friendship. But your Excellency must not be the sufferer. The Count of Moncade is, most assuredly, the person whom you wished to serve; he is bound to repay what your generous friendship hastened to advance, in order to procure him a happiness which he would have felt most deeply. I hope, therefore, Marquis, that your Excellency will have no hesitation in accepting the remittance contained in this letter, of three thousand louis of France, of the disbursal of which you sent me an account.' "

The manner in which the Comte de St. Germain spoke, in the characters of the young adventurer, his mistress, and the Ambassador, made his audience weep and laugh by turns. The story is true in every particular, and the adventurer surpasses Gusman d'Alfarache in address, according to the report of some persons present. Madame de Pompadour thought of having a play written, founded on this story; and the Count sent it to her in writing, from which I transcribed it.

M. Duclos came to the Doctor's, and harangued with his usual warmth. I heard him saying to two or three persons, "People are unjust to great men, Ministers and Princes; nothing, for instance, is more

common than to undervalue their intellect.  I astonished one of these little gentlemen of the corps of the
*infallibles,* by telling him that I could prove that
there had been more men of ability in the house of
Bourbon, for the last hundred years, than in any
other family."  " You prove that? " said somebody,
sneeringly.  " Yes," said Duclos; " and I will tell you
how.  The great Condé, you will allow, was no fool;
and the Duchesse de Longueville is cited as one of the
wittiest women that ever lived.  The Regent was a
man who had few equals, in every kind of talent and
acquirement.  The Prince de Conti, who was elected
King of Poland, was celebrated for his intelligence,
and, in poetry, was the successful rival of La Fare
and St. Aulaire.  The Duke of Burgundy was learned
and enlightened.  His Duchess, the daughter of Louis
XIV., was remarkably clever, and wrote epigrams
and couplets.  The Duc du Maine is generally spoken
of only for his weakness, but nobody had a more
agreeable wit.  His wife was mad, but she had an ex-
tensive acquaintance with letters, good taste in poetry,
and a brilliant and inexhaustible imagination.  Here
are instances enough, I think," said he; " and, as I
am no flatterer, and hate to appear one, I will not
speak of the living."  His hearers were astonished at
this enumeration, and all of them agreed in the truth
of what he had said.  He added, " Don't we daily
hear of *silly D'Argenson,* because he has a good-
natured air, and a *bourgeois* tone? and yet, I believe,
there have not been many Ministers comparable to
him in knowledge and in enlightened views."  I took
a pen, which lay on the Doctor's table, and begged
M. Duclos to repeat to me all the names he had
mentioned, and the eulogium he had bestowed on
each.  " If," said he, " you show that to the Marquise,
tell her how the conversation arose, and that I did

not say it in order that it might come to her ears,
and eventually, perhaps, to those of another person.
I am an historiographer, and I will render justice, but
I shall, also, often inflict it." " I will answer for
that," said the Doctor, " and our master will be represented as he really is. Louis XIV. liked verses, and
patronised poets; that was very well, perhaps, in his
time, because one must begin with something; but
this age will be very superior to the last. It must
be acknowledged that Louis XV., in sending astrono-
mers to Mexico and Peru, to measure the earth, has a
higher claim to our respect than if he directed an
opera. He has thrown down the barriers which
opposed the progress of philosophy, in spite of the
clamour of the devotees: the Encyclopædia will do
honour to his reign." Duclos, during this speech,
shook his head. I went away, and tried to write
down all I had heard, while it was fresh. I had the
part which related to the Princes of the Bourbon race
copied by a valet, who wrote a beautiful hand, and
I gave it to Madame de Pompadour. But she said
to me, " What! is Duclos an acquaintance of yours?
Do you want to play the *bel esprit,* my dear good
woman? That will not sit well upon you." The
truth is, that nothing can be further from my
inclination. I told her that I met him accidentally
at the Doctor's, where he generally spent an hour
when he came to Versailles. " The King knows him
to be a worthy man," said she.

Madame de Pompadour was ill, and the King came
to see her several times a day. I generally left the
room when he entered, but, having stayed a few
minutes, on one occasion, to give her a glass of chic-
ory water, I heard the King mention Madame d'Egmont. Madame raised her eyes to heaven, and said,
" That name always recalls to me a most melancholy

and barbarous affair; but it was not my fault."
These words dwelt in my mind, and, particularly,
the tone in which they were uttered. As I stayed
with Madame till three o'clock in the morning, reading to her a part of the time, it was easy for me
to try to satisfy my curiosity. I seized a moment,
when the reading was interrupted, to say, "You
looked dreadfully shocked, Madame, when the King
pronounced the name of D'Egmont." At these
words, she again raised her eyes, and said, "You
would feel as I do, if you knew the affair." "It
must, then, be deeply affecting, for I do not think
that it personally concerns you, Madame." "No,"
said she, "it does not; as, however, I am not the
only person acquainted with this history, and as I
know you to be discreet, I will tell it you. The last
Comte d'Egmont married a reputed daughter of the
Duc de Villars; but the Duchess had never lived with
her husband, and the Comtesse d'Egmont is, in fact,
a daughter of the Chevalier d'Orléans. At the death
of her husband, young, beautiful, agreeable, and
heiress to an immense fortune, she attracted the suit
and homage of all the most distinguished men at
Court. Her mother's director, one day, came into
her room and requested a private interview; he then
revealed to her that she was the offspring of an
adulterous intercourse, for which her mother had been
doing penance for five-and-twenty years. 'She could
not,' said he, 'oppose your former marriage, although
it caused her extreme distress. Heaven did not grant
you children; but, if you marry again, you run the
risk, Madame, of transmitting to another family the
immense wealth, which does not, in fact, belong to
you, and which is the price of crime.'

"The Comtesse d'Egmont heard this recital with
horror. At the same instant, her mother entered,

and, on her knees, besought her daughter to avert
her eternal damnation. Madame d'Egmont tried to
calm her own and her mother's mind. 'What can I
do?' said she, to her. 'Consecrate yourself wholly
to God,' replied the director, 'and thus expiate your
mother's crime.' The Countess, in her terror, promised whatever they asked, and proposed to enter the
Carmelites. I was informed of it, and spoke to the
King about the barbarous tyranny the Duchesse de
Villars and the director were about to exercise over
this unhappy young woman; but we knew not how
to prevent it. The King, with the utmost kindness,
prevailed on the Queen to offer her the situation of
Lady of the Palace, and desired the Duchess's friends
to persuade her to endeavour to deter her daughter
from becoming a Carmelite. It was all in vain; the
wretched victim was sacrificed."

Madame took it into her head to consult a fortune-
teller, called Madame Bontemps, who had told M. de
Bernis's fortune, as I have already related, and had
surprised him by her predictions. M. de Choiseul,
to whom she mentioned the matter, said that the
woman had also foretold fine things that were to happen to him. "I know it," said she, "and, in return,
you promised her a carriage, but the poor woman goes
on foot still." Madame told me this, and asked me
how she could disguise herself, so as to see the woman
without being known. I dared not propose any
scheme then, for fear it should not succeed; but, two
days after, I talked to her surgeon about the art,
which some beggars practise, of counterfeiting sores,
and altering their features. He said that was easy
enough. I let the thing drop, and, after an interval
of some minutes, I said, "If one could change one's
features, one might have great diversion at the opera,
or at balls. What alterations would it be necessary

to make in me, now, to render it impossible to recognise me?" "In the first place," said he, "you must
alter the colour of your hair, then you must have a
false nose, and put a spot on some part of your face,
or a wart, or a few hairs." I laughed, and said,
"Help me to contrive this for the next ball; I have
not been to one for twenty years; but I am dying to
puzzle somebody, and to tell him things which no one
but I can tell him. I shall come home, and go to bed,
in a quarter of an hour." "I must take the measure
of your nose," said he; "or do you take it with wax,
and I will have a nose made: you can get a flaxen
or brown wig." I repeated to Madame what the
surgeon had told me: she was delighted at it. I took
the measure of her nose, and of my own, and carried
them to the surgeon, who, in two days, gave me the
two noses, and a wart, which Madame stuck under
her left eye, and some paint for the eyebrows. The
noses were most delicately made, of a bladder, I think,
and these, with the other disguises, rendered it impossible to recognize the face, and yet did not produce any shocking appearance. All this being accomplished, nothing remained but to give notice to the
fortune-teller; we waited for a little excursion to
Paris, which Madame was to take, to look at her
house. I then got a person, with whom I had no connection, to speak to a waiting-woman of the Duchesse
de Ruffèc, to obtain an interview with the woman.
She made some difficulty, on account of the Police; but
we promised secrecy, and appointed the place of meeting. Nothing could be more contrary to Madame de
Pompadour's character, which was one of extreme
timidity, than to engage in such an adventure. But
her curiosity was raised to the highest pitch, and,
moreover, everything was so well arranged that there
was not the slightest risk. Madame had let M. de

Gontaut, and her *valet de chambre*, into the secret.
The latter had hired two rooms for his niece, who
was then ill, at Versailles, near Madame's hotel. We
went out in the evening, followed by the *valet de
chambre*, who was a safe man, and by the Duke, all
on foot. We had not, at farthest, above two hundred
steps to go. We were shown into two small rooms,
in which were fires. The two men remained in one,
and we in the other. Madame had thrown herself on
a sofa. She had on a night-cap, which concealed
half her face, in an unstudied manner. I was near
the fire, leaning on a table, on which were two candles. There were lying on the chairs, near us, some
clothes, of small value. The fortune-teller rang—a
little servant-girl let her in, and then went to wait in
the room where the gentlemen were. Coffee-cups,
and a coffee-pot, were set; and I had taken care to
place, upon a little buffet, some cakes, and a bottle
of Malaga wine, having heard that Madame Bontemps
assisted her inspiration with that liquor. Her face,
indeed, sufficiently proclaimed it. " Is that lady ill? "
said she, seeing Madame de Pompadour stretched
languidly on the sofa. I told her that she would
soon be better, but that she had kept her room for a
week. She heated the coffee, and prepared the two
cups, which she carefully wiped, observing that nothing impure must enter into this operation. I affected
to be very anxious for a glass of wine, in order to
give our oracle a pretext for assuaging her thirst,
which she did, without much entreaty. When she had
drunk two or three small glasses (for I had taken
care not to have large ones), she poured the coffee
into one of the two large cups. " This is yours," said
she; " and this is your friend's; let them stand a
little." She then observed our hands and our faces;
after which she drew a looking-glass from her pocket,

into which she told us to look, while she looked at the reflections of our faces. She next took a glass of wine, and immediately threw herself into a fit of enthusiasm, while she inspected my cup, and considered all the lines formed by the dregs of the coffee she had poured out. She began by saying, "*That is well—prosperity—but there is a black mark—distresses. A man becomes a comforter. Here, in this corner, are friends, who support you. Ah! who is he that persecutes them? But justice triumphs—after rain, sunshine—a long journey successful. There, do you see these little bags? That is money which has been paid—to you, of course, I mean. That is well. Do you see that arm?*" "*Yes.*" "*That is an arm supporting something: a woman veiled; I see her; it is you. All this is clear to me. I hear, as it were, a voice speaking to me. You are no longer attacked. I see it, because the clouds in that direction are passed off* (pointing to a clearer spot). *But, stay—I see small lines which branch out from the main spot. These are sons, daughters, nephews—that is pretty well.*" She appeared overpowered with the effort she was making. At length, she added, "*That is all. You have had good luck first—misfortune afterward. You have had a friend, who has exerted himself with success to extricate you from it. You have had lawsuits—at length fortune has been reconciled to you, and will change no more.*" She drank another glass of wine. "Your health, Madame," said she to the Marquise, and went through the same ceremonies with the cup. At length, she broke out, "*Neither fair nor foul. I see there, in the distance, a serene sky; and then all these things that appear to ascend— all these things are applauses. Here is a grave man, who stretches out his arms. Do you see?—look attentively.*" "*That is true,*" said Madame de Pompadour, with surprise (there was, indeed, some appearance of the kind). "*He points to something square—that is an open coffer.—Fine weather.—But, look! there are clouds of azure and gold, which surround you. Do you see that ship on the high sea? How favourable the wind is! You are on board; you land in a beautiful country, of which you become the Queen. Ah! what do I see? Look there—look at that hideous, crooked, lame man, who is pursuing you—but he is going on a fool's errand. I see a very great man, who supports you in his arms. Here, look! he is a kind of giant. There is a great deal of gold and silver—a few clouds here and there. But you have nothing to fear. The vessel will be sometimes tossed about, but it will not be lost. Dixi:*" Madame said, "When shall I die, and of what disease?" "I never speak of that," said she; "*see here, rather—but fate will not permit it. I will shew you how fate confounds everything*"—shewing her several confused lumps of the coffee-dregs. "Well, never mind as to the time, then, only tell me the kind of death." The fortune-teller looked in the cup, and said, "*You will have time to prepare yourself.*" I gave her only two louis, to avoid doing anything remarkable. She left us, after begging us to keep her secret, and we rejoined the Duc de Gontaut, to whom we related everything that had passed. He laughed heartily, and said, "Her coffee-dregs are like the clouds—you may see what you please in them."

There was one thing in my horoscope which struck me, that was the comforter; because one of my uncles had taken great care of me, and had rendered me the most essential services. It is also true that I afterwards had an important lawsuit; and, lastly, there was the money which had come into my hands through Madame de Pompadour's patronage and bounty. As for Madame, her husband was represented accurately enough by the man with the coffer; then the country of which she became Queen seemed to relate to her present situation at Court; but the most remarkable thing was the crooked and lame man, in whom Madame thought she recognized the Duc de V——, who was very much deformed. Madame was delighted with her adventure and her horoscope, which she thought corresponded very remarkably with the truth. Two days after, she sent for M. de St. Florentin, and begged him not to molest the fortune-teller. He laughed, and replied that he knew why she interceded for this woman. Madame asked him why he laughed. He related every circumstance of her expedition with astonishing exactness; but he knew nothing of what had been said, or, at least, so he pretended. He promised Madame that, provided Bontemps did nothing which called for notice, she should not be obstructed in the exercise of her profession, especially if she followed it in secret. " I know her," added he, " and I, like other people, have had the curiosity to consult her. She is the wife of a soldier in the guards. She is a clever woman in her way, but she drinks. Four or five years ago, she got such hold on the mind of Madame de Rufféc, that she made her believe she could procure her an elixir of beauty, which would restore her to what she was at twenty-five. The Duchess pays high for the drugs of which this elixir is compounded; and sometimes they are bad: sometimes, the sun, to which they were exposed, was not powerful enough; sometimes, the influence of a certain constellation was wanting. Sometimes, she has the courage to assure the Duchess that she really is grown handsomer, and actually succeeds in making her believe it." But the history of this woman's daughter is still more curious. She was exquisitely beautiful, and the Duchess brought her up in her own house. Bontemps predicted to the girl, in the Duchess's presence, that she would marry a man of two thousand louis a year. This was not very likely to happen to the daughter of a soldier in the guards. It did happen, nevertheless. The little Bontemps married the President Beaudouin, who was mad. But, the tragical part of the story is, that her mother had also foretold that she would die in child-birth of her first child, and that she did actually die in child-birth, at the age of eighteen, doubtless under a strong impression of her mother's prophecy, to which the improbable event of her marriage had given such extraordinary weight. Madame told the King of the adventure her curiosity had led her into, at which he laughed, and said he wished the Police had arrested her. He added a very sensible remark. " In order to judge," said he, " of the truth or falsehood of such predictions, one ought to collect fifty of them. It would be found that they are almost always made up of the same phrases, which are sometimes inapplicable, and sometimes hit the mark. But the first are rarely mentioned, while the others are always insisted on."

I have heard, and, indeed, it is certainly true, that M. de Bridge lived on terms of intimacy with Madame, when she was Madame d'Etioles. He used to ride on horseback with her, and, as he is so handsome a man that he has retained the name of *the handsome man*, it was natural enough that he should be thought the lover of a very handsome woman. I have heard something more than this. I was told that the King said to M. de Bridge, " Confess, now, that you were her lover. She has acknowledged it to me, and I exact from you this proof of sincerity." M. de Bridge replied, that Madame de Pompadour was at liberty to say what she pleased for her own amusement, or for any other reason; but that he, for his part, could not assert a falsehood; that he had been her friend; that she was a charming companion, and had great talents; that he delighted in her society; but that his intercourse with her had never gone beyond the bounds of friendship. He added, that her husband was present in all their parties, that he watched her with a jealous eye, and that he would not have suffered him to be so much with her if he had conceived the least suspicion of the kind. The King persisted, and told him he was wrong to endeavour to conceal a fact which was unquestionable. It was rumoured, also, that the Abbé de Bernis had been a favoured lover of hers. The said Abbé was rather a coxcomb; he had a handsome face, and wrote poetry. Madame de Pompadour was the theme of his gallant verses. He sometimes received the compliments of his friends upon his success with a smile which left some room for conjecture, although he denied the thing in words. It was, for some time, reported at Court that she was in love with the Prince de Beauvau: he is a man distinguished for his gallantries, his air of rank and fashion, and his high play; he is brother to the little Maréchale: for all these reasons, Madame is very civil to him, but there is nothing marked in her behaviour. She knows, besides, that he is in love with a very agreeable woman.

Now that I am on the subject of lovers, I cannot avoid speaking of M. de Choiseul. Madame likes him better than any of those I have just mentioned, but he is not her lover. A lady, whom I know perfectly well, but whom I do not choose to denounce to Madame, invented a story about them, which was utterly false. She said, as I have good reason to believe, that one day, hearing the King coming, I ran to Madame's closet door; that I coughed in a particular manner; and that the King having, happily, stopped a moment to talk to some ladies, there was time to adjust matters, so that Madame came out of the closet with me and M. de Choiseul, as if we had been all three sitting together. It is very true that I went in to carry something to Madame, without knowing that the King was come, and that she came out of the closet with M. de Choiseul, who had a paper in his hand, and that I followed her a few minutes after. The King asked M. de Choiseul what that paper was which he had in his hand. He replied that it contained the remonstrance from the Parliament.

Three or four ladies witnessed what I now relate, and as, with the exception of one, they were all excellent women, and greatly attached to Madame, my suspicions could fall on none but the one in question, whom I will not name, because her brother has always treated me with great kindness. Madame de Pompadour had a lively imagination and great sensibility, but nothing could exceed the coldness of her temperament. It would, besides, have been extremely difficult for her, surrounded as she was, to keep up an intercourse of that kind with any man. It is true that this difficulty would have been diminished in the case of an all-powerful Minister, who had constant pretexts for seeing her in private. But there was a much more decisive fact—M. de Choiseul had a charming mistress—the Princesse de R——, and Madame knew it, and often spoke of her. He had, besides, some remains of liking for the Princesse de Kinski, who followed him from Vienna. It is true that he soon after discovered how ridiculous she was. All these circumstances combined were, surely, sufficient to deter Madame from engaging in a love affair with the Duke; but his talents and agreeable qualities captivated her. He was not handsome, but he had manners peculiar to himself, an agreeable vivacity, a delightful gaiety; this was the general opinion of his character. He was much attached to Madame, and though this might, at first, be inspired by a consciousness of the importance of her friendship to his interest, yet, after he had acquired sufficient political strength to stand alone, he was not the less devoted to her, nor less assiduous in his attentions. He knew her friendship for me, and he one day said to me, with great feeling, " I am afraid, my dear Madame du Hausset, that she will sink into a state of complete dejection, and die of melancholy. Try to divert her." What a fate for the favourite of the greatest monarch in existence! thought I.

One day, Madame de Pompadour had retired to her closet with M. Berryer. Madame d'Amblimont stayed with Madame de Gontaut, who called me to talk about my son. A moment after, M. de Gontaut came in and said, " D'Amblimont, who shall have the Swiss guards?" " Stop a moment," said she; " let me call my council——, M. de Choiseul." "That is not so very bad a thought," said M. de Gontaut, " but I assure you, you are the first person who has suggested it." He immediately left us, and Madame d'Amblimont said, " I'll lay a wager he is going to communicate my idea to M. de Choiseul." He returned very shortly, and, M. Berryer having left the room, he said to Madame de Pompadour, " A singular thought has entered d'Amblimont's head." " What absurdity now?" said Madame. " Not so great an absurdity neither," said he. " She says the Swiss guards ought to be given to M. de Choiseul, and, really, if the King has not positively promised M. de Soubise, I don't see what he can do better." " The King has promised nothing," said Madame, " and the hopes I gave him were of the vaguest kind. I only

told him it was possible. But though I have a great
regard for M. de Soubise, I do not think his merits
comparable to those of M. de Choiseul." When the
King came in, Madame, doubtless, told him of this
suggestion. A quarter of an hour afterwards, I went
into the room to speak to her, and I heard the King
say, "You will see that, because the Duc du Maine,
and his children, had that place, he will think he
ought to have it, on account of his rank as Prince
(Soubise); but the Maréchal de Bassompièrre was
not a Prince; and, by the bye, the Duc de Choiseul is
for him to be. Her name was Romans. She was
Majesty is better acquainted with the history of France
than anybody," replied Madame. Two days after
this, Madame de ——— said to me, "I have two great
delights; M. de Soubise will not have the Swiss guards,
and Madame de Marsan will be ready to burst with
rage at it; this is the first: and M. de Choiseul will have
them; this is the greatest."

There was a universal talk of a young lady with
whom the King was as much in love as it was possible
for him to be. Her name was Romans. She was
said to be a charming girl. Madame de Pompadour
knew of the King's visits, and her confidantes brought
her most alarming reports of the affair. The Maréchale de Mirepoix, who had the best head in Madame's
council, was the only one who encouraged her. " I
do not tell you," said she, "that he loves you better
than her; and if she could be transported hither by
the stroke of a fairy's wand; if she could entertain him
this evening at supper; if she were familiar with all his
tastes, there would, perhaps, be sufficient reason for
you to tremble for your power. But Princes are,
above all, pre-eminently the slaves of habit. The
King's attachment to you is like that he bears to your
apartment, your furniture. You have formed your-

self to his manners and habits; you know how to listen
and reply to his stories; he is under no constraint
with you; he has no fear of *boring* you. How do you
think he could have resolution to uproot all this in a
day, to form a new establishment, and to make a public exhibition of himself by so striking a change in
his arrangements?" The young lady became pregnant; the reports current among the people, and even
those at Court, alarmed Madame dreadfully. It was
said that the King meant to legitimate the child, and to
give the mother a title. "All that," said Madame de
Mirepoix, " is in the style of Louis XIV.—such dignified proceedings are very unlike those of our master." Mademoiselle Romans lost all her influence over
the King by her indiscreet boasting. She was even
treated with harshness and violence, which were in no
degree instigated by Madame. Her house was
searched, and her papers seized; but the most important, those which substantiated the fact of the
King's paternity, had been withdrawn. At length she
gave birth to a son, who was christened under the
name of Bourbon, son of Charles de Bourbon, Captain of Horse. The mother thought the eyes of all
France were fixed upon her, and beheld in her son a
future Duc du Maine. She suckled him herself, and
she used to carry him in a sort of basket to the Bois de
Boulogne. Both mother and child were covered with
the finest laces. She sat down upon the grass in a
solitary spot, which, however, was soon well known,
and there gave suck to her royal babe. Madame had
great curiosity to see her, and took me, one day, to the
manufactory at Sèvres, without telling me what she
projected. After she had bought some cups, she said,
" I want to go and walk in the Bois de Boulogne,"
and gave orders to the coachman to stop at a certain
spot where she wished to alight. She had got the

most accurate directions, and when she drew near the young lady's haunt she gave me her arm, drew her bonnet over her eyes, and held her pocket-handkerchief before the lower part of her face. We walked, for some minutes, in a path, from whence we could see the lady suckling her child. Her jet black hair was turned up, and confined by a diamond comb. She looked earnestly at us. Madame bowed to her, and whispered to me, pushing me by the elbow, "Speak to her." I stepped forward, and exclaimed, "What a lovely child!" "Yes, Madame," replied she, "I must confess that he is, though I am his mother." Madame, who had hold of my arm, trembled. and I was not very firm. Mademoiselle Romans said to me, "Do you live in this neighbourhood?" "Yes, Madame," replied I, "I live at Auteuil with this lady, who is just now suffering from a most dreadful tooth-ache." "I pity her sincerely, for I know that tor-menting pain well." I looked all around, for fear any one should come up who might recognise us. I took courage to ask her whether the child's father was a handsome man. "Very handsome, and, if I told you his name, you would agree with me." "I have the honour of knowing him, then, Madame?" "Most probably you do." Madame, fearing, as I did, some rencontre, said a few words in a low tone, apologizing for having intruded upon her, and we took our leave. We looked behind us, repeatedly, to see if we were followed, and got into the carriage without being per-ceived. "It must be confessed that both mother and child are beautiful creatures," said Madame—"not to mention the father; the infant has his eyes. If the King had come up while we were there, do you think -he would have recognised us?" "I don't doubt that he would, Madame, and then what an agitation I should have been in, and what a scene it would have

been for the bystanders! and, above all, what a surprise to her!" In the evening Madame made the
King a present of the cups she had bought, but she
did not mention her walk, for fear Mademoiselle Romans should tell him that two ladies, who knew him,
had met her there such a day. Madame de Mirepoix
said to Madame, " Be assured, the King cares very
little about children; he has enough of them, and he
will not be troubled with the mother or the son. See
what sort of notice he takes of the Comte de L——,
who is strikingly like him. He never speaks of him,
and I am convinced that he will never do anything
for him. Again and again I tell you, we do not live
under Louis XIV." Madame de Mirepoix had been
Ambassadress to London, and had often heard the
English make this remark.

Some alterations had been made in Madame de
Pompadour's rooms, and I had no longer, as hereto-
fore, the niche in which I had been permitted to sit,
to hear Caffarelli, and, in later times, Mademoiselle
Fel and Jeliotte. I, therefore, went more frequently
to my lodgings in town, where I usually received my
friends: more particularly when Madame visited her
little hermitage, whither M. de Gontaut commonly accompanied her. Madame du Chiron, the wife of the
Head Clerk in the War-Office, came to see me. " I
feel," said she, " greatly embarrassed, in speaking to
you about an affair, which will, perhaps, embarrass
you also. This is the state of the case. A very poor
woman, to whom I have sometimes given a little assistance, pretends to be a relation of the Marquise de
Pompadour. Here is her petition." I read it, and
said that the woman had better write directly to Madame, and that I was sure, if what she asserted was
true, her application would be successful. Madame
du Chiron followed my advice. The woman wrote she

was in the lowest depth of poverty, and I learnt that
Madame sent her six louis until she could gain more
accurate information as to the truth of her story.
Colin, who was commissioned to take the money, made
inquiries of M. de Malvoisin, a relation of Madame,
and a very respectable officer. The fact was found
to be as she had stated it. Madame then sent her
a hundred louis, and promised her a pension of sixty
louis a year. All this was done with great expedition,
and Madame had a visit of thanks from her poor relation, as soon as she had procured decent clothes to
come in. That day the King happened to come in
at an unusual hour, and saw this person going out.
He asked who it was. "It is a very poor relation of
mine," replied Madame. "She came, then, to beg
for some assistance?" "No," said she. "What
did she come for, then?" "To thank me for a
little service I have rendered her," said she, blushing
from the fear of seeming to boast of her liberality.
"Well," said the King; "since she is your relation,
allow me to have the pleasure of serving her too. I
will give her fifty louis a year out of my private purse,
and, you know, she may send for the first year's allowance to-morrow." Madame burst into tears, and
kissed the King's hand several times. She told me
this three days afterwards, when I was nursing her in
a slight attack of fever. I could not refrain from
weeping myself at this instance of the King's kindness. The next day, I called on Madame du Chiron
to tell her of the good fortune of her protégée; I
forgot to say that, after Madame had related the affair to me, I told her what part I had taken in it. She
approved my conduct, and allowed me to inform my
friend of the King's goodness. This action, which
showed no less delicate politeness towards her than
sensibility to the sufferings of the poor woman, made

a deeper impression on Madame's heart than a pension of two thousand a year given to herself.

Madame had terrible palpitations of the heart. Her heart actually seemed to leap. She consulted several physicians. I recollect that one of them made her walk up and down the room, lift a weight, and move quickly. On her expressing some surprise, he said, " I do this to ascertain whether the organ is diseased; in that case motion quickens the pulsation; if that effect is not produced, the complaint proceeds from the nerves." I repeated this to my oracle, Quesnay. He knew very little of this physician, but he said his treatment was that of a clever man. His name was Rénard; he was scarcely known beyond the Marais. Madame often appeared suffocated, and sighed continually. One day, under pretence of presenting a petition to M. de Choiseul, as he was going out, I said, in a low voice, that I wished to see him a few minutes on an affair of importance to my mistress. He told me to come as soon as I pleased, and that I should be admitted. I told him that Madame was extremely depressed; that she gave way to distressing thoughts, which she would not communicate; that she, one day, said to me, " The fortune-teller told me I *should have time to prepare myself;* I believe it, for I shall be worn to death by melancholy." M. de Choiseul appeared much affected; he praised my zeal, and said that he had already perceived some indications of what I told him; that he would not mention my name, but would try to draw from her an explanation. I don't know what he said to her; but, from that time, she was much more calm. One day, but long afterwards, Madame said to M. de Gontaut, " I am generally thought to have great influence, but if it were not for M. de Choiseul, I should not be able to obtain a Cross of St. Louis."

The King and Madame de Pompadour had a very high opinion of Madame de Choiseul. Madame said, " She always says the right thing in the right place." Madame de Grammont was not so agreeable to them; and I think that this was to be attributed, in part, to the sound of her voice, and to her blunt manner of speaking; for she was said to be a woman of great sense, and devotedly attached to the King and Madame de Pompadour. Some people pretended that she tried to captivate the King, and to supplant Madame: nothing could be more false, or more ridiculously improbable. Madame saw a great deal of these two ladies, who were extremely attentive to her. She one day remarked to the Duc d'Ayen, that M. de Choiseul was very fond of his sisters. " I know it, Madame," said he, " and many sisters are the better for that." " What do you mean? " said she. " Why," said he, " as the Duc de Choiseul loves his sister, it is thought fashionable to do the same; and I know silly girls, whose brothers formerly cared nothing about them, who are now most tenderly beloved. No sooner does their little finger ache, than their brothers are running about to fetch physicians from all corners of Paris. They flatter themselves that somebody will say, in M. de Choiseul's drawing-room, " How passionately M. de ⸺ loves his sister; he would certainly die if he had the misfortune to lose her." Madame related this to her brother, in my presence, adding, that she could not give it in the Duke's comic manner. M. de Marigny said, " I have had the start of them all, without making so much noise; and my dear little sister knows that I loved her tenderly before Madame de Grammont left her convent. The Duc d'Ayen, however, is not very wrong; he has made the most of it in his lively manner, but it is partly true." " I forgot," replied Madame, " that the Duke said, ' I want extremely to be in the fashion, but which sister shall I take up? Madame de Caumont is a devil incarnate, Madame de Villars drinks, Madame d'Armagnac is a bore, Madame de la Marck is half mad.' " "These are fine family portraits, Duke," said Madame. The Duc de Gontaut laughed, during the whole of this conversation, immoderately. Madame repeated it, one day, when she kept her bed. M. de G—— also began to talk of his sister, Madame du Roure. I think, at least, that is the name he mentioned. He was very gay, and had the art of creating gaiety. Somebody said, he is an excellent piece of furniture for a favourite. He makes her laugh, and asks for nothing either for himself or for others; he cannot excite jealousy, and he meddles in nothing. He was called the White Eunuch. Madame's illness increased so rapidly that we were alarmed about her; but bleeding in the foot cured her as if by a miracle. The King watched her with the greatest solicitude; and I don't know whether his attentions did not contribute as much to the cure as the bleeding. M. de Choiseul remarked, some days after, that she appeared in better spirits. I told him that I thought this improvement might be attributed to the same cause.

# THE MEMOIRS OF
# CATHERINE DE MEDICI

### BY THE
### ABBÉ BRANTÔME

# INTRODUCTION

THE figure of Catherine de Medici is remarkable in history as being the pivotal point for more controversy than has ever centred about any other Queen of France. Of Italian descent, she became the wife of one French monarch, the mother of three others, and the dominant force behind that glittering Court which Brantôme eulogises. Both of her daughters likewise ascended thrones,—Elisabeth, became the wife of Philip II. of Spain; while Marguerite (whose memoirs are found elsewhere in this volume) wedded Henry of Navarre, the life-long rival of the ambitious Queen Mother, who was destined to become Henry IV., displacing her tottering dynasty.

Brantôme's tribute to this famous Queen will be read with great interest, but it is unnecessary to caution the reader to accept it *cum grano salis;* for Brantôme's likes and dislikes are at all times apt to run away with his historical judgment. Says Louis Moland in an introduction to the French edition of the Abbé's works: "The admiration which he professes for these grand princesses whom he has the honour of depicting so influences him that, despite his notorious credulity on this point, he shows them all, or nearly all, as perfectly virtuous." Nevertheless, his portraits, though coloured with the most favourable tints, are of great value as portraits from life. "I saw it," "I was there," are his favourite expressions in narrating an incident.

The study of Catherine is a typical example of his

work. He had lived at her Court and received many favours at her hands. He now sets himself the task of answering her calumniators and paying a tribute to her memory. This spirit of chivalry is certainly admirable, albeit the results may show as more partisan than accurate. It is interesting to compare this with Honoré de Balzac's more extended work, "Sur Catherine de Medicis," which is designated as a romance but is actually a careful historical portrait of the Queen.

Catherine's whole life may be said to have combined romance with history. She was the daughter of Lorenzo de Medici, that famous ruler of Florence for whom Machiavelli wrote his "Prince." Having been left an orphan at an early age, she was sent to a convent to be educated, but left there at fourteen to become the wife of the Dauphin, afterwards Henry II. of France. Her royal father-in-law was the celebrated Francis I., the life-long rival of Henry VIII. of England, on the one hand, and the Emperor Charles V., on the other. During his reign Catherine remained in obscurity, and was even threatened with divorce, as for ten years she remained childless. On hearing that Francis was considering this decree for state reasons, she planned her first bold stroke. With Italian finesse she made her way to the King at a favourable moment, threw herself at his feet, and expressed her willingness to submit to the royal will. "Do with me as you choose, sire," she said; "let me remain the dutiful wife of your son; or if it may please you to choose another, let me serve as one of her humblest attendants." Her speech won the heart of Francis, she was reinstated in favour, and finally had the happiness of bringing him grandchildren ere he died. This was one reason for the great veneration in which Catherine always held his memory, and to which Brantôme alludes.

Indeed, the dominant trait with her throughout her long life was loyalty to her family and their interests, —a loyalty fine in the abstract, but which was to lead her along many doubtful and devious ways. It caused her to match prince against prince, party against party, religion against religion, until the culminating horror of St. Bartholomew's Massacre was reached,—chargeable directly to her, despite the strenuous denials of Brantôme. Henry IV., the royal son-in-law who suffered so much at her hands, was broad-minded enough to palliate her offences on the ground of this family loyalty. Claude Grouard quotes him as saying to a Florentine ambassador in regard to Catherine: "I ask you what a poor woman could do, left by the death of her husband, with five little children on her arms, and two families in France who were thinking to grasp the crown,—ours and the Guises. Was she not compelled to play strange parts to deceive first one and then the other, in order to guard, as she has done, her sons who have successively reigned through the wise conduct of that shrewd woman? I am only surprised that she never did worse.

Sainte-Beuve in his "Causeries du Lundi" gives us additional glimpses of this Queen, basing his views upon those of Mézeray, author of an older "History of France": Mézeray, who never thinks of the dramatic, nevertheless makes known to us at the start his principal personages; he shows them more especially in action, without detaching them too much from the general sentiment and interests of which they are the leaders and representatives, while, at the same time, he leaves to each his individual physiognomy. . . . Catherine de Medici is painted there in all her dissimulation and her network of artifices, in which she herself was often caught; ambitious of sovereign power without possessing either the force or the genius for it; striving

to obtain it by craft, and using for this purpose a continual system of what we should call today 'see-saw-
ing'—'rousing and elevating for a time one faction,
putting to sleep or lowering another; uniting herself
sometimes with the feeblest side out of caution, lest
the stronger should crush her; sometimes with the
stronger from necessity; at times standing neutral when
she felt herself strong enough to command both sides,
but without intention to extinguish either.' Far from
being always too Catholic, there are moments when
she seems to lean to the Reformed religion and to
wish to grant too much to that party; and this with
more sincerity, perhaps, than belonged to her naturally. The Catherine de Medici, such as she presents
herself and is developed in plain truth on the pages of
Mézeray is well calculated to tempt a modern writer."

It is precisely to this temptation that Balzac has
yielded, in his book already mentioned. His summing-
up of her character is as follows: "Catherine de Medici
has suffered more from popular error than almost any
other woman . . . and yet she saved the throne of
France, she maintained the royal authority under circumstances to which more than one great prince would
have succumbed. Face to face with such leaders of
the factions, and ambitions of the houses of Guise and
of Bourbon as the Cardinals de Lorraine and the two
'Balafrés,' the two Princes de Condé, Henry IV.,
Montmorency, the Colignys, she was forced to put
forth the rarest fine qualities, the most essential gifts
of statesmanship, under the fire of the Calvinist press.
These, at any rate, are indisputable facts. And to the
student who digs deep into the history of the sixteenth
century in France, the figure of Catherine de Medici
stands out as that of a great king . . .

"Hemmed in between a race of princes who proclaimed themselves the heirs of Charlemagne, and a

factious younger branch that was eager to bury the
Constable de Bourbon's treason under the throne;
obliged too, to fight down a heresy on the verge of de-
vouring the monarchy, without friends, and aware of
treachery in the chiefs of the Catholic party and of
republicanism in the Calvinists, Catherine used the
most dangerous but the surest of political weapons—
Craft. She determined to deceive by turns the party
that was anxious to secure the downfall of the house
of Valois, the Bourbons who aimed at the Crown, and
the Reformers. . . . Indeed, so long as she lived, the
Valois sat on the throne. The great M. de Thou understood the worth of this woman when he exclaimed
on hearing of her death: 'It is not a woman, it is
Royalty that dies in her'!"

On the contrary, if one will follow the genial Dumas
through the pages of his Valois Romances, he will find
a French writer who, while loyal to the kingly line,
does not hesitate to paint this woman in unlovely
colors. She is here the low intriguer who does not
stop at assassination to gain her ends. On only one
point, indeed, do historians and romancers seem to
agree: she is always interesting—never commonplace.
She fills a definite niche in an important period, and
her personal reputation must be handled as a thing
apart.

This portrait of her by Brantôme is one of a series
of papers comprising his "Lives of Illustrious Ladies,"
—or as he preferred to call it, "Book of the Ladies."
Brantôme himself lived an adventurous life. Born in
Perigord in 1537, he was only eighteen years younger
than the queen he here discusses. His family, the de
Bourdeilles, was one of the oldest and most respected
in that province. "Not to boast of myself," he says,
"I can assert that none of my race has ever been home-
keeping; they have spent as much time in travels and

wars as any, no matter who they be, in France." The young Pierre had his first experience in Court life, at the Court of Marguerite, sister of Francis I., to whom his mother was lady-in-waiting.  As he was the youngest of the family, he was destined for the priesthood—which he always regarded from the militant, rather than the spiritual side—and when only sixteen King Henry II. bestowed upon him the Abbey of Brantôme.

The record of his life thereafter is one of travel and adventure in many lands.  It is the period of the Renaissance, when wars and conquests, intrigues and romances, poetry and song flourish,—in all of which our Abbé is equally at home!  He goes with the Duc de Guise to escort the young widowed Queen, Mary, back to her Scottish throne.  He visits Marguerite de Valois in her retirement and is so smitten by her beauty that he dedicates all his books to her.  And during his busy, adventurous life he finds time to set down many things which he sees and hears.  Some of these stories smack of the scandalous, but all undoubtedly reflect the spirit and manners of the time.

After a long life, Brantôme passed away in 1614, and although a clause in his will expressly related to the publication of his works they were left in MS. form, in his castle of Richemont, for half a century. They were finally published in Leyden, in 1665, and have been frequently reprinted since.

# THE MEMOIRS OF
## CATHERINE DE MEDICI

I HAVE wondered a hundred times, and been astonished, that, with so many good writers as we have had in France in our day, none of them have been inquisitive enough to bring out some sketches on the life and deeds of the Queen-Mother, Catherine de Medici, since she has given ample material, and did as much fine work as ever was done by a queen—as once said the Emperor Charles to Paolo Giovio on his return from his triumphant voyage in the "Goulette," when wishing to declare war against King Francis, that it was only necessary to be provided with paper and ink, to supply him with any amount of work.

True it is that this Queen cut out so much work, that any clever and industrious writer might build from it a complete Iliad; but the writers have all proven lazy or ungrateful, although she was never niggardly to learned men, or those writers of her times. I could name several who derived favors from the Queen, and for this reason do I accuse them of ingratitude.

There was one, however, who did attempt to write of her, and who brought out a little book which he called "The Life of Catherine," but it is an imposture and not worthy of belief, since it is more full of lies than truth, as she herself said, when she saw the book. The errors are so glaring as to be apparent to all, and are thus easily noted and rejected.

The author wished her mortal harm, and was inimical to her name, to her station, to her life, to her honor and to her nature, and for this reason he should be rejected.

As for myself, I would that I could speak well, or that I had a fluent pen at my command that I might exalt and praise her as she deserves.

At any rate, be my pen what it may, I shall use it at all hazards.

This Queen is descended, on her father's side, from the race of the Medici, one of the noblest and most illustrious families, not only in Italy but in Christendom.

Whatever may be said, she was a foreigner to these parts, since the alliances of the royal houses cannot commonly be made with those within their kingdoms. Nor is it often for the best, since foreign marriages are often more advantageous than those made nearer home.

The House of the Medici has ever been allied with the Crown of France, and still bears the *fleur-de-lys* that King Louis XI granted that house as a token of alliance and perpetual confederation.

On her mother's side she is descended from one of the noblest houses of France; a house truly French in race, in heart and in affection, that great house of Boulogne and of the County of Auvergne.

Thus it is difficult to say or to decide which of these two houses is the grander, or which is the more memorable by its deeds.

Here is what is said of them by the Archbishop of Bourges, he of the house of Beaune, as great a scholar and as worthy a prelate as there is in Christendom (although there are some who say that he was a trifle unsteady in belief, and of little worth in the scales of M. Saint-Michel, who weighs good Christians for the day of judgment, or so 'tis said). It is found in the funeral oration which the Archbishop made upon the said Queen at Blois.

In the days when that great captain of the Gauls, Brennus, led his forces through Italy and Greece, there were in his troop two French nobles, one named Felsinus, the other named Bono, who seeing the wicked designs of Brennus to invade and desecrate the temple of Delphos, after his great conquests, withdrew their forces and passed into Asia with their ships and followers.

They pushed on until they entered the sea of Medes, which is near Lydia and Persia.

Thence, after gaining many victories and obtaining many conquests, they retired, and while returning through Italy on their way to France, Felsinus stopped on the site of what is now Florence, beside the river Arno, a place which he saw was beautiful and commanding and situated much as another place which had pleased him much in the country of the Medes.

There he built the city which to-day is Florence.

His companion, Bono, built a second, and neighboring city which he called Bononia, the modern Bologna.

Henceforth Felsinus was called Medicus by his intimates, in commemoration of his victories and conquests among the Medes, a name that became the family name, just as we read of Paulus being surnamed Macedonicus, on account of his conquest of Macedonia from Perseus, and of Scipio being called Africanus for doing the like in Africa.

I do not know from what source M. de Beaune got his history, but it is very probable, that, speaking as he did before the King and such an august assembly, there convened for the funeral of the Queen, M. de Beaune would not have made the statement without good authority.

This descent is very different from the modern story invented and attributed without cause to the Medici family, according to that lying book on the life of the Queen, which I have mentioned.

Furthermore, continues the aforementioned Sieur de Beaune, one reads in the chronicles that a certain Everard de Medici, Sieur of Florence, many years afterwards, went with many of his subjects to the assistance of Charlemagne in his expedition in Italy against Didier, king of the Lombards, and having courageously succoured and assisted him was granted and invested with the lordship of Florence.

Many years later, one Anemond de Medici, also a Sieur of Florence, accompanied, with many of his subjects, Godefroy de Bouillon to the Holy Land, where he died at the siege of Nicæa in Asia.

Such greatness continued in that family down to the time when Florence was reduced to a republic by the internecine wars in Italy between the emperors and the people, the illustrious members of this family continually manifesting their valour and grandeur from time to time, as we see in these later days, how Cosmo de Medici, with his arms, his navy and ships struck terror into the Turks on the Mediterranean and even in the distant East; so that none since his time, no matter how great he may have been, has surpassed him in strength, valour and wealth, as has been recorded by Raffaelle Volaterano.

The temples and sacred shrines built by him, the hospitals founded by him, even as far as Jerusalem, all give ample proof of his piety and magnanimity.

Then there was Lorenzo de Medici, surnamed the Great on account of his virtuous deeds, and the two great popes, Leo and Clement, besides many cardinals and great personages of the name, including the Grand

Duke of Tuscany, Cosmo de Medici, a wise and wary man, if there ever was one.

He succeeded in retaining his duchy, which he found invaded and in great distress when he inherited it.

In short, nothing can rob this house of the Medici of its lustre, and of its nobleness and grandeur in all ways.

As to the house of Boulogne and Auvergne, who can deny its greatness, descending as it does from that noble Eustache de Boulogne, whose brother, Godefroy de Bouillon, who bore his arms and escutcheons with that vast number of princes, seigneurs, chevaliers, and Christian soldiers even to Jerusalem and to the sepulchre of our Saviour, where he would have made himself, by his sword and by the favour of God, king, not only of Jerusalem, but also of the greater part of the East, to the confusion of Mahomet, the Saracens, and the Mahometans, to the amazement of all the rest of the world, and would have replanted Christianity in Asia when it had fallen to the lowest depths?

Besides this house had ever been sought in alliance by all the monarchies of Christendom and by the great families, such as those of France, England, Scotland, Hungary, and Portugal, which latter kingdom belonged to it of right, as I have heard President de Thou say, and as the Queen herself did me the honor to tell me at Bordeaux, when she heard of the death of King Sebastian. The Medici were even allowed to argue the justice of their claims at the last Assembly of States previous to the death of King Henry.

And it was for this reason that she armed M. de Strozzi for an invasion of Portugal, where the King of Spain had usurped the kingdom. She was prevented from carrying out her well-chosen plans by reasons which I will explain at another time.

I will leave it to you, therefore, whether the house of Boulogne was great: yea, so great it is that I once heard Pope Pius IV say, while sitting at table at a dinner he gave after he had made Ferrara and Guise cardinals, that the house of Boulogne was so great and noble he knew none in France, no matter which, that could surpass it in antiquity, valour, and grandeur.

All this is much against those malicious detractors, who have said that this Queen was a Florentine of lowly birth, as one can see the contrary to be the case.

Moreover, she was not so poor since she brought to France as portion of her marriage estates which are valued to-day twenty-six thousand livres, such as the Counties of Auvergne and Lauragais, the seigneuries of Leverons, Donzenac, Boussac, Gorrèges, Hondecourt, and other lands—all inherited from her mother.

Her dowry included also more than two hundred thousand ducats, which are worth to-day over four hundred thousand; as well as great quantities of furniture, precious stones, jewels, including the finest and the largest pearls ever seen in such quantities, pearls that she afterwards gave to the Queen of Scotland [Mary Stuart], her daughter-in-law, whom I have seen wearing them. Besides all this, many manors, houses, deeds, and claims which she possessed in Italy.

But, more than all else, her marriage caused a strengthening in the fortunes of France, which had been so shaken by the imprisonment of the King and by his losses at Milan and Naples.

King Francis, it is well known, knew that such a marriage greatly helped his interests. Therefore there was given to this Queen, as a device, a rainbow, which she bore as long as she was married, with these words in Greek, φως φέρει ἠδὲ γαλήνην, which is the equivalent of saying that just as this fire and bow in the heavens brings and signifies good weather, just so this Queen was a true sign of clearness, of serenity and of the tranquillity of peace. The Greek is thus translated: *Lucem fert et serenitatem* — she brings light and serenity.

After that the Emperor [Charles V] no longer dared to push forward his ambitious motto: "Ever farther." For, notwithstanding the truce which existed between himself and King Francis, he was nursing his ambition with the plan of gaining always from France whatever he could; and he was much surprised at this alliance with the Pope [Clement VII], yet recognising the latter as an able, a courageous man, but vindictive on account of his imprisonment by the imperial troops at the sack of Rome.

Such a marriage was displeasing to him so much that I have heard a truthful lady of the Court say that if he had not been married to the Empress, he would have made an alliance with the Pope himself, and espoused his niece [Catherine de Medici], as much for the help of so strong a party as because he feared the Pope would help in losing for him Naples, Milan and Genoa; for the Pope had promised King Francis, in an authentic document, when he had delivered the money of his niece's dowry and her rings and jewels, that he would make the dowry worthy of such a marriage by adding to it three pearls of inestimable value, the excessive splendour of which caused envy and covetousness among the greatest of kings, meaning the three cities of Naples, Milan and Genoa. And it cannot be doubted that if the Pope had lived the natural span of his life he would have sold out the Emperor too, and made him pay well for that imprisonment, in order to enrich his niece and the kingdom to which she was joined. But Clement VII died too soon and all these expected gains could not withstand this blow. So that our Queen, having lost her mother, Magdelaine de Boulogne, and Lorenzo de Medici, Duke of Urbino, her father, in her early life, was given in marriage to France by her uncle, Pope Clement VII, and was brought by sea in great triumph to Marseilles, where at the age of fourteen she was wedded with great ceremony.

She made herself so beloved by the King, her father-in-law, and by King Henry, her husband, that after ten years had passed and still no heir being born to her, and though many persons endeavoured to persuade the King and the Dauphin, her husband, to divorce her, neither one would consent, so greatly did they love her. But after ten years, in accordance with the nature of the women of the Medici family, who were ever slow in conceiving, she began to furnish heirs, the first being King Francis II.

After him was born the Queen of Spain, and then consecutively, that fine and illustrious progeny whom we have all seen, besides others who were no sooner born than they died, by great misfortune and fatality. For this reason the King, her husband, loved her more and more, and in such manner that he, who was naturally of an amorous temperament, and who greatly liked to make love and to vary his loves, often said that of all the women in the world there was none who excelled his wife for love-making, nor did any equal her.

He had good cause for saying this, for she truly was a princess beautiful as well as lovable. She was of fine and stately presence; of great majesty, at the same time gentle when occasion required it; of noble appearance and good grace, her face handsome and agreeable, her bosom full, beautiful, and exquisitely fair, her body also very fair, the flesh firm, the skin smooth, as I have heard from several ladies-in-waiting; of a good plumpness as well, the leg and thigh well formed (as I have heard too from the same ladies).

She also took great pride in being well shod and in having her stockings tightly drawn up without wrinkles. Besides all this she possessed the most beautiful hand that was ever seen, as I believe. The poets once praised Aurora for her fine hands and tapering fingers; but I think our Queen would surpass her in that; and she carefully guarded and maintained this beauty to her dying day.

King Henry III, her son, inherited much of this beauty of the hand.

Moreover she always dressed herself well and superbly, often with some new and pretty conceit. In short, she had many charms in herself to make her well loved. I remember that at Lyons one day she went to see a painter named Corneille who had painted and exhibited in a spacious room portraits of all the great seigneurs, princes, cavaliers, queens, princesses, ladies and maids of honour of the Court, and she being in this room with us we all saw there her portrait painted true to life, showing her in all her beauty and perfection, apparelled as a Frenchwoman with a cap, showing her great pearls, and a gown whose wide sleeves of silver tissue were trimmed with lynx—the whole picture, which also showed the portraits of her three daughters, was so perfect that speech alone seemed lacking.

The Queen took great pleasure in seeing the portrait, and the assembled company did likewise, and praised and admired her beauty above all.

She herself was so ravished at the sight of the portrait that she could not take her gaze from it, until M. de Nemours came to her and said, "Madame, I think you are so well portrayed there that there remains nothing more to be said, and it seems to me, too, that your daughters do you great honour, for they do not excel you, nor surpass you."

To this the Queen replied, "My cousin, I think you
can remember the period, the age, and the dress represented in this portrait, so that you can judge better
than any one present, you who have seen me dressed
as I am represented in this portrait, and can say
whether I was esteemed as much as they say, and
whether I ever looked as I am portrayed there."

There was not one in the whole company who did
not lavish praise and estimate her beauty highly, and
who did not say that the mother was worthy of the
daughters and the daughters of the mother. And this
beauty remained her portion through life, while married and while widowed, until her death; not that she
had the freshness of her more blooming and younger
years, but still she remained well preserved, always
agreeable, always desirable.

Besides she was very good company, always of a
good humour; loving any becoming exercise, such as
dancing, in which she exhibited great grace and
dignity.

She also greatly loved hunting; about which I heard
a lady of the Court tell this tale: King Francis having
chosen and gathered a few of his Court whom he
called "the little band of Court ladies," which included
the handsomest, daintiest and most favoured, often escaped from the Court and went to other estates to
hunt deer and while away the time, sometimes staying thus in retreat eight days, ten days, sometimes
more, sometimes less, just as the humour took him.

Our Queen (who was then simply Madame la
Dauphine) seeing that such parties were made up without her, and that even Mesdames her sisters-in-law were
included while she was left at home, begged the King
to always take her with him, and to further honour
her by never allowing her to go about without being
accompanied by him.

It's said that she, who was always shrewd and clever, did this as much or more to watch the King's movements and to learn his secrets and to be able to hear and know all that went on, as she did it from pure liking for the chase.

King Francis was so pleased with this request, showing, as it seemed, the love she had for his company, that he heartily granted her request. He loved her more now than ever before and showed delight in giving her the pleasures of the hunt, which she followed, riding at full speed and ever by his side.

She was a good and fearless horseback rider, sitting her horse with easy grace, and was the first to ride with the leg around the pommel, which was more graceful and becoming than the former mode of sitting with feet upon a board. She loved to ride horseback even up to the time she was sixty years old and over, and when her growing feebleness prevented her riding she pined for it. It was one of her greatest pleasures to ride far and fast, though she had many falls, even breaking her leg and bruising her head so severely that it had to be trepanned. After she became a widow and had charge of the King and the kingdom, she accompanied the King everywhere and took all her children with her; and when the King, her husband, was still living she generally accompanied him to the stag and other hunts. If he played pall-mall she often watched him, and sometimes played herself. She was also fond of shooting baked clay balls with a cross-bow, and she shot well too; so that she always took with her her cross-bow when riding, in order if any game was seen she could shoot it. When she was kept indoors by bad weather she was forever devising some new dance or beautiful ballet. She invented games as well and passed her time by these devices, being quite unreserved, but knowing how to be grave and austere when occasion demanded it.

She was fond of seeing comedies and tragedies enacted, but after "Sophonisbe," a tragedy written by M. de Saint-Gélais, was well·presented at Blois by her daughters, maids-of-honor and other ladies as well as gentlemen of her Court during the celebration attendant on the marriages of M. du Cypière and the Marquis d'Elbœuf, she took the notion that tragedies were unlucky for state affairs and so would not let them be played again. But she still listened readily enough to comedies and tragi-comedies, even such as "Zani" and "Pantaloon" and took great pleasure in them, laughing as heartily as any one, for she liked laughter, being naturally of a happy disposition, loving a witty word and being ever ready with a witty rejoinder, knowing well when to cast a jest or a stone, and when to withhold it.

In the afternoons she passed her time at work on her silk embroideries, in which she was as perfect as possible.

In short the Queen liked and practiced all healthy exercises, and there was not one that was worthy of herself or her sex that the Queen did not wish to essay and practice.

This is a brief description, avoiding prolixity, of the beauty of her person and of her various exercises.

When she called any one "my friend" it was because she either thought him a fool or was angry with him. This was so well known that once when she had thus addressed one of her attendant gentlemen, named M. de Bois-Fevrier, he made reply, "Alas, Madame, I would rather have you call me 'enemy,' for to call me your friend is the equivalent of saying either I am a fool or that you are angry with me, for I have long known your nature."

As for her mind, it was great and admirable, as is shown by so many fine and striking acts, by which her life has been made illustrious forever.

The King, her husband, as well as his Council of State esteemed her so highly that when the King left the kingdom on his journey to Germany, he established and placed her as Regent and Governor throughout his dominions during his absence by royal declaration solemnly made before the Houses of Parliament in Paris. This trust she exercised so wisely that there was no disturbance, change, nor alteration in the State because of the King's absence; but, on the contrary, the Queen so carefully saw to affairs that she was able to assist the King with money, means, and men, and other kinds of aid; which greatly aided him in his return and for the conquest which he made of cities in the duchy of Luxembourg, such as Yvoy, Montmedy, Dampvilliers, Chimay and others.

I leave it to you what must be thought of him who wrote that fine life when he slanders her by saying that never did the King, her husband, allow her to put her nose into matters of state.

Was not this making her Regent in his absence giving her ample opportunities to have full knowledge of them? And she did this during all the trips he made yearly in going to his armies.

What did she do after the battle of Saint-Laurens, when the state was so shaken and the King had hastened to Compiègne to raise a new army?

She became so wrapped up in state affairs that she so aroused and stirred up the gentlemen of Paris that they gave prompt aid to their King, which came at a good time, and included money and other things very necessary in war.

Furthermore, when the King, her husband, was wounded, persons who were there and saw it cannot be uninformed of the great care she took for his cure, and the vigils she kept by his bedside; the prayers she offered continuously; the processions and visitations she made to the churches; and the hurried journeys she made in all directions for doctors and surgeons. But the King's hour had come; and when he passed from this world to the next, her grief was so great and she shed so many tears that it would seem she never could control them, and ever after, whenever his name was spoken the tears welled up from the depths of her eyes. For this reason she assumed a device in keeping and suitable to her tears and mourning, namely, a mound of quicklime over which the drops from heaven fall abundantly, with these words in Latin as a motto: *Adorem extincta testantur vivere flamma* (Although the flame is extinguished, this testifies that the fire still lives). The drops of water, like her tears, show ardour, though the flame has been extinguished. This device is allegorical of the nature of quicklime, which when watered burns strangely and shows its fire though the flame is wanting. Thus did our Queen show her zeal and affection by her tears, though the flame, which typified her husband, was now extinct. And this was the same as saying that, although he was dead, she wished to show by her tears that she could never forget him, but would love him always.

A similar device was formerly borne by Madame Valentine de Milan, Duchess d'Orléans, after the death of her husband, who was killed in Paris, for whom she grieved so much, that as a solace and comfort in her mourning, she assumed as device a watering pot, above which was an S, meaning, it is said, *Seule, souvenir, soucis, soupirer* (Lonely, remembrance, solicitude, sighing). And around the watering-pot were inscribed these words, *Rien ne m'est plus; plus ne m'est rien* (Nought is more to me; more is to me nothing). This device is still to be seen in her chapel in the Church of the Franciscans at Blois.

Good King René of Sicily having lost his wife Isabel, Duchess de Lorraine, suffered such great grief that he never was happy afterwards; and when his intimate friends and favourites tried to console him he was wont to lead them to his bedroom and there show them a picture, painted by himself (for he was an excellent painter), depicting a Turkish bow unstrung, beneath which was written, *Arco per lentare piaga non sana* (The bow although unstrung heals not the wounds).

Then King René would thus address them: "My friends, with this picture I answer all your arguments. By unstringing a bow, or by breaking the string, the harm done by the arrow can quickly be prevented, but the life of my dear spouse being broken and extinguished by death, the wound to the loyal love that ever filled my heart for her while she lived cannot be cured." In various places in Angers these Turkish bows with broken strings can be seen, with these words inscribed beneath, *Arco per lentare piaga non sana* (The loosened bow does not heal the wound). The same is seen on the Franciscan church, in the Chapel of Saint-Bernardin, which he decorated. He assumed this device after the death of his Queen, although during her lifetime he had used another one.

Our Queen, around her device, which I have described, placed many trophies, such as cracked mirrors, fans, rumpled plumes, pearls, broken quivers, precious stones and jewels scattered about, bits of broken chains, the whole to signify the abandoning of all worldly pomp, since, now that her husband was dead, her mourning for him was never to cease, and without the grace of God and the courage which He had given her, she would have succumbed to her great grief and distress. But she saw that her young chil-

dren, as well as France, needed her aid, as we ourselves
have seen since by experience; for, like a Semiramis,
or a second Athalie, she foiled, saved, guarded and
preserved these same young children from many enterprises planned against them during their early years;
and accomplished this with so much prudence and in-
dustry that all thought her wonderful.

She was Regent of this kingdom after the death of
King Francis, her son, and during the minority of our
kings by the ordinance of the Estates of Orléans, and
this, which well might have been given to the King of
Navarre, who as premier prince of the blood wished to
be Regent in her place, and to be Governor over all.
But she won over so easily and dexterously the said
Estates that if the King of Navarre had not gone elsewhere, she would have had him attainted of the crime
of lèse-majesté.

And it is possible that but for Madame de Montpensier, who had great influence over her, she would
still have done so on account of the intrigue against
the Estates into which he forced the Prince de Condé.

So the aforementioned King was obliged to content
himself to serve under her, and this was one of the
shrewd and subtle moves she made in the beginning
of her management of affairs. Afterwards she knew
how to maintain her rank and authority so imperiously
that no one dared deny it, no matter how grand or
how strenuous he might be, as was shown after a
period of three months when, during a stay of the
Court at Fontainebleau, this same King of Navarre,
wishing to show the resentment still in his heart, took
offence because M. de Guise had the keys of the King's
palace brought to him each night, and kept them all
night in his room exactly like a grand master of the
household (for that was one of his appointments), so
that no one could go out without his permission.

This angered greatly the King of Navarre, who himself wished to keep the keys. On being refused the keys, he grew spiteful and rebellious to such an extent that one morning he suddenly came to the King and Queen and announced his intention of taking leave of the Court, and of taking with him all the princes of the blood, whom he had won over, including M. le Connétable de Montmorency, his children and nephew.

The Queen, who did not expect this move, was astounded at first, and did all in her power to avert the blow, giving assurances to the King of Navarre that if he would but be patient he would some day be satisfied with affairs.

But fair words gained her nothing with the King, who was determined to leave.

It was then that our Queen decided on this shrewd plan: She sent orders to M. le Connétable, as principal, first and oldest officer of the crown, to remain near the person of the King, his master, as then his office demanded, and not to take his departure.

M. le Connétable, being a wise and judicious man, and being zealous for his master's interests as well as alert to his grandeur and honour, after reflecting on his duty and the orders sent him, went to the King and announced himself ready to fulfil his office.

This greatly astonished the King of Navarre, who was on the point of mounting his horse, waiting only the arrival of M. le Connétable to depart.

M. le Connétable when he came explained his duty and the responsibility of his office and endeavoured to persuade the King of Navarre himself not to budge or take his departure. This he did so well that the King of Navarre at his urging went to see the King and Queen, and after conferring with their majesties he gave up his journey and countermanded his orders for his mules, they having by that time arrived at Melun.

So peace once more reigned, to the great joy of the King of Navarre.

Not that M. de Guise diminished any of his claims pertaining to his office, or yielded one atom of his honour, for he retained his pre-eminence and all that belonged to him, without being shaken in the least, although he was not the stronger; but in such affairs he was a man of the world and was never bewildered, but knew well how to face things courageously and to keep to his rank, and to hold what he had.

It cannot be doubted, as all the world knows, but that, if the Queen had not bethought herself of this scheme regarding M. le Connétable, all that party would have gone to Paris and stirred up trouble for us, for which reason great credit should be given the Queen for her makeshift.

I know, for I was there, that many said that the plan was not of her invention, but rather that of Cardinal de Tournon, a wise and judicious prelate; but this is false, for, old hand as he was for prudence and counsel, my faith, the Queen knew more tricks than he, or all the Council of the King put together.

For often, when he was at fault, she would help him and put him on the track of what he ought to know, of which I might give many examples; but it will be enough to cite this one instance, which is recent, and about which the Queen herself did me the honour to disclose.

It is as follows:

When she went to Guyenne, and, later, to Coignac to reconcile the princes of the Religion and those of the League, and so give peace to the kingdom again—for she saw that it would soon be ruined by this division— she determined to declare a truce in order to formulate this peace; because of which the King of Navarre and the Prince de Condé became very discontented and mutinous—for the reason, they said, that this proclamation did them great harm because of their foreign troops, who, having heard of it, might repent of their coming, or might delay in coming, thinking that the Queen had made it with that very intention.

And they declared and resolved not to see the Queen nor to treat with her until the said truce was revoked.

Her Council, whom she had with her, though composed of able men, she found to be without much sense and weak, because they could find no means by which this truce could be rescinded.

The Queen then said to them, "Truly, you are very stupid as to finding a remedy. Don't you know any better? There is only one solution to this. You have at Maillezais the Huguenot regiment of Neufvy and of Sorlu. Send for me from here, from Niort, all the arquebusiers you can muster and cut the regiment to pieces and so you will have the truce broken and rescinded without any further trouble."

And as soon as she commanded it, it was done, the arquebusiers started, led by Captain l'Estelle, and forced their fort and barricades so well that the Huguenot regiment was defeated, Sorlu killed, who was a valiant man, Neufvy taken prisoner and many others killed. Their flags were all captured and brought to the Queen at Niort. She showed her accustomed clemency by pardoning all, and sent them away with their ensigns and flags, which, as regards flags, is a very rare thing.

But she wished to make this concession, she told me, on account of its very rarity, so that the princes would now know that they had to deal with a very able princess, and that they should not apply to her such mockery as to make her revoke a truce by the very heralds who had proclaimed it. For while they were planning to give her this insult, she had fallen upon them, and now sent word to them by the prisoners that it was not for them to affront her by demanding of her unseemly and unreasonable things, since it remained in her power to do them good or evil.

In this manner this Queen knew how to give and drill in a lesson to her Council. I might tell of other instances, but I have other points to treat upon, the first of which will be to answer those whom I have often heard accuse her of being the first to fly to arms, thus being the cause of our civil wars.

Whoever will look to the source of the thing will not believe it; for, the triumvirate being created, with the King of Navarre at its head, she (seeing the plots that were being concocted, and knowing the change of faith made by the King of Navarre—who from being Huguenot and very strict, had turned Catholic—and knowing by this change she had cause to fear for the King, for the kingdom, and for herself, and that he might move against them, she reflected and wondered to what tended such plots, such numerous meetings, colloquies and secret audiences; and, not being able to fathom the mystery, it is said that one day she bethought herself to go to the room above which the secret session was being held, and there, by means of a tube which she had caused to be surreptitiously inserted under the tapestry, she listened unperceived to all their plans.

Among other things she heard one that was very terrible and bitter for her, and that was when Maréchal de Saint-André, one of the triumvirate, proposed that the Queen be taken, put in a sack and flung into the river, since otherwise they would never succeed in their plans.

But the late M. de Guise, who was always fair and generous, said that such a thing must not be, for it was going too far, and was too unjust to thus cruelly slay the wife and mother of our kings, and that he was utterly opposed to the plan.

For this the said Queen has always loved him, and proved it by her treatment of his children, after his death, by giving them his entire possessions.

I leave to your imagination what such a sentence meant to the Queen, hearing it as she did with her own ears, and also whether she did not have cause for fear, notwithstanding her defence by M. de Guise.

From what I have heard told by one of the Queen's intimates, the Queen feared, as indeed she had cause to, that they would strike the blow without the knowledge of M. de Guise. For, in a deed so detestable, an upright man is to be distrusted, and should never be informed of the act. She was thus compelled to look out for her own safety, and to employ for it those who were already under arms (the Prince de Condé and the leaders of the Protestant party), imploring them to have pity for a mother and her children.

Such as it was, this was the sole cause of the Civil War.

For this reason she would never go, with the others, to Orléans, nor allow them to have the King and her children, as she could have done; and she felt glad, and with reason, that amongst the uproar and rumour of strife, she and the King, her son, and her other children were in safety.

Moreover she begged and obtained the promise from others, that when she should summon them to lay down their arms that they would do so, but this they would not do when the time came, notwithstanding the appeals she made to them, and the trouble she took, and the great heat she endured at Talsy, trying to induce them to listen to terms of peace which she could have made favourable and lasting for France had they only listened to her. And this conflagration, and others which we have seen lighted from this first brand, would have been stamped out forever in France had they but believed in her. I know the zeal she showed, and I know what I myself have heard her say, with tears in her eyes.

This is why they cannot tax her with the first spark of the Civil War, nor yet with the second, which was that day's work at Meaux, for at that time she was thinking only of the hunt, and of giving pleasure to the King at her beautiful house at Monceaux.

The warning came that M. le Prince and those of the Religion were under arms and in the field to surprise and seize the King under pretext of presenting a request.

God knows who was the cause of this new disturbance, and had it not been for the six thousand Swiss troops, newly raised, no one knows what might not have happened.

This levy of Swiss troops was the pretext for them to take up arms, and of saying and spreading broadcast that it was done to force them into war.

But it was they themselves who requested this levy of troops from the King and Queen, as I know from being then at Court, on account of the march of the Duke of Alva and his army, fearing that, under pretext of marching on Flanders, he might descend upon the frontiers of France, and besides urging that it was always the custom to strengthen the frontiers whenever a neighbouring state was arming.

No one can be uniformed of how urgently they pressed this upon the King and Queen, both by letters and by embassies. Even M. le Prince himself and M. l'Admiral (Coligny) came to see the King on this subject, at Saint-Germain-en-Laye, where I saw them.

I should also like to ask (for all that I write here I saw myself), who it was who took up arms on

Shrove Tuesday, and who bribed and begged Monsieur, the King's brother, and the King of Navarre to listen to the schemes for which Mole and Coconas were executed in Paris?

It was not the Queen, for it was by her wisdom that she prevented them from uprising, holding Monsieur and the King of Navarre so imprisoned in the forest of Vincennes that they could not break out, and on the death of King Charles she held them as tightly in Paris and the Louvre, even barring their windows one morning—at least those of the King of Navarre, who was lodged on the lower floor (this I know from the King of Navarre, who told it me with tears in his eyes), and kept such strict watch over them that they could not escape as they intended.

Their escape would have greatly embroiled the state and prevented the return of Poland to the King, a thing for which they were striving.

I know this from having been invited to the fracas, which was one of the finest strokes of policy ever made by the Queen.

Starting from Paris, she carried them to the King at Lyons so watchfully and skilfully that no one who saw them would think that they were prisoners.

They journeyed in the same coach with her, and she herself presented them to the King, who pardoned them soon after their arrival.

Again, who was it that enticed Monsieur, the King's brother, to leave Paris one fine night, casting off the affection of his brother who loved him so much, and to take up arms and embroil all France?

M. de La Noue knows all this, and the plots which began at the siege of La Rochelle, and what I told him about them.

It was not the Queen Mother, for on this open and abrupt departure by her son, she felt such grief to

see one brother banded against another brother, his
King, that she swore she would die of grief if she
could not reunite them as they were before, which
she accomplished.   I have heard her say at Blois, in
conversation with Monsieur, that she prayed for nothing so much as that God would grant the favour of
this re-union, after which He might send her death
and she would accept it with the best of heart.   Or
else she would retire to her houses of Monceaux and
Chenonceaux and never again meddle with the affairs
of France, willing to end her days in tranquillity.

In fact she really wished to do this, but the King
begged her to refrain, for both he and his kingdom
had great need of her.

I am assured that had she not gained peace by this
re-union, all would have been up with France, for
there were then fifty thousand foreigners scattered
over France who would have gladly helped to humble
and destroy her.

It was not, therefore, the Queen who brought about
this taking up of arms, nor was it the State Assembly
at Blois, who wanted but one religion and proposed
to abolish all contrary to their own, and who demanded that, if the spiritual sword did not suffice to
abolish it, recourse should be had to the temporal.

Some have stated that the Queen bribed them; this
was wrong, for in each province there were authorities
who would not have yielded to her wishes.   I do not
say that she did not win them over later; that was a
fine stroke of policy, showing her resourcefulness.
But it was not she who summoned the Assembly.   On
the contrary, she laid all the blame on it, because it
lessened both the King's authority and her own.   It
was the Church party which had long demanded the
Assembly, and voluntarily called it together, and required by the articles of the last peace that it should

be convened and held; to which the Queen strongly objected, foreseeing this abuse of power. Nevertheless, to quiet their incessant clamour, they were allowed to convoke it, to their own confusion and injury, not to their profit and contentment as they had thought; and for this reason they resorted to arms. Again it was not the Queen who did so.

Neither was it she who caused certain of them to be seized when they captured Mont-de-Marsan, La Fere in Picardy, and Cahors. I recall what the King said to M. de Moissans, who came to him on behalf of the King of Navarre. He repulsed him roughly, telling him that while these men were cajoling him with fine speeches, they were taking up arms and seizing cities.

This, then, is the way in which the Queen was the fomenter of all our wars and civil fires, the which she not only did not light but employed all her energies and efforts to extinguish, abhorring to see the death of so many nobles and landed gentlemen. And without that and her commiseration, those who bore against her a mortal enmity would have found themselves in dire straits, themselves laid beneath the sod, and their party not flourishing as it now is. All this must be imputed to her goodness of heart, of which we now stand in sore need—so everybody agrees and the poor people cry: "We no longer have the Queen Mother to make peace for us!" It was not through lack of her efforts that she did not succeed when she went to Guienne recently to treat for peace, at Coignac and Jarnac, with the King of Navarre and the Prince de Condé. I know that which I have witnessed—the tears in her eyes and the regret in her heart to which these princes would not yield; and the result we possibly see in the evils which afflict us to-day.

They have wished to accuse her of having been implicated in the War of the League. Why, then, should she have undertaken to conclude the peace I have just mentioned, if she had been? Why should she have appeased the riots of the barricades of Paris; and why reconciled the King with the Duc de Guise, as we have seen, if it were only to destroy the latter?

In short, no matter how much they slander her, never shall we have in France another so active in peace.

But the chief accusation against her is the massacre of Paris [of Saint Bartholomew]. All that is a sealed book to me, for I was just then setting out by boat from Brouage; but I have heard it said on good authority that she was not the prime mover in it. Three or four others, whom I might name, were much more active in it than she, pushing her forward and making her believe, from threats made upon the wounding of Admiral Coligny, that the King was to be killed, with herself and all her children, or else that the country was to be still worse involved in arms. Certainly the Church party were very wrong to utter such threats as they are said to have made, for they hastened the downward steps of the poor Admiral and procured his death. If they had kept their own counsel and uttered no word, and allowed the Admiral's wounds to heal, he could have left Paris in safety and quiet, and nothing else would have happened. M. de La Noue has been strongly of this opinion. Indeed, he and M. de Strozze and I have talked it over more than once, and he has never approved the bravados, the bold threats and the like which were openly made in the King's Court and his city of Paris. And he blamed no less strongly his brother-in-law, M. de Theligny, who was one of the hottest heads of them all, calling him a downright fool and blockhead. The Admiral never was guilty of this loud talk, at least not in public. I do not say that in secret or with his closest friends he did not say things. And this was the true cause of his death and of the massacre of his friends, and not the Queen, as was charged, although there are many who never have been able to get the idea out of their heads that this was a train long laid and a fuse well concealed. It is false. The least passionate agree with me, and the more violent and obstinate think otherwise; and thus very often we credit to kings and great princes the ordering of the natural course of events, and say afterwards how prudent and provident they were and how well they could dissimulate; when all the while they knew nothing more about it than a plum.

To return again to the Queen, her enemies have given it out that she was not a good Frenchwoman. God knows with what zeal she urged that the English be driven from Havre de Grâce, and what she said about it to M. le Prince, and how she made him go, with many cavaliers of his party, with the crown-companies of M. Andelot, and other Huguenots, and how she herself led this army, usually on horseback, like a second beautiful Queen Marfisa, exposing herself to the arquebusades and the cannonades like one of her captains, always watching the batteries, and saying that she would never be at ease until she had taken this city, and driven the English out of France, and hating worse than poison those who had sold it to them. And she accomplished so much that finally she restored it to France.

When Rouen was besieged I saw her in the greatest of fury, when she saw enter English reinforcements, by means of a French galley captured the year before, fearing that this place, failing to be captured by us, might fall into the control of the English. For this reason she "pushed hard at the wheel," as the saying is, to capture it, and never failed to come each day to the fort Sainte-Catherine to hold council and to watch the bombardment.

I have often seen her passing along the covered way to Sainte-Catherine, while the arquebusades and cannonades rained shot around her, and her paying no attention to them. Those who were there saw it as well as I. There are living to-day ladies who accompanied her, to whom the firing was not pleasant (I know this for I saw them there), and when M. le Connétable and M. le Guise remonstrated with her, telling her some accident might happen to her, she merely laughed and said that she saw no reason why she should spare herself more than they, since her courage was as good as theirs, although her sex had denied her the same strength. As for hardship, she endured that very well, either on foot or horseback. I think that for a long time there never was a better queen or princess on horseback, nor one who sat her mount with better grace; not seeming for all that like a masculine woman, formed like some fantastic Amazon, but a noble princess, beautiful, gracious and sweet.

It was said of her that she was strongly Spanish. Certainly while her good daughter was alive [Elizabeth, wife of Philip II of Spain] she loved the Spanish. But after her daughter died we knew—at least some of us—whether she had cause to love either the land or the people. It is true that she was always so prudent that she desired to receive the Spanish King always as a good son-in-law, to the end that he should treat her daughter the better, as is the way with good mothers; and also that he might never come to trouble us in France, nor make war here according to his warlike tastes and natural ambition.

Others have charged that she never liked the nobles of France and was always glad to shed their blood. I refute that by the many times she made peace and spared bloodshed; and in addition to this one should take notice of the fact that while she was Regent and her children in their minority, there were not seen at Court so many quarrels and duels as we have seen since, for she would not countenance them, giving express orders against such things and punishing those who disobeyed her. At other times, I have often seen her at Court when the King had gone away for some time leaving her absolutely alone, at a time when quarrels were rife and duels common—which she never would permit—I have seen her suddenly give orders to the captain of the guards to make arrests, and to the marshals and officers to regulate all such quarrels; so that, to speak the truth, she was more feared than the King, for she well knew how to deal with the disobedient and unruly and could reprimand them severely.

I remember once, when the King had gone to the baths at Bourbon, that my late cousin La Chastaignerie had a quarrel with Pardailhan. She sent to seek him, warning him on his life not to fight a duel; but being unable to find him for two whole days she had him shadowed so well that, on a Sunday morning, the Grand Provost found him on the island of Louviers, where he was awaiting his enemy, arrested him there, and took him as a prisoner to the Bastille, by the Queen's orders. But he remained there only overnight, and then she sent for him and gave him a reprimand partly sharp, partly gentle, for she was naturally of good heart, and harsh only when she wished to be. I know very well what she said to me also, inasmuch as I was to be my cousin's second: that as I was older I ought to know better.

The year that the King returned from Poland, a quarrel began between De Grillon and D'Entaigues, both brave and valiant gentlemen, who being called

out and ready to fight, the King gave orders for their
arrest of M. de Rambouillet, one of his Captains of the
Guards on duty; and also ordered M. de Nevers and
Marshal de Retz to reconcile the two men, which they
failed to do. The Queen thereupon summoned them
both, that evening, to her room; and as their quarrel
was in regard to two great ladies of her household,
she commanded them sternly and then besought them
gently to leave to her the settlement of their differences; for since she had done them the honour to meddle in it, and the princes, marshals, and captains had
failed to bring them together, she wished to have the
credit and honour for so doing. By this means she made
them friends, and they embraced unreservedly, taking
all from her; so that by her prudence the subject of
the quarrel, which touched upon the honour of the two
ladies and was rather delicate, was never known publicly. This shows the great goodness of the Princess!
And then to charge that she never liked the nobility!
Ha! If the truth were known she liked and esteemed
it too much. I believe that there was not a house in
her kingdom with whom she was not personally acquainted. It is said that she learned all about them
from the great King Francis, who knew all the
genealogies of the great families of his kingdom;
while as for her husband, the King, he had this faculty
that after he had once seen a gentleman he recognised
him ever after, knowing not only his face but also his
deeds and his reputation. I have seen this Queen, frequently and as a usual thing, when her son the King
was a minor, take the trouble to present to him personally the gentlemen of his realm, reminding him that
'This one has rendered good service to the King, your
grandfather," and such and such things "to the King,
your father," and so on; and commanding him to be
mindful of them, to cherish them, look after their in-

terests, and remember them by name. And that he heeded her advice was seen later, for, through this instruction, the King was thoroughly informed of the gentlemen of rank and honourable race who resided in his kingdom.

These detractors have also said that she never loved her people. This does not appear. Did she ever levy as many taxes, subsidies, imposts and other duties, while she directed the Government during the minority of her children, as has been levied since in a single year? Have they ever discoverd any hoards of money here or in the banks of Italy, as has been believed? On the contrary, after her death they never found a solitary coin; and I have heard some of her creditors and ladies say that after her death she was found to be in debt to the sum of eight thousand crowns, the wages of her ladies, gentlemen, and officers of her household for an entire year, and the income of a year spent in advance; so that, some months before her death, her bankers remonstrated with her over this deficit. But she laughed and said that one must praise God for everything and enjoy it while one was alive.

This, then, was her avarice, and the great wealth which she is said to have amassed. She never saved anything, for she had a heart wholly noble, liberal and magnificent, in every way the equal of that of her great-uncle, the Pope Leo, and of the celebrated Lorenzo de Medici. She spent and gave everything away; erecting buildings or applying it to memorable spectacles; and taking delight in giving entertainments to her people or Court, such as festivals, balls, dances, combats, and tourneys, three specially superb events being given during her lifetime. The first was at Fontainebleau, a carnival after the first troubles, where there were tourneys, and breaking of lances, and combats at the barrier; in brief, all sorts of joustings, followed by a comedy on the subject of the beautiful Genevra of Ariosto which was played by Madame d'Angoulême and her most beautiful and virtuous princesses and ladies and demoiselles of her Court, who certainly played it very well, so that nothing more beautiful was ever seen. The next was at Bayonne, at the interview between the Queen and her daughter, the Queen of Spain, where the magnificence was such in all things that the Spaniards, who are very disdainful of other countries besides their own, swore that they had never seen anything more splendid, and that their King could hardly rival it; and so they returned home greatly edified.

I know that many in France blamed this expense as quite unnecessary. But the Queen said she had done it to show other nations that France was not so totally ruined and poverty-stricken by reason of her recent wars as was supposed; and that, since she was able to spend so much for frivolity, she would be able to do far more for affairs of consequence and importance; and that France was all the more to be esteemed and feared, whether through the sight of so much wealth and richness, or the spectacle of so great an array of gentlemen, so brave and adroit at arms—for certainly there was a goodly number and worthy to be admired. And so it was for good and sufficient reason that our most Christian Queen made this splendid festival; for be assured that if she had not done so, the visitors would have derided us and returned home with a poor opinion of France.

A third exceedingly fine entertainment was given by her on the arrival of the Polish envoys in Paris, whom she dined superbly at the Tuileries; and afterwards in a grand ball-room made especially for the spectacle and entirely enclosed by a countless number of torches, she presented the most beautiful ballet ever seen on earth (if I may say so), which comprised sixteen ladies and demoiselles who were best suited to it. They appeared in a great grotto of silver, being seated in niches and clad as though in vapour about its sides. These sixteen ladies represented the sixteen provinces of France, with the most melodious music possible; and after having made, in this grotto, the round of the hall like a review of troops, giving an opportunity for all to see them, they descended from the grotto and formed themselves into a little company fantastically arranged, while an orchestra of thirty violins discoursed sweet music, and marched to the melody of these violins by a beautiful dance step, approaching and halting before their majesties. After this they danced their ballet, so fantastically invented, with so many turns and convolutions, twinings and twistings, in which no lady failed to find her own place again, that all the spectators were amazed at the accuracy and grace of the evolutions. This unique ballet lasted for at least an hour, after which the ladies representing, as I have said, the sixteen provinces advanced to the King, the Queen, the King of Poland, Monsieur his brother, the King and Queen of Navarre, and other notables of France and Poland, tendering to each a golden salver as large as the palm of the hand, finely enamelled and engraved, showing the fruits and products peculiar to each province, as for example: In Provence, citrons and oranges; in Champagne, cereals; in Burgundy, wines; in Guienne, soldiers—certainly a great honour to Guienne!—and so on through the various other provinces.

At Bayonne similar gifts were bestowed, and a combat was fought which I would willingly describe, but it would take too much space. But at Bayonne the men presented gifts to the ladies, while here it was the ladies giving to the men. And note that all these inventions were derived from no other bounty and brain than that of the Queen. She was mistress and deviser of everything. She had such a knack that, no matter what spectacles were offered at Court, hers surpassed all the others. So they had a saying that only the Queen Mother knew how to do fine things. And if such shows were expensive, they also gave great pleasure, and people used to say that she wished to imitate the Roman emperors, who studied how to exhibit games to the people and give them pleasure, and so amuse them that they had no time to get into mischief.

In addition to the fact that she delighted to give pleasure to her people, she gave them much money to earn; for she greatly preferred all kinds of skilled workmen and paid them well. Each was kept busy at his own work, so that they never lacked employment, especially masons and architects, as will be seen in her beautiful mansions—the Tuileries (still unfinished), Saint Maur, Monceaux, and Chenonceaux. Also she favoured men of genius and gladly read, or had read to her, the works which they presented to her or which she knew they had written, even the high-flown invectives which they launched against her, at which she scoffed and laughed, but took no other notice of, calling the writers prattlers and penny-liners.

She wished to know everything. On the journey to Lorraine, during the second uprising, the Huguenots took with them a very fine culverin which they nicknamed the "queen mother." They were obliged to bury it at Villenozze as they were unable to drag it further because of its excessive weight and poor harness; and they were never able to find it again. The Queen Mother was curious to know why they had named the gun for her, when she heard about it. Finally some one, after being strongly pressed by her for the reason, replied: "Because, Madame, she has a greater calibre and is larger than any of the others." The Queen was the first to laugh at this reply.

The Queen spared no pains to read anything which struck her fancy. On one occasion I saw her embarking at Blaye on her way to dine at Bourg, and occupying the whole journey by reading from a parchment, like some reporter or lawyer, a deposition made by Derdois, favourite secretary of the late M. le Connétable, concerning certain actions and information of which he had been accused and for which imprisoned at Bayonne. She never lifted her eyes until she had finished reading the whole thing, and there were more than ten pages of it. When she was not prevented she herself read all letters of importance addressed to her, and often wrote the reply with her own hand, whether to the most exalted or insignificant person. I saw her once, after dinner, indite twenty such letters of considerable length.

She wrote and spoke French very well, although an Italian. She even addressed those of her own nation often in French, so much did she honour it, making special effort to exhibit its fine diction to strangers and ambassadors who came to pay her their respects after seeing the King. She would reply to them very pertinently, with grace and dignity, just as I have heard her speak to the courts of parliament both publicly and privately; often keeping them well in hand when they were extravagant or over-cautious, and did not wish to yield to the royal edicts or to the wishes of the King or herself. You may be sure that she spoke as a Queen and made herself feared as such. I saw her once at Bordeaux when she took her daughter, the Queen of Navarre, to her husband. She had commanded the Court to come with her and spoke urgently on the subject to these gentlemen, who did not wish to abolish a certain fraternity which they had founded and adhered to, and which she wished to dissolve, foreseeing that it might lead to some end prejudicial to the state. They came to visit her in the Bishop's garden, where she was walking one Sunday morning. One of them, the spokesman, showed to her the usefulness of this fraternity and its good offices for the people. She, without preparation, responded so well, with such apt words and cogent reasons to show why it was badly founded and odious, that there was none present who could help but admire the spirit of the Queen or remain astonished and confused at her logic. She concluded with these words: "No, I wish it, and the King my son wishes that this order shall be abolished and that the subject may never again be discussed, for secret reasons which I shall not give you, in addition to those which I have given; otherwise I shall make you sensible of what it means to disobey the King and me." After that they all went their way, and nothing more was heard of the matter.

She assumed this manner very often and kept in line the princes and haughty lords when they had committed some large indiscretion and made her angry. Then she put on her grandest air, and no other living person could be so proud and disdainful as she, when it was necessary, sparing the truth to no one. I have seen the late M. de Savoie, who was a friend of the Emperor, the King of Spain, and many notables, fear and respect her more than if she had been his mother; and M. de Lorraine the same—in short, all the great people of Christendom. I could cite many instances, which at another time and in their own place I may do, but at present what I have said will suffice.

Among all her other fine qualities, she was a good Christian and very devout, always observing her fast days and never failing to attend daily service, either

mass or vespers, which she made very agreeable to\
worshippers by the good singers in her chapel, being
careful to select the finest artists. She had a natural
taste for music and often entertained the Court in her
own apartment, which was never closed to right-
minded ladies and gentlemen. She saw each and every
one, not denying admittance as was the custom in
Spain and also in her own country, Italy; nor yet as
our other Queens, Elizabeth of Austria and Louise of
Lorraine, have done; but saying, like King Francis, her
father-in-law, whom she greatly honoured as he had
raised her to her high position, that she wished to
maintain the true French spirit as the King her
husband had also desired. So her rooms were always
accessible to the Court.

Generally, she had very beautiful and virtuous maids
of honour, who could be seen every day in her antechamber chatting with us and entertaining us so
sensibly and modestly that none of us would have
dared do otherwise; for the gentlemen who fell short
of this were denied admittance, or warned of even
worse punishment, until she pardoned them and extended her favour again, which out of her good heart
she was ready to do.

In a word, her company and her Court were a real
Paradise in this world, and a school of honesty and
virtue, the ornament of France, as was well known
and spoken of by its visitors; for they were all well
received, and in their honour her ladies were commanded to adorn themselves like goddesses and devote
themselves to these guests instead of elsewhere; otherwise she would scold and reprimand them severely.

Indeed, such was her Court, that when she died all
said that we would never have such another, and that
never again would France have a real Queen Mother.
What a Court it was! Its equal, I believe, was never

held by an Emperor of Rome, in respect to its ladies,
nor by any of our Kings of France. It is true that the
great Emperor Charlemagne took great delight in
maintaining a splendid and overflowing Court, with
many peers, dukes, counts, paladins, barons, and
chevaliers of France, with their wives and daughters,
and many from other countries to keep their company
at Court—as we read in many of the old romances of
the time—and that there were many jousts, tourneys
and magnificent pageants. But what of that? These
gorgeous assemblages did not come together more
than three or four times a year, and at their close they
departed and retired to their own estates, to remain
until the next time. Moreover, others say that
Charlemagne in his old age was much given to
women, although they were always of good family,
and that Louis the Debonair on ascending the throne
was obliged to banish some of his sisters from Court,
by reason of scandalous love affairs which they had
with men; and also that he dismissed a large number
of ladies who were of the joyous band. These courts,
moreover, of Charlemagne were never long maintained in comparison to his long reign, for he was
chiefly devoted to his wars, as we read in the old
romances; and in his old age the Court was too dis-
solute, as I have said. But the Court of our King,
Henry II, and the Queen his wife, was an established
thing both in war and peace, and whether held in one
place or another for months at a time, either in the
pleasure houses or castles of our kings who were
never lacking in them, having more than any other
sovereigns. This elegant and distinguished company
always kept together, at least for the greater part of
the time, going and coming with the Queen; so that
as a usual thing her Court contained at least three
hundred ladies and maids of honour.

The chiefs of households and royal stewards affirmed that they always occupied at least one-half of all the apartments, as I myself have seen during the thirty-three years that I lived at Court, except during time of war, or while in foreign countries. But upon my return I was habitually there, for life there was most agreeable to me, and I never saw anything so attractive elsewhere. And I think that the world, since then, has never seen its equal; and as the list of those fair dames who assisted our Queen to ornament the Court should not be slighted, I shall mention some of them here as they occur to me, whom I saw after the Queen's marriage and during her widowhood. Before that time I was too young.

First of all, there were Mesdames, the daughters of France [the Royal Princesses]. I head the list with them because they never lost their high rank, and belong before all the others, so grand and noble was their house, viz.: Madame Elizabeth of France, afterwards Queen of Spain.

Madame Claude, since Duchess of Lorraine.

Madame Marguerite, afterwards Queen of Navarre.

Madame, the King's sister, afterwards Duchess of Savoie.

Mary Queen of Scots, afterwards Dauphiness and Queen of France.

The Queen of Navarre, Jeanne d'Albret.

Madame Catharine, her daughter, now Madame, the King's sister.

Madame Diane, natural daughter of King Henry II, afterwards legitimatised and made Duchess d'Angoulême.

Madame D'Enghien, heiress of Estouteville.

Madame the Princess of Condé.

Madame de Nevers.

Madame de Guise.

Madame Diane de Poitiers [the King's favourite].

Mesdames, the Duchesses d'Aumale and de Bouillon, and their daughters.

Madame de Montpensier.[1]

But why name any others? No, for my memory could not supply them all. Indeed, there are so many other ladies and maidens that I beg of them to excuse me if I pass them by with a stroke of the pen. Not that I do not hold and esteem them highly, but I should dream over them and devote myself to them too much. I will say, to conclude this, that in all this company I can name none who might be found fault with, for beauty abounded everywhere, and all was majesty, gentleness and grace. Lucky was the man who might be touched with the love of such fair ones, and very lucky he who could escape it. I swear to you that I have named none who were not very beautiful, agreeable and accomplished, and so endowed as to fire the whole world with passion. Indeed, some of them in their zenith did set fire to a good part of it, including those of us gentlemen of the Court who approached too close to the flames. Also to many were they sweet, amiable, favourable, and courteous. I allude now to certain ones of whom I wish to relate good stories in this book before I have ended it, and of others who are not included. But all will be told so quietly and without scandal that none can take offence, for the curtain of silence will cover their names; so that if any of them should happen to read stories of themselves they will not be displeased. For although the pleasures of love cannot last forever, on account of too many hindrances, accidents and changes, the memories of past joys delight us none the less.

[1] The author here continues with a long catalogue of names including some one hundred and fifty other ladies of the Court, belonging to various noble houses of France.

Now, in order to give proper consideration to them, it would be necessary to see for oneself all this lovely array of dames and demoiselles, creatures more divine than human; it would be necessary to represent them in their entrances into Paris and other cities, or at the holy and splendid nuptials of the royal family— such as those of the Dauphin, King Charles, King Henry III, the King of Spain, Madame de Lorraine, the Queen of Navarre, as well as other grand weddings of princes and princesses, such as that of M. de Joyeuse, which would have surpassed them all if the Queen of Navarre had been present.  Nor must we forget the interview at Bayonne, the Polish embassy, and an infinite number of similar spectacles which I should never be able to finish counting, where could be seen an array of these ladies, each seemingly more beautiful than the rest, and some more handsomely apparelled than others, since at such festivities, in addition to their own wealth, the King or the Queen gave them splendid liveries of different kinds.

In a word, no one ever saw anything finer, more dazzling, attractive, superb.  The glory of Niquée [in the enchanted palace of "Amadis"] never approached it; for one could see all this glowing in the ballrooms at the Palace or the Louvre, like the stars of heaven in the clear sky.  The Queen desired and commanded that they should always appear in lovely and expensive apparel, although she herself, during her widowhood, never dressed in worldly silks, unless of subdued tints, but always in good taste and well-fitting, so that she looked the Queen above all others. It is true that on the wedding days of her sons Charles and Henry she wore robes of black velvet, wishing, she said, to solemnise these occasions in this way beyond all others.  But while her husband the King was alive, she dressed very richly and superbly, and looked the great lady that she was. It was a privilege to see and admire her, in the general processions which were held both at Paris and elsewhere, such as that of the Fête Dieu, and that of Palm Sunday, carrying palms and torches with such grace, and that of Candlemas Day, when all carried lighted candles whose flame vied with their own splendour. In these three processions, which are the most noteworthy, assuredly one could see nothing but beauty, grace, noble bearing, stately marching and fine array—at sight of which all the by-standers were spellbound.

It was also a fine sight in the earlier days to see the Queen going about in her litter, or on horseback, when she was attended by forty or fifty ladies all well mounted on handsome steeds finely caparisoned and sitting their mounts with such ease that the men could not exceed them, either in horsemanship or accoutre-ment. Their hats were richly decorated with plumes which floated back in the air seeming to offer a chal-lenge of love or war. Virgil, who attempted to write of the beautiful apparel of Queen Dido when she went hunting, does not rival in description the luxury of our Queen and her ladies, whom I do not wish to displease, as I have already said.

This Queen, established by the hand of the great King Francis, who introduced this beautiful pag-eantry, did not wish to forget or neglect anything that she ever learned, but always wished to imitate it, to see if she could surpass it. I have heard her talk on this subject three or four times. Those who have seen all the things that I have will feel the same delight of the soul that I do, for what I say is true and I have seen it myself.

This, then, was the Court of our Queen. How un-fortunate was the day she died! I have heard it re-lated that our present King [Henry IV], some eighteen months after he saw his prospects brightening to become King, one day began to talk over with the late Marshal de Biron the designs and projects which he would set on foot to make his Court well established, elegant, and closely similar to that which our Queen maintained; for it was then in the heyday of its lustre and splendour. The Marshal replied: "It is not in your power, nor in that of any King who is to succeed, unless you make a compact with God that He resuscitate the Queen Mother and bring her back to your aid." But that was not what the King desired, for there was no one, at the time she died, whom he hated so much, and without reason that I could see. But he ought to know better than I.

How unlucky indeed was the day when such a Queen died, and at the time when we had the greatest need of her, as we still have!

She died at Blois from melancholy over the massacre which occurred there, and the sad tragedy which was enacted, seeing that unthinkingly she had caused the princes to come there, thinking to do the right thing; whereas, on the contrary, as the Cardinal de Bourbon said to her: "Alas, Madame! you have led us all to the slaughter, without intending it." That so touched her heart, and also the death of these poor gentlemen, that she took to her bed, having been previously ill, and never again rose from it.

They say that when the King told her of M. de Guise's death, saying that now he was King indeed, without rival or master, she asked him if he had put the affairs of his kingdom in order before striking the blow. He replied that he had. "God grant it, my son!" said she. Very prudent that she was, she foresaw clearly what might happen to him and to all the kingdom.

Various reports have gone about concerning her

death, some even saying that it was from poison.
Possibly so, possibly not; but she is believed to have
died of despair of soul, as she had reason for.  She
was placed upon her bed of state, as I have heard
said, by one of her ladies, in pomp neither more nor
less than Queen Anne, of whom I have spoken elsewhere, and clad in the same royal vesture, which has
not served since her death for any others; and was
then carried into the church of the castle, in the same
pomp and solemnity as at the funeral of Queen Anne,
where she still lies and reposes.  The King had wished
to carry her body to Chartres, and thence to Saint
Denis, to place it by the side of the King her husband,
in the same imposing vault which he had caused to be
built, but the ensuing war prevented him.

This is what I can say at this time of our great
Queen, who has assuredly given us so worthy a subject
to speak in praise of her, that this brief essay is not
long enough to sing her praises.  I know it well, and
also that the quality of my mind does not suffice,
since better speakers than I would still be inadequate.
However, such as it is, I lay this discourse in all
humility and devotion at her feet.  And also I wish to
avoid too great prolixity, for which indeed I feel myself liable.  But I earnestly hope that in my discourse
I shall not defraud her of much, although I am silent
on many things, speaking only of essential matters
and those which her beautiful and unequalled virtues
demand of me; giving me ample material since I have
seen all that I write concerning her; while as for that
which took place before my day, I received it from
very illustrious persons.

> This queen the mother of so many kings,
>   And queens as well, within our realm of France,
> Died when we needed her in many things,
>   For none save she could give us such assistance.

CPSIA information can be obtained
at www.ICGtesting.com
Printed in the USA
BVHW040820190620
581364BV00009B/79

9 781297 703706